The Last
Yankee Dodger

Fred Kipp
from Brooklyn to LA
and the Bronx

by Fred Kipp and Scott Kipp

www.fredkipp.com

ISBN: 0692952489
ISBN-13: 978-0692952481

Front Cover Pictures:

Top Left: Fred Kipp with Brooklyn Dodgers in Wrigley Field — 1957

Top Right: Fred Kipp with Los Angeles Dodgers in Wrigley Field — 1958

Bottom: Kent Hadley, Joe DeMaestri, Roger Maris, Elmer Valo, and Fred Kipp in Yankee Stadium — 1960

Endorsements

Good luck with the book Fred!
Tommy Lasorda, Brooklyn Dodger pitcher, legendary LA Dodger Manager

If you are a true baseball fan, Fred Kipp's book is one of the best stories ever about what it was like playing with the two best teams of that era. He takes you through his experiences from the minor leagues, winter leagues, and major leagues. This is a rare insight into what it was like being a professional baseball player in the fifties and sixties.
— Ralph Terry, New York Yankee and 1962 World Series MVP

Fred Kipp, my teammate, is one of the quality left hand pitchers in a long line of left handers for the Dodgers. This includes Sandy Koufax, Preacher Roe & Johnny Padres. When you read this book you will feel the excitement of the Jackie Robinson years in Brooklyn.
Carl "Oisk" Erskine – Brooklyn/LA Dodger Pitcher and All Star

From Piqua, Kansas, to Tokyo, Japan, with stops along the way in Ebbets Field, LA Coliseum, and Yankee Stadium, Fred touched them all. You will be touched too when you read this book.
— Vin Scully, The Voice of Baseball and the Dodgers for 67 years

Credit Fred Kipp with the "save" for preserving and sharing priceless insight and images from his remarkable baseball journey.
— Mark Langill, Team Historian for Los Angeles Dodgers

Fred was a battler on the mound and fun to play behind. This book is great at bringing back memories from the old days. He was also a fun teammate.
— Randy "Handsome Ransom" Jackson, Chicago Cub and Brooklyn/LA Dodger

Fred's work ethic made him a tremendous competitor. He was determined to do things the old fashioned way, "work on it!" Fred Kipp was one of the good guys.
— Don Demeter – Brooklyn/LA Dodger

CONTENTS

ACKNOWLEDGMENTS

I would like to thank the people who supported me throughout my baseball career and life. From my parents supporting me when I went off to play baseball in the Great Plains in my youth to the Queen of the Holy Rosary parish who supported my family while my wife suffered from cancer, I was given a solid foundation upon which to build my life and support during the hard times.

I would also like to thank my wife, Lorraine, for her support in making this book, and my family, who collected pictures and memorabilia to put in this book. I also want to thank the fans who cheered me on over the decades and made the game exciting.

1. BEATING STAN "THE MAN" MUSIAL

Five years after I signed as a free agent with the Brooklyn Dodgers, I got my first pitching start, in front of over sixty thousand fans in the Los Angeles Coliseum, on April 25, 1958. Friday nights were sports nights in LA, and a small prize fight could draw a crowd of twenty-five thousand. The largest night crowd in the history of the National League was ready to watch me throw my knuckleball to Stan "the Man" Musial and his Cardinals. Fans were on the edges of their seats to see the Man's first appearance in LA. They didn't know much about this rookie pitcher from Kansas, but they soon would.

LA was the perfect place to play baseball. Everything was fresh. Pacific Ocean breezes blew in from about ten miles away and kept the air crisp at about sixty degrees—perfect baseball weather. The fans were excited to see us play in only our seventh game at the coliseum. The Dodgers were the hottest ticket in town, and the city was buzzing. The players were fresh at the beginning of the season. Most importantly, I was fresh and ready to pitch.

This was the biggest chance I'd gotten to this point in my career. I figured Walter Alston, the Dodgers' manager, had seen me work my way through the Dodger system and was giving me my day on the mound. If it didn't work out, well, then he'd send me back to the minors again. I'd worked a long time to get where I was, but Montreal was never far away. We were off to a slow start in '58, with a record of 3–6, and had just gotten walloped 15–2 the night before by the Cubs. Our best pitcher, Don Drysdale, was 0–3, and we needed to turn things around. Walt decided to try someone new and go with me. They were giving me an opportunity, and I wasn't going to let it slip by.

The problem was that I was facing one of the legends of the game. Stan was considered the most consistent hitter in baseball at that time. He was thirty-seven and hotter than ever—batting over .500 when he came into the ninth game of the season. I didn't know how to stop him—no one did. Our strategy was to control the damage. In the 3,026 games that he would eventually play, he had over 3,600 hits. He hit .331 lifetime—almost one hit for every three times at the plate. He was a first-ballot Hall of Famer—no questions asked.

I was the rookie facing the veteran in the best duel in sports. I would have to outmaneuver Stan, and his henchmen, multiple times that evening and many more times throughout the year. I had the ball, and he had the bat. I had to get inside his head and keep one step ahead. I had to bait him with balls and tease him with curves. If he figured out a pitch, I had to change it up and throw him off. I had to mix it up and hopefully get my first win.

The Red Birds had a solid lineup with several veterans. Their top four stars, Stan, Al Dark, Ken Boyer, and Del Ennis, would end up with almost ten thousand hits between them. Stan had led them to second place in '57, but they hadn't won the pennant since '46. Stan was the only one left over from the Redbirds' golden era that had started during World War II, when they won the Series in '42, '44, and '46 and lost in '43.

Cardinal Stars

Player	G	Hits	2B	3B	HR	RBI	BB	SO	BA	SLG
Stan Musial 1942–63	3,026	3,630	725	177	475	1,951	1,599	696	.331	.559
Al Dark 1946–60	1,828	2,089	358	72	126	757	430	534	.289	.411
Ken Boyer 1955–69	2,034	2,143	318	68	282	1,141	713	1,017	.287	.462
Del Ennis 1946–59	1,903	2,063	358	69	288	1,284	597	719	.284	.472

The Dodger fans were coming to see their new team too. They wanted to see the legends who had mainly played on the East Coast until this year. Most people didn't have the means to see the pros. People came out to see us whether we won or lost, and we knew the owner, Walter O'Malley, liked that. Back in Brooklyn, we had had to win, or the fans would get mad or sad and call us bums. The LA fans, at least this early in the season, reflected the weather—almost constant sunshine with positive outlooks through the rest of the summer.

The fans also wanted to see the LA Coliseum as a baseball stadium. They knew it as the football stadium or a track field. How would they turn an elliptical track into a baseball diamond? They basically couldn't. They had to cut corners. All the players and fans couldn't help but notice the weakness of the stadium—the short left field that everyone called the China Wall.

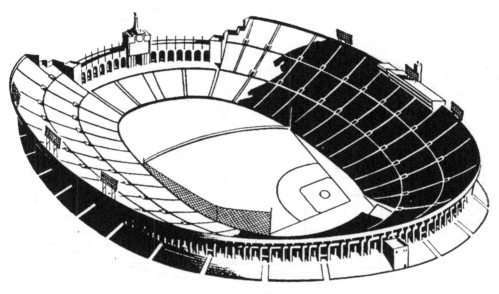

Memorial Coliseum, Los Angeles—First N. L. Game Played in April, 1958

Turning a track into a baseball diamond was never going to be pretty. The China Wall, shown as the net in left field, kept my first double from turning into a home run.

The China Wall was a 42-foot-tall screen that was supposed to prevent pop flies from turning into home runs. Some people thought a lefty like me shouldn't be pitching in the Coliseum because right-handed hitters could pull it over the screen at only 251 feet. It was the new joke of the baseball world, and some called it "O'Malley's Chinese Theater" or "the House that Charlie Chan Built." Those terms wouldn't go over too well today.

The problem was that we didn't have anywhere else to play. Dodger Stadium was just a dream and wouldn't open until four years later, in '62. I didn't get to pitch in Dodger Stadium until 2015—and that was only a ceremonial opening pitch! I was at the Coliseum when they filled it up with

115,300 fans to celebrate the fiftieth anniversary of the move out to LA. That set the Guinness and MLB attendance records for an exhibition game on March 29, 2008. On this day in 1958, with 60,000-plus fans, the stadium was only a little over half full.

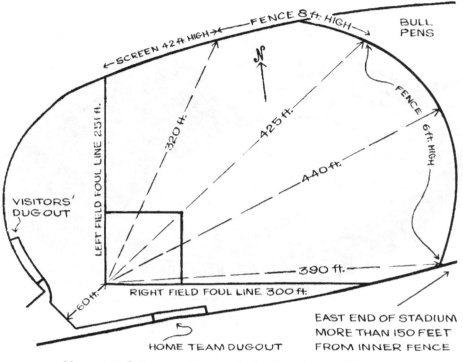

Memorial Coliseum, Home of the Los Angeles Dodgers

The dimensions of the field were very distorted, and many minor-league fields I played on had better proportions than this squashed diamond that bulged out into right field.

After the warmups, they sang the national anthem, and I walked onto the mound. I looked over my right shoulder, and the China Wall loomed only about two hundred feet away. I could have thrown the ball over it from the mound. We'd been talking a lot about that wall in the bull pen. Don Drysdale said we should pitch outside to right-handed hitters so that they'd have to pull it hard to get to the wall. It was one more problem to throw on the log pile in my mind. As if I didn't have enough things going on in my head—now I had to reduce the strike zone further and pitch outside to right handers and inside to lefties because of that wall.

4

I looked over my left shoulder and saw the far-off row of arches beyond right field. As easy as it was to hit to the China Wall, the right-field home-run fence stood way out there at 440 feet. It was a safe bet that there wouldn't be many home runs in that direction. I could barely see some fans out in the stands in far right field. They said they were 710 feet from home plate. They didn't need binoculars; they needed a telescope!

Umpire Ed Sudol called out, "Play ball!" Rube Walker was catching that night. Rube was a farm boy like me and knew how to set batters up. Don Blasingame was the first Card to bat, and Rube had told me that he didn't swing at the first pitch too often — especially at the start of the game. Rube called for a fastball, and I threw it in for the first strike and a good start. On the second pitch, I threw a curve, and Don popped out to Charlie Neal at second for an easy out. One down, but many more to come.

The veteran Al Dark came up next. They called Al the Swamp Fox because of his strong Louisiana accent. He had been a football star at Louisiana State and gotten drafted by the Philadelphia Eagles. He chose baseball instead and won Rookie of the Year in '48. Joe DiMaggio said Al was the perfect number-two hitter because of his uncanny ability to get on base. He could bunt and place the ball well and was an All Star with the New York Giants for a few years. I got behind in the count with two balls to start, and then I threw a low fastball that was just low enough. Al grounded it right back at me, and I made the routine play for an easy out — this time.

Then, up came the legend. Stan was on a hitting streak. He had gone three for four the night before in Seals Stadium versus the Giants. Stan was on fire in his seventeenth year in the majors. He looked menacing at the plate. Stan was known for his kindness off the field, but he was all business with the bat. Rube called for a curve, but I wanted my best pitch. I shook my head no and called off the next pitch too, until he called for my knuckleball. I gripped my knuckleball with my fingernails instead of my knuckles and wound up and threw a nice floater — almost no spin. The stitches caught the cool air, and I saw the ball wobble and drop right below his bat as he swung hard for the first strike.

His swing was fluid and different from others. The Man held his feet close together at the start and had a rhythmic progression from feet to hips to shoulders to arms and finally to his powerful wrists. If he could turn that fluidic motion from foot to bat, he had power. If I could keep him out of his rhythm, if I could make him hesitate in his swing, I could reduce his extra-base hits to singles. That was how I wanted to control the damage. I had to throw Stan out of his rhythm.

Rube called for a fastball. I threw it hard but too low for a ball. I always tried to pitch low, as my Asheville Tourists coach Ray Hathaway had encouraged me—pitch low and get grounders. I tried again and threw two more balls in a row. Stan just watched them go by, and when he did that, the umpire would rarely call a strike. Stan seemed to know right where the ball was going before I threw it. The count was now at 3–1. We decided to go back to my knuckleball again, but I didn't fool the Man the second time. Musial tracked it with his eyes and lined one out to deep right field for an easy double.

With Stan on base, Del Ennis, another veteran All Star from his time in Philly, walked to the plate. He lined the first pitch to left field. Stan ran around and scored, but Del got a little greedy and tried to turn a nice single into a double. Charlie Neal and Gil Hodges wouldn't have anything to do with that. They got him in a rundown between first and second and tagged him out. That ended the inning with us down 1–0. Musial had drawn first blood fast.

We didn't do anything in the bottom of the first, and I got through the second inning with a couple of grounders and a pop fly. In the third, their pitcher, Herm Wehmeier, walloped a double off the China Wall. I bet he had been thinking about that screen like I was. That screen was always in the corner of my mind. I had to protect against it.

Well, the Cards went back to the top of their order, and Blasingame came up again. It's a lot different pitching when a man's on second in the third inning than when he's the leadoff batter in the first. Blazer was a good hitter, and '58 turned out to be an All-Star season for him as well. On the fourth pitch, he hit a grounder toward me, and I fielded it quickly. I saw Wehmeier going for third, and I knew he wasn't that fast. It was an easy fielder's choice. I threw the ball to Randy "Handsome Ransom" Jackson at third.

Randy made the tag, but Wehmeier slid through the tag and cleated Randy on the ankle with metal spikes. Randy fell to the ground, and I ran over and saw blood gushing into his sock and dripping on the ground. The metal spikes back then were dangerous, and Randy had to leave the game because of the gash. I remember Jim Gilliam replacing Randy then, but the box score shows he replaced him in the fourth. That left Blazer on first. Al Dark was back up, and he swung at the first pitch and grounded to Jim for an easy out. We were still down 1–0, and I was coming up first to bat in the bottom of the third.

Stan had the fastest bat that I ever saw. His concentration and competitiveness put him ahead of everyone else.

This was only my first at bat for the season and my second in the majors. I hit pretty well for a pitcher, but that wasn't what I was on the team for. I couldn't make a living off my hitting. I walked into the batter box and looked out forever to right field, and then I saw that China Wall just 251 feet away. That wall called to me. On the fourth pitch, Herm threw a changeup, and I knew it. I saw it coming and hit it to the opposite field — right at the China Wall — right where I wanted to.

The sixty thousand fans got up on their feet and started cheering. What a rush! I wasn't a power hitter, but I could hit the ball 251 feet! I started running and looked up to see the ball climbing toward that China Wall. I can imagine Vin Scully eloquently announcing, in his delicious drawl, "A high fly ball toward the China Wall. It falls just a couple feet short of a nice home run." The ball bounced high off the screen, and I got an easy standup double. With all the great Dodger hitters, I got the first extra-base hit for the team that night. I was on cloud nine! A standup double was a great way to start the season and the inning. It was good to get that hit off Wehmeier, who had done the same thing to me.

Gino Cimoli, our center fielder and leadoff hitter, came up to the plate with no outs and a runner in scoring position — me! Gino had been an All Star in '57 in Brooklyn and was a nice Italian guy from San Francisco. When we were at Seals Stadium, he got a lot of North Beach fans to cheer for him that year — his last year with the Dodgers. After I retired in '63, I pitched batting practice to Gino in Kansas City, and we'd relive the old times in Brooklyn and LA.

Anyway, Gino came up and hit a couple foul balls before he hit one right in front of me. Since the ball was hit in front of me, I should have gone back to second, but I was so excited that I ran. That was my mistake, and they made an easy out at third. I should have learned from how I'd gotten Wehmeier out in the same situation in the top of the inning. Both pitchers hit doubles off the China Wall but got thrown out at third.

Stan was the leadoff batter in the top of the fourth. He'd already beaten my best pitch, the knuckler. In the dugout, I talked to Rube about using my second-best pitch — the curve, which is a type of changeup because it's slower. While I closed with a knuckleball, my bread-and-butter pitch was the curve ball. To throw a curve, I needed to establish my fastball. I later read that Stan said he would remember the speed of a pitcher's fastball and set his rhythm accordingly. I bet I could throw a fastball in the nineties on a good day with the wind to my back. We didn't have radar guns back then, so nobody really knew how hard we were pitching.

I threw my first fastball low and outside, right where I wanted to, but Sudol called a ball. I tried my fastball again to set the pace in Stan's mind. My control felt good, and I thought it went to the same exact place. To my surprise, Sudol called a strike. With my speed established, it was time to throw Stan a curve. I threw my first breaking ball, which might come in at a slow seventy-five miles per hour.

Hitting is all about timing, and I think that was one thing that Stan could do better than anyone else. I could see that Stan took the bait and started his rhythmic swing as usual. The difference between him and most hitters was that he could tell the ball was coming in slow, and he would break his rhythm in his arms and wrist to match the slower pitch. While his body was rotating normally, his arms slowed up, and he hit the fourth pitch for a line drive to left field for his second hit.

Stan made it to first and got off the base pretty far. I had to throw to first a couple of times to check him. Del Ennis was back up, and I got him to pop out to center field for the first out. Next up was Ken Boyer. Ken was another All Star—six years in a row in the early sixties. He was a talent, and it wasn't fun facing him. I got ahead of him in the count, and then I threw this wicked knuckleball that Rube just couldn't catch. The ball got loose and rolled back behind the umpire, and Stan advanced to second.

My knuckler was hard to catch, and Rube would only reluctantly call for it. Roy Campanella would call for it all day long. Campy had such good hands. Even if Campy didn't catch it, he was great at keeping it in front of him. He'd scoop it out of the dirt if it was a low ball and keep it in the field of play. It was frustrating for everyone if the ball got loose behind the catcher and runners advanced. At least my knuckleball was a challenge to hit too.

The count was 2–2 now, and Ken was kicking dirt and looking like a bull, ready to pound that ball into oblivion. I knew he wanted it, so Rube signaled for a changeup, and I consented. I was known as a change-of-speed pitcher and wasn't overpowering. I pitched from the stretch and laid the pitch in there nice and slow. Ken swung early, as if it were my normal pitch, and the bat went by, and the ball landed smack dab in the middle of Rube's glove.

That was the effect I was looking for. I couldn't hear it over the radio, but I imagine Vin Scully calling, "Strike three. The batter is out." That was my first strikeout of the game, and it couldn't have come at a better time.

Two outs now, and their right fielder Gene Green was coming up to bat. I had played with Gene in the minors and winter ball. He was a tough out and a free swinger. I threw a swinging strike and a ball, and then he hit a slow dribbler to Don Zimmer at short. Zimmer had been playing back because of Musial being on second, and he ran in to get the ball. Musial ran for third with two outs and ran in front of the ball on the way to third. Don charged the ball and got a quick release to first, but the throw came in too late and low. Gil came off the base and dug the low ball out of the dirt and saw Stan running for home. Stan never stopped at third and was hightailing it to home.

Gil found his footing and made a quick throw to Rube. Everything was happening so fast that I just spun around looking from short to first and then to home. Rube was in position, and Gil made a great throw. Stan slid, and Rube made a swinging tag that I couldn't see with the dirt flying up in the air and Rube's position. Sudol threw his thumb in the air to call Stan out at home to end the inning. What a close call. Phew!

In the bottom of the fourth, Jim Gilliam hit Gil Hodges in to tie the game at 1–1. The top of the fifth went quickly—three up and three down—and I got my second strikeout of the game. In the bottom of the fifth, I got walked in five pitches. Frank Barnes, their new pitcher, must have seen my double in the third and was worried about my power. Ha! Ha! Anyway, I was on first when Gino Cimoli came up and hit to the gap between the first and second basemen. That walk set the hit up because Stan had to play closer to first because I was there. Gino saw that hole and drove the ball right through it. I ran off the crack of the bat, of course, and the ball came right at me. I had to duck, and it whistled by my head and out into right field. I was on second again with Gino on first when Norm Larker came up to bat.

Norm was a solid hitter and was pinch hitting well for us quite a bit. He got ahold of the second pitch and sent it to deep center. The crowd got on their feet and roared. I ran to third with my long legs going as fast as they ever had. The third-base coach waved me on, and I hightailed it home. I crossed the plate and turned around and looked back to see Gino cruising home not far behind me for the second score, putting us up 3–1. Norm ran to third. He slid, but the throw wasn't even coming yet. Deep right-center field was so far out there that they didn't have a chance. It was exhilarating to score a run, and all I'd done was get walked. I didn't even swing the bat that inning. Sometimes, I was at the right place at the right time. It was nice to have great teammates who pushed me to home and to new levels.

In the top of the sixth, the Cards were at the top of their order. It's always the top of the order that's hard. The top of the fifth had been easy because it was batters seven, eight, and nine. Feast or famine. The sixth started off well when I struck Blasingame out with a knuckleball. My high from scoring was about to end. This roller coaster of a night was about to take another turn. Al Dark came up, and it was a long series. Al hit three foul balls, and I threw three balls, and the count got to 3–2. I could tell he was getting used to my pitching, and he seemed to know what I was going to throw. On the eighth pitch, he got ahold of the ball, and it sailed right over the China Wall.

Here's what Frank Finch of the *LA Times* reported comically:

Chinese Homer?

And now we take you to our Far Eastern headquarters for a direct report on the Chinese home-run situation:

There was only one-round tripper slugged last night — by the Cards' Al Dark in the sixth inning. It was a right, smart rap, but press box observers couldn't agree whether it was on the legit or slightly Oriental. The ball struck about halfway up in the lower left field seats, so we'll call it a Eurasian home run and let it go at that.

We were now down 2–3, and Stan was coming up to the plate. Musial was so hard to pitch to. The pitching staff talked a lot about him, since we faced him so often for so many years. Brooklyn had given him the nickname "the Man." One story goes that during an All-Star Game, the American League coach Charlie Dressen was reviewing the opposing hitters and making suggestions on how to pitch to them. As if he were saying something brilliant, Charlie said, "Pitch him high and tight or low and away."

Stan went around third base three times that day, but he only made it home one time. Throwing him out at home twice made the difference in the game.

This caused some of the players to laugh and say, "They've been trying that strategy for twenty years, and it doesn't work!" Nothing worked—except trying to control the damage. I think I blocked the third at bat out of my head, but the scorecard said that Stan singled a line drive to center field for his third hit on my fifth pitch.

When it rained, it poured. As if that third single weren't bad enough, Ennis came up and hit a deep ball to left field. Stan held up at first until it bounced off the China Wall. Norm made a good throw, and we held Musial up on third. Well, I thought Alston would pull me, but he gave me the thumbs up and let me sit in my own mess. I've always remembered a shortstop named John Buckley whom I played with in Emporia during the summer of 1950. He came to the mound and said, "Now, let's see what you're made of!" Now I was staring at Ken Boyer with runners on second and third.

The pressure was getting to me, and I was sweating bullets out there. Ken Boyer hadn't gotten a hit that night, but I knew he had gone two for three the night before. I eyed Stan on third and looked back at Ennis on second. I had to focus. I told myself this was my night. This was when I needed to perform. I focused on my pitches and threw my breaking ball to Ken. He grounded it down the third baseline toward Jim Gilliam. Now, Jim was a great athlete and all-around good defender, but he was our third-string third basemen. Randy Jackson had started for us, but he was in for Dick Gray, who was out with an injury. Anyway, the ball was drilled at third, and Jim stepped up and made a great play. He threw Stan out at home again! Stan steamed off the field for the second time. Two missed scores at home.

That was the kind of team we were. Our third-string guys were as good as many starters on other teams. Pee Wee was nursing an injury too—that was why Zimmer was playing.

Runners were at first and third, and Gene Green was back up to bat. First pitch, he grounded to shortstop, and it was an easy force out to second. The longest inning in my life was over. I was so happy to get off the field with only one run scored, and we were still up 3–2.

As if our team weren't banged up enough, Barnes hit Charlie Neal with a pitch to start off the bottom of the sixth. Charlie's wrist swelled up bad, so Pee Wee came into the game to pinch run and play for him. Barnes struck out Gilliam and then walked two of our guys, so the bases were loaded when I came up to bat. Barnes threw a strike that looked like a ball to me for the first pitch. Then he threw a fastball, and I swung way late and missed. I was down in the count, and then he finally threw a ball to make the count 1–2.

1958 LOS ANGELES DODGERS

Front Row left to right: Charlie Neal, Ed Roebuck, Don Demeter, Arnold Tesh, Batboy; Larry Sherry, Jackie Collum, Jim Gilliam.

Second Row: Charlie DiGiovanna, Equipment Mgr.; Dick Gray, Joe Pignatano, Pee Wee Reese, Joe Becker, Coach; Greg Mulleavy, Coach; Walt Alston, Manager; Charlie Dressen, Coach; Roger Craig, Carl Erskine, Gino Cimoli.

Third Row: John Griffin, Clubhouse Attendant; Lee Scott, Traveling Secretary; Randy Jackson, Elmer Valo, Norm Larker, Fred Kipp, John Roseboro, Ron Negray, Danny McDevitt, Duke Snider, Dr. Harold Wendler, Trainer.

Back Row: Carl Furillo, Sandy Koufax, Clem Labine, Don Zimmer, Al Walker, Coach; Gil Hodges, Don Newcombe, Johnny Podres, Don Bessent, Don Drysdale, Bill Buhler, Trainer.

The 1958 Dodgers were a team in transition. Besides changing cities, we lost Roy Campanella that year to his paralyzing car crash and Don Newcombe midseason.

It was so nerve wracking, standing there. One more strike, and I would have to take that long walk to the bench. The count was 1–2, and he threw another fastball. I swung and hit it late and fouled into the crowd. I had to hold my ground. I couldn't let a ball go by unless I knew it was a ball. The next pitch was an inside ball, evening the count out. Watching a pitch go by was a true test of patience and split-second judgment—hoping the ump agreed with what I saw. Another pitch and another ball made it a full count.

I knew Vin was up there saying, "Full count, bases loaded, bottom of the sixth." The pressure was on, and Barnes threw an inside pitch that looked like a ball to me. Ed Sudol didn't agree, though, and called that bloody third strike. There was no way that was a strike. It's always a game of inches, and I just got cut short. My batting average dropped to .500! I wished I could have repeated my first at bat and hit the first "Chinese Grand Slam" in the park. Not today.

Gino followed me with two outs and the bases loaded. He popped out to end the inning with no runs. I hated to leave three guys stranded on base. No one got a hit that inning, though, so it's not as if we were playing that great. It was a shame to let those chances go by, but we did our best.

In the seventh, I went back to the mound and took Ray Katt to a full count before he popped a foul ball up to Rube. Then I struck the next two out to end the inning. For our side, Norm Larker was up, and he got a quick single. Then Gil Hodges hit a double, and Norm scored to put us up 4–2 at the end of the seventh.

I went back on the mound to face the top of the order in the eighth. Blasingame started it off with a sharp one to Zimmer. Don made a bad throw for the first error of the game. Dark flied out to left, and then who came up but the guy who had already gotten three hits on me. Musial was up to his usual work of killing rookies like me. Life just wasn't fair when I had to face a guy like Stan over and over. He fouled the first one off and then singled to left field—a short blooper that sent Blasingame to third.

These images were taken with an eight-millimeter camera that Topps baseball cards gave me for taking my picture. My sidearm throws in the bottom right were used to confuse lefty batters.

Well, Walt had finally seen enough, and he walked out to me and said, "Good work, Kipp. Into your eighth inning for your first start. Why don't you have a seat on the bench and relax."

I nodded and walked off with my head held high. The crowd gave me a good cheer. With sixty thousand of 'em making noise, I felt it in my chest, and it warmed me. Back in Brooklyn, I'd seen many of our pitchers get booed off the mound after eight innings of hard work. Those Brooklyn fans were edgy and expected a lot more. LA was easy and carefree compared to them.

I felt good about my first start, and it was the most exhilarating experience of my twenty-six years. I'd played in a lot of games, but this was the first time I'd started in the big leagues. I had gone eight innings and given it all I had. I made it back to the bench, sat down, and let out a big sigh. The pressure was so intense and I was immersed in it so far that I didn't realize the magnitude of my effort. I like how Frank Finch of the *LA Times* wrote about my performance on the mound:

L.A. BEATS CARDS, 5–3, BEFORE 60,635
Los Angeles, CA, Frank Finch, *Los Angeles Times*, April 26, 1958
National Night Game Record Set; Musial Raps Out Four Hits

Fred Kipp, a lanky drink of water from Piqua, Kan, making his first major league start, subdued the Redbirds with some relief help from Fireman Ed Roebuck. The 26-year-old southpaw did it, moreover, with a patchwork line-up behind him.

Musial came to town owning a .500 batting average and boosted it to .553 with a double and three singles. Do your son and heir a favor and take him out to see this future hall-of-famer swing a bat.

Stan had worked me over, but he didn't get an RBI or a homer. He worked over everyone he faced at one time or another. The .553 batting average was the highest it would get in 1958. In other years, he would hit over .600 early in the season. He started many seasons off hot, and tonight was normal for him.

The pitching was in Ed Roebuck's hands now. Of course, he didn't walk into a good situation, like most relief situations. One out and runners on first and third. Ed gave up a sacrifice fly to Del Ennis, and Blasingame scored. Boyer was up next and grounded out to end the inning with the score at 3–4.

In the bottom of the eighth, Ed singled, and then Gino hit a double off the China Wall to score Ed. Two hits and scores by the Dodger pitchers ended up making the difference in the game. Ed did a good job and shut them down in the ninth, so we won the game 3–5, and I got my first win!

In summary of my first start, I threw five strikeouts and didn't give up a walk. Looking back, maybe I should have walked Stan a couple times. Without the walks, I gave up nine hits, including three doubles and a Eurasian homer. The high hit count was pretty painful, but my ERA was only 1.93. I was pleased with my control and felt I put up some pretty good pitches. Stan had my number for sure by going four for four, but I'll take the win every day of the week and twice on Sunday!

Fred Kipp's First Major Start Is a Winner — 5–3 Over Cardinals

Los Angeles CA, Ed Wilks, Associated Press, April 26, 1958
5–3 Over Cardinals, Before Record 60,000 at L.A.

The rookies are really giving those rookie crowds a treat in San Francisco and Los Angeles. At Los Angeles, Norm Larker drove in a pair of runs while rookie southpaw Fred Kipp won his first as a NL record night game crowd of 60,636 sat in on the Dodger's 5–3 victory over the Saint Louis Cardinals.

Kipp, who had a brief fling last year, also didn't walk a man, although he gave way to Ed Roebuck when the Cardinals scored an unearned run in the eighth that made it 4–3.

Highlights

- I'd gone coast to coast with the Dodgers and gotten my first start in the awkward LA Coliseum. The sixty thousand fans set a record for the largest night game in National League history.

- I gave up three runs and nine hits in seven and one-third innings to get the win over the St. Louis Cardinals.

- Despite Stan going four for four, our excellent fielding stopped the Man at home plate twice, and we won by two runs.

- In my first at bat in the Coliseum, I hit a double that was almost a Chinese home run, and I scored after a walk in the fifth inning.

- The Dodgers and I got the win from good offense and defense and scored five runs to the Cardinals' three.

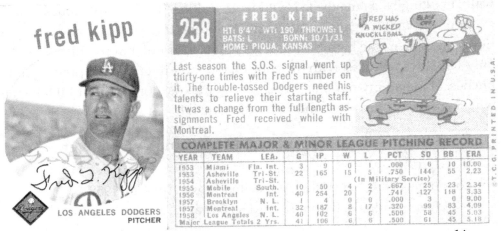

YEAR	TEAM	LEA.	G	IP	W	L	PCT	SO	BB	ERA
1953	Miami	Fla. Int.	3	9	0	1	.000	6	10	10.00
1953	Asheville	Tri-St.	22	165	15	5	.750	144	55	2.23
1954	Asheville	Tri-St.					(In Military Service)			
1955	Mobile	South.	10	50	4	2	.667	25	23	2.34
1956	Montreal	Int.	40	254	20	7	.741	127	148	3.33
1957	Brooklyn	N. L.	1	4	0	0	.000	3	0	9.00
1957	Montreal	Int.	32	187	8	17	.320	99	83	4.09
1958	Los Angeles	N. L.	40	102	6	6	.500	58	45	5.03
Major League Totals 2 Yrs.			41	106	6	6	.500	61	45	5.18

This is Topps #258 card released in 1959 for the 1958 season. I was never as big as the illustration on the back suggests, but I like that they called out my knuckleball.

2. FROM PIQUA TO SUPERIOR — 1931–53

I was born on a family farm near the small town of Piqua in southeastern Kansas during the Great Depression on October 1, 1931. I was the third and youngest child of Chuck and Ida Kipp, born two years after the stock market crash. In good times, Catholic families like mine have the usual six, eight, or ten children, but times were hard and less fruitful in that era. My family lived relatively well on a typical small farm, and we worked hard and didn't take anything for granted. Other future ballplayers grew up not far from where I lived. Mickey Mantle grew up about a hundred miles away and was born the same month I was. We both grew up in hard times, and our paths would eventually cross on the field as opponents and teammates.

Pre–World War II Kansas was a sedate place. My family never went hungry like other people of that era. We had a big garden, fruit trees, and livestock. Dinner was always running around in our backyard — chickens were right outside our porch, and pigs were in their sty. My mom made some mean fried chicken, and we regularly had veal steaks and thick beefsteaks. We'd slaughter a pig and roast pork and cure sausage in our basement. We had dairy cows, so my father got up early to feed and milk them. I helped do the chores every day, and there was always something to do. Farming was hard work, and I knew I didn't want to be a farmer.

My great-grandfather John Kipp was a blacksmith and wagonmaker, and he was born on the Isle of Rugen in Germany. He immigrated to the United States and had a son, John, who also became a blacksmith. My grandfather John started the small town of Piqua with a few other German immigrants in 1880. He moved from near Chicago to the rich farmland in the Neosho River valley near Iola, Kansas. My mother's side of the family, the Konens, came from

> Hall of Famer Red Schoendienst of the St. Louis Cardinals is my second cousin once removed. My great-grandfather John Herman Westerman is Red's great-great grandfather. Red was born in Germantown, Illinois, and my family would talk about his exploits on the field. I pitched to him once while he played for the Milwaukee Braves in 1958.

Germantown, Illinois, near Saint Louis in 1884. Farmland was getting scarce for their growing family in those parts, so they moved on to new lands.

Hall-of-Famers Stan Musial and Red Schoendienst were good friends and productive teammates who propelled the Cards to the 1946 World Series victory over the Red Sox. Red was my second cousin, and I faced him once while he was the second baseman for the Milwaukee Braves in 1958.

They took the train out to Piqua with a bag of cash to buy farmland. There weren't any banks then to transfer the money, so they pooled their money, and a few of my great uncles took a train with the cash in hand to buy their new home. The oral history said that the bag contained $37,000—about $1 million in 2016 money. They only bought a quarter section of land, or 160 acres, in a very remote area of Kansas, so I think it was $3,700. We didn't live high on the hog, but we ate well.

We didn't have indoor plumbing until I was a teenager. We had a wagon and a team of horses to get around the farm and a 1936 Chevy—not a coupe de ville. We bought our first tractor right before the war, but we still used a team of horses most of the time to save gas. We used the team of horses for light chores such as feeding the cows and getting supplies from town. We used the tractor for the hard work of plowing the fields or harvesting.

My mother, Ida, was a strong-willed woman, and she never moved out of the house where she was born in 1899. My brother, sister, and I were born right there as well. We lived directly across the street from St. Martins Catholic church. The steeple could be seen from miles around, and its shadow fell on our house at sunset. My mother was very protective of me and my siblings—especially my sister.

My sister, Donna, fell in love with Dick Riddle, a non-Catholic, and they knew my mother wouldn't accept that. They ended up eloping when Donna was nineteen. I never saw my mother as mad as when she found out about that. My father was hurt that she would do something like that without their consent. When they came home after a honeymoon in Arkansas a few days later, my mother took them across the street to have the marriage blessed in the Catholic church. Their marriage lasted for sixty-three years, and they raised a nice family.

Catholic nuns taught grade school in a two-room schoolhouse next to the church. About ten to twelve kids were in one room for first through fourth grades, and the other room held about the same number of kids from fifth through eighth grades. Woodson County took over the administration while I was there and began paying the nuns for teaching us. We would go to mass or be taught religion in the hour before school since the county wouldn't pay for that. When I graduated from grade school, we had to drive seven miles to Iola for high school.

On the left, I wore my work uniform on my first birthday. I was almost three when my family was in our Sunday best by our back porch. My mother, Ida, was born in this house in 1899, and I was born there too in 1931.

Since I was the youngest child, my mother adored me, and she was always my number-one fan. From an early age, she started collecting newspaper clippings about me and my family. By high school, I would get in the paper regularly for my baseball and basketball games, and she would clip the articles out and post them in a scrapbook. By the time I left high school, she already had a full photo album of clippings. She kept saving articles about me throughout my career. In the end, she had collected over a thousand articles and clippings about me.

I reviewed these articles to help me write this book, and I've worked with my son Scott to make the best ones available online at www.fredkipp.com/articles. I'm amazed at how much was written about me. My mom and the local newspaper—the *Iola Register*—had a network of people who would send in clippings from the places I played around the United States, Canada, and the Caribbean. Wherever I played, far-flung friends and family collected articles about me, and my mother saved them in an archive. I didn't read most of them back in the day, so it was really interesting to read many of them for the first time while writing this book. From regular op-ed pieces about my career to full-length articles, I was the Pride of Piqua—at least that was what they called me.

Growing up in small-town Piqua, we didn't have much to do except work, play sports, and shoot the breeze. We didn't have video games, computers, TVs, or even a radio when I grew up. It wasn't until I was twelve that we got a radio, and we could only tune in a couple of stations. That left us kids with few options for what to do in the afternoons — cause trouble and drive my parents crazy or play sports. I mainly played sports.

In the summer, we'd play baseball. In the winter, we'd play basketball. I remember my first glove was a Lonny Frey edition, and I wore it out. We played everywhere — in the field, in barns, and in the gravel streets downtown. I always went to the earliest morning mass in the summer so that I'd have more time to play baseball. Most afternoons in the summer, we'd gather downtown and commandeer a side street and hit a rubber ball around. We broke some windows, though, so they sent us out to a field. On rainy days, we'd go play in the boxcars that were left on the tracks behind the house and bounce the ball around in there. We spent our childhood days like most kids — hitting and throwing balls.

As I got older, we played in the field next to the church. During summer, the men of the town scraped an infield out of a pasture, and eventually we put up a backstop. We played most evenings in the summer until it got dark. After World War II, we led a drive to raise money to light the baseball field so that we could play after dark on special nights. Playing baseball on warm summer evenings was splendid.

I liked to pitch, and my catcher was my cousin Archie Specht. Archie lived down the street about two hundred yards, and we'd finish our chores and go play catch and practice almost every day. He might have been only 140 pounds by the time we graduated high school, but he had great hands and could have easily played in the minor leagues with me. He helped me grow into a good pitcher. We played great together for the Piqua town team.

The relationship between the pitcher and catcher is a special one, and I don't think catchers get enough credit. A good catcher is like a secret weapon or inside man who gets a unique and close-up perspective on the batter. No one gets closer to the batter than the catcher, and they can feel what the batter is up to and sometimes even smell them. Where are they standing in the batter's box? How are they holding the bat? Are they having trouble swinging low? Are they crowding the plate? What did they eat for lunch?

The catcher called the pitch, and I agreed with the call or not. I always got along well with my catchers, and I played with some of the best over a long career, outlined in the summary table below. I worked with all of them to get batters out and keep our team on the winning side. If I got them out, I got to stay in the game. I owe a lot of credit for my success to these catchers.

Great Catchers I Played With

Name	Year	Team
Archie Specht	1947–49	Piqua
Earl Woods	1949	Kansas State College
Joe Pignatano	1953	Asheville Tourists
John Roseboro	1956–57	Montreal Royals
Roy Campanella	1956–57	Japan and Brooklyn Dodgers
Joe Pignatano	1957	Montreal Royals
Rube Walker	1958	Los Angeles Dodgers
John Roseboro	1958–59	Los Angeles Dodgers
Joe Pignatano	1958–59	Los Angeles Dodgers
Yogi Berra	1960	New York Yankees
Elston Howard	1960	New York Yankees
Billy Shantz	1960–62	Richmond Virginians

One Christmas during World War II, my mother bought me the book *How to Pitch Baseball*, by Lew Fonseca. It was the best gift I ever got. I read the whole book Christmas Day, and I read it many times after that. The book showed me how to throw curves — sidearm, underhand, and overhand — and the fastball. Fonseca also wrote about change-of-speed pitching, and I really liked that. After I read the book on that Christmas Day, Archie came over and pitched in the barn to stay warm. I worked on my changeup and different delivery techniques as described in the book. Come spring, I was throwing some pretty good curve balls, and my fastball was getting faster.

One source of frustration from Lew's book was that he left out advanced pitches such as the curve ball and knuckleball. The book showed a picture of how to hold a knuckleball but said that knuckleballs should be left for "the more experienced pitcher." I wanted to be that experienced pitcher, and it made me more curious about "advanced pitches." I talked to other pitchers about how to throw them and read articles about the odd pitches. I was looking for anything to keep me ahead of the batters, who were often twice my age when we played teams from other nearby towns.

I searched the Internet for YouTube videos on how to grip and throw the ball. OK, I made that up. Ha! Ha! I just kept throwing the ball to Archie, and we figured out how to do it. He'd tell me whether it broke well and whether it was a strike. Pretty soon, I could get the ball to move pretty well, and we worked on my repertoire of pitches until I was feeling good about my game.

We didn't have a town baseball team during World War II because most of the men were away fighting. That all changed after the war ended in 1945. By the spring of 1946, I was fourteen and started pitching on our town team. By '48, I was the main pitcher on the team, and I liked making those thirty-year-old farmers swing at air. Archie and I were the youngest on the team, and we were right in the middle of the game. We'd drive to nearby towns such as Chanute, Bronson, Burlington, and Iola on Sunday afternoons after church. We played the other town teams and mainly played for bragging rights.

I started getting known as the "young gun" for striking out full-grown men and throwing shutouts. I had a lot of fun playing with my brother, Tom; my cousins; and my friend Mo Riley on the Piqua team. By the time I was sixteen and a junior in high school, I was being asked to play for the Burlington, Kansas, town team for twenty-five dollars a game. That was pretty good money for a game in '47, but it would make me ineligible for high school sports. I wanted to play basketball, and I hoped that would be my ticket to college. I should have worked something out like having the team donate the money to the town team, but I didn't think of that at the time. I stuck with the town baseball team throughout high school.

I was very competitive, and I think that was the root of my success. We didn't have coaches or anyone who could instruct me, but I was driven to get the batter out. I usually found a way to get guys out, and that was my goal. If I couldn't do that, then I'd try to keep them on the bases. I'd watch the batters and remember what pitches they had trouble with and which ones they were swatting at like flies. I kept working on new pitches with Archie, and we had a great thing going. We would always smile at each other when the batters walked back to the bench after a strikeout.

I tried to keep pitching simply—high and tight or low and away. High and tight would jam the batter up so that he couldn't get any power. Low and away would make him reach down for it and rob him of power unless he could pull it down the line. I learned a lot in those days from just playing hour after hour. One weekend, I hitchhiked to Cassville, Missouri, about four hours away, for a scouting tryout with the New York Giants. The scout wanted to sign me. I considered it, but college was more in my plans.

I put myself through college on my basketball scholarship and was the captain of the team during my junior and senior years at Iola High School and Emporia Teachers College, which turned into Emporia State.

While baseball was a great sport when school was out, basketball was the sport I excelled at in high school. I was too skinny for football and didn't want to get hurt on the gridiron. I focused on basketball and played after school each day. My sophomore year, I played on the Iola High basketball team with Archie and Herb Trout. Iola High didn't have a baseball team.

I lettered in basketball three years and was the captain of the team on occasion in my junior and senior years. Probably because of my basketball prowess, I was elected vice president of our class too, but I didn't care too much about that. I was all about sports. I helped lead the Iola basketball team to a victory in the Southeast Kansas League championship and took third in the Class A State Tournament in the spring of 1949. Life was good.

I guess word got around about my basketball skills, and I started getting recruited. The first recruiter who showed interest was Tex Winter, who eventually became Phil Jackson's right-hand man through all of those championships with the Chicago Bulls and then the Los Angeles Lakers. Tex was a big innovator of the triangle offense and later taught the techniques to Michael Jordan, Scottie Pippen, Shaquille O'Neal, and Kobe Bryant—to name a few. In the fifties and sixties, Tex was known for leading the KSU Wildcats to two Final Four games. That wasn't easy to do with the small budgets of KSU.

Tex was the freshman coach from Kansas State College, which would eventually become Kansas State University (KSU), so I'll call it KSU for convenience. KSU had a solid Division I basketball team at the time and regularly beat Kansas University (KU) in the 1940s. These two teams played the Sunflower Showdown for bragging rights, and both were top-ranked national teams in the Big 7 Conference, which later become the Big 8 and Big 12.

Kansas had a rich basketball tradition all the way back to James Naismith, the founder of basketball. Naismith was the coach at KU at the turn of the century. One of Naismith's students, Dr. Forrest "Phog" Allen (the namesake for Allen Fieldhouse), was coaching at KU at the time. KSU was in their golden era of basketball when I was growing up because of their Hall of Fame coach Jack Gardner. K-State had gotten to the Final Four in 1948 and ended up losing to Kentucky in the national championship game in 1951. The KU-KSU basketball rivalry peaked in the 1950s, and I wanted to be a part of it.

My cousin Hank Specht told the KSU coaches about me, and Tex Winter came calling to our little farmhouse in Piqua that summer of '49. My mother served her famous fried chicken to Tex on our screened-in porch. Tex and Hank were there to persuade me to join them at KSU.

Anyway, Tex was an impressive man—even in those days—and did most of the recruiting. Hank and Tex pushed me pretty hard to sign, but I was troubled about not being able to play baseball if I went to KSU. The local newspaper, the *Iola Register*, even wrote about my decision:

Kipp Chooses

Kipp has been wavering between several colleges, as against a baseball career. The fact that his close Piqua friend, Hank Specht, is at K-State may have been the chief influence in his selection of Manhattan. Freddie, 6'4," should be able to make any basketball squad.

Now or Later

His problem has been whether to throw in with baseball right away. He probably could sign with about any of the farm systems after a lookover. The New York Giants were ready to give him a contract among a very few picked out of a recent try-out camp in Missouri two weeks ago.

Kipp can pitch and play first base. He could have joined up with organized baseball and played basketball in the Central conference. Instead, he has chosen K-State—and no baseball temporarily—at the behest of his family.

Fred figures that in another year he could change his mind, maybe give up basketball and go into baseball, or change schools and go into baseball. The latter is quite unlikely, it can be assumed. Meanwhile, he could develop in college baseball.

I moved up to Manhattan (that's Manhattan, Kansas) in the fall of '49 and settled into the Phi Kappa fraternity, but I was still uncertain of my decision. When I got there, things just didn't feel right. While Manhattan was a nice city of about nineteen thousand, the campus had about six thousand students, and it was overwhelming. I didn't fit in well, and I just felt as if I was in the wrong place, since I couldn't play baseball while on a basketball scholarship.

I did some soul searching in Manhattan and knew that I wanted to play baseball. Some afternoons, I would go over to the baseball fields and pitch to Earl Woods—Tiger's father. Earl had grown up in Manhattan and was a good catcher. I'll always remember him saying, "Hot damn! That's the best goddamn knuckleball I've ever seen. Hoo wee!" I liked hearing that, and I liked playing baseball. I knew KSU wasn't going to work out for me if I couldn't play baseball.

After some senseless hazing in the fraternity, I started looking to move on in the new year. I made a call to the New York Giants scout who had been recruiting me, but I couldn't reach him. I later found out that he had left the Giants. I also put feelers out to Emporia Teachers College, which would eventually become Emporia State University. Emporia was a smaller school of about fifteen hundred students, and the basketball coach, Gus Fish, worked out a full-ride scholarship for me if I played baseball and basketball. I switched over to Emporia in the new year and the new decade—1950.

Emporia was a nice little quiet town of about fifteen thousand people and was closer to my hometown. My parents liked that because they could come and see me play. Instead of playing on the freshman basketball team at KSU, I got to play a little on the varsity basketball team my freshman year. Since KSU was in the NCAA, freshmen weren't allowed to play on the varsity team. More importantly, I'd be able to pitch baseball as soon as the basketball season ended.

Playing baseball turned out to be a good decision. I got to pitch right away, and I'd play first base when I wasn't pitching. I got a lot of playing time and got to work on my hitting. I hit .356 that first year and was pitching well. We only had a sixteen-game season, and on the last game of the year, I got to start against Washburn University. I threw a no-hitter and struck out fourteen—over half of the batters. Here's what the papers said:

Kipp Throw No-Hitter at Ichs in Last Contest

Kipp's performance was a masterpiece of pitching as he gave up only one walk, saw two runners reach first base on errors and he struck out 14 (Washburn) Ichabod batters. He finished strong, getting Russell Moody, Bill Ransom and Ike Crabaugh, the first three batters in the lineup, on strikeouts in the ninth to insure finishing up with his no-hit job.

The no-hitter basically made me at Emporia. Everyone congratulated me, and a couple weeks later, I was playing on the semipro Emporia city team. The Emporia Rangers were the local town team, and we played other teams from larger towns and cities such as Fort Riley, Wichita, Topeka, and Coleman. We even played the Kansas City Monarchs. I hurled the first game and pitched well. I won quite a few games and would usually strike out ten or more players and give up five or six hits. In the state tournament, I pitched the win and set a tournament record by hitting five batters. Not that proud of that stat, but sometimes I was wild.

The 1950–1951 academic year went fast, and I lettered in basketball and baseball and played well. In the summer of '51, I played for the Chamberlain Chiefs up in South Dakota. I bagged groceries during the day and played baseball at night against other local teams and some traveling teams. I was able to save enough money that summer to buy a one-year-old Buick for $1,500 and drive it home at the end of the season. They paid me $300 a month to play ball, and I made about half as much bagging groceries. In one game, I faced the Cuban Stars, a traveling all-star team, and they beat me up pretty good by scoring nine runs on twelve hits. We didn't believe much in relievers in those days, and I just kept pitching. I was 8–7 for the summer and again played first base when I wasn't pitching.

In the spring of '52, I pitched a one-hitter at Emporia and played for the Superior Knights in the Nebraska Independent League during the summer. One of the other players in the league was Russ Snyder, the future Yankee. He was only eighteen, but I could see he was gifted and could hit really well. He ended up playing for quite a few major-league teams and almost had a thousand hits in the majors. I pitched a lot of games that summer, but there was nothing much to speak about until I hurt my knee toward the end of the season.

I was pitching well in a game in Kearney, and we knew that a scout was in the stands. I went up to bat and swung at a pitch, and my knee locked up. A lightning bolt of pain went up my leg, and I couldn't move my darn knee. It wouldn't move until the next day when they gave me some ether in a hospital in Superior. The ether was strong and opened my mind and my knee. I ended up having surgery in St. Elizabeth's Hospital in Lincoln, where Dr. Farcot removed some cartilage on the outside of my knee. I did some rehabilitation work to strengthen my quadriceps to compensate and wore a small knee brace through the rest of my career. My knee never affected my play and would be the only significant injury of my career.

My knee healed well, and I was back in time for the basketball season. I averaged about twenty points for the basketball team and was the captain. Because so few children were born in rural Kansas during the Depression and because the Korean War was going on, the student population dropped at Emporia to below a thousand students in 1952. Many activities dried up, and they canceled the baseball team in '53 from lack of new players. It didn't bother me very much, though, because I got a letter from the Dodgers to try out for their team at Vero Beach.

The effect of Jackie Robinson breaking into the majors had repercussions throughout the baseball world. Here was a promotional picture with the Nebraska Superior Knights crossing over the racial divide in 1952.

Highlights

- I was born on a small farm in Piqua, Kansas, during the Depression, and we didn't have running water until I was in high school.

- I started pitching for the town baseball team when I was a teenager and excelled in basketball.

- Tex Winters recruited me to play basketball for Kansas State University. But they wouldn't let me play baseball, so I transferred to Emporia State, where I could play two sports and get a degree in education.

- I pitched a no-hitter against Washburn and played summer leagues in the Great Plains and was recruited to Dodgertown.

3. TO VERO BEACH — 1953

How I got the letter to go to Dodgertown is a typical small-town Kansas story. The Kansas sporting world was rather small back in the early 1950s, and word got around pretty quick. We didn't have Twitter or the Internet, but the grapevine worked well. The connection to the Dodgers went back to my no-hitter at Washburn. The Washburn Ichabod baseball coach Marion McDonald turned out to be a bird dog for Burt Wells, a Dodger scout for the Midwest.

McDonald was also the assistant basketball coach for Washburn, so I faced Marion quite a bit on the basketball court over the years. Besides my no-hitter against his team in Topeka, Coach McDonald saw me on the basketball court as the captain of the Emporia Hornets. He saw that I was a good competitor, so Marion recommended me to Burt and got a signing bonus for getting me to Dodgertown.

I was in my senior year in college and didn't have much time to take a forty-hour train ride to Florida to try out for the Dodgers. We did have an Easter break for a few days, and if I missed a couple days of school, I could leave on a Friday and get there Sunday. I could play six days and get back to school in about ten days. I had to give it the old college try to play with the Dodgers. This was 1953, and the Dodgers had been in three of the last five World Series but had lost them all to the Yankees. This was the team of Jackie Robinson, Pee Wee Reese, Gil Hodges, and Duke Snyder, to name a few. I thought for sure I'd get to see them, so it was worth the trip just for that. My friends and I were so excited that I had to find a way to get there.

The Dodgers sent a set of train tickets, and I was off. Emporia was on a main line of the Atchison, Topeka, Santa Fe line, and it took me straight to Kansas City. I hadn't been to Kansas City on the train before, and Union Station was teeming with people. Union Station was a grand train station and was built in 1914, when train travel was expected to be the future of transportation. Union Station was notorious for the Kansas City Massacre, when four unarmed FBI agents were gunned down in 1933 by Pretty Boy Floyd and other gangsters. Union Station is still an icon of Kansas City and was the location of the huge celebration for the Royals' World Series victory in 2015.

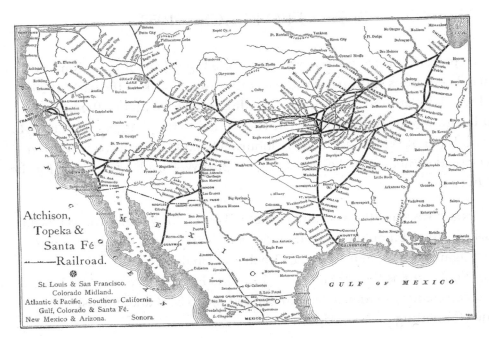

The railroads were the main way to get between cities in the early 1950s. Interstate highways didn't exist yet, and air travel was prohibitively expensive. I took the Santa Fe train from Emporia to Kansas City, where I transferred onto the Southern Railway.

Train travel was very popular in the early fifties because construction of the interstate highway system wouldn't start until 1956. Most people didn't fly or drive long distances yet, so trains were the way to get around back then. This was a long time before Amtrak, which started in 1971, and the nation was made up of a patchwork of railways. I had to change railways several times to get from central Kansas to southern Florida. In Kansas City, I changed to Southern Railways and went south through Kansas, Missouri, Arkansas, and finally to Memphis, Tennessee. I remember crossing over the Mississippi River for the first time, and I started noticing people talking funny with their southern accents.

I remember having dinner with a couple from the South in the dining car. "Ware ya goin', young maiyan?" asked the gentleman. When I told him the Dodgers' spring training, his eyes lit up, and he said he was a Dodger fan. He started talking about the World Series losses and his favorite players. We talked for a couple hours, and I felt the world was opening up to me. It was a special time, and my eyes were wide open, and I was taking it all in.

I changed trains again in Memphis that night and got on a sleeper that went through Birmingham and on to Atlanta. I didn't sleep well because I was so excited. I watched the small towns and farms and thought the tryouts were my job interview, because I hadn't been looking for any other work since I had gotten the invitation to Dodgertown.

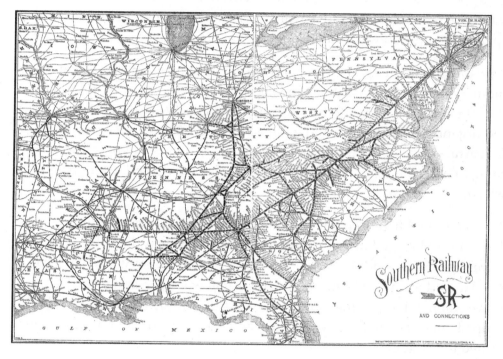

From Kansas City, I traveled to Memphis and on to Birmingham and Atlanta. In Atlanta, I transferred to the Ponce de Leon train to Jacksonville, where I changed trains again and went to Vero Beach.

I changed trains again in Atlanta in the morning and got on the Ponce de Leon train, which took me over to Jacksonville, Florida. In Jacksonville, I got on one of the many East Coast lines that were popular. The Eastern Seaboard was covered by trains that went down the coast from Boston to Miami. After about forty hours of train travel, I finally arrived in Vero Beach at about four in the morning. I'd left the day before at noon and arrived in the middle of the night. I didn't sleep that much on the train either, because I didn't want to miss my stop. I was exhausted.

I got off the train, and a dozen other young men like me got off too. We all kind of looked at one another and realized that we were all going to Dodgertown. Someone said a Dodger bus would come around for us in front of the station. We paraded through the little station and hadn't been there but a few minutes when an old blue bus pulled up that had "Dodgers" painted in white across the side. We all got on and didn't say much. I was dog tired. The town was dead quiet, and the night was cool — probably in the upper forties or low fifties. We didn't drive more than five minutes before we pulled into the old Naval Air Station, with rows of buildings lined up. A sign at the entrance said Dodgertown. I had arrived.

A predawn calm hung in the air, and we got off the bus and looked at one another. The bus driver got out and showed us to the barracks. They put four of us in one room with two sets of bunk beds. We each went to our beds and organized our luggage and got ready for bed. The temperature inside the barracks was about the same temperature as outside. I knew it was going to be a cold night. I brushed my teeth, lay down, and instantly fell asleep.

It seemed as if I had been out only for a minute when a knock came on the door. A middle-aged man let himself in and said he was the scout in charge of free agents. He said we each needed to report to the front desk by 8:00 a.m. He said it was 7:00 a.m. and the mess hall was open and we could eat all we wanted. His parting words were "It's time for Dodger baseball!" I jumped out of bed with the other guys and shook off the cold. We were all excited to get going.

I started talking to one of my bunkmates, who was only nineteen years old. His name was Lonny, and he had played shortstop for some town teams up in Ohio. He'd been here last year and knew his way around more than the rest of us. He led us to the mess hall and showed us around. I was shocked to see hundreds and hundreds of men eating in the mess hall. He pointed out some minor-league players and guessed that the Brooklyn Dodgers had already taken off for some exhibition games in Miami. I guessed I wouldn't be eating with the stars that day.

Everyone was chatting and saying hi to one another. It seemed like a reunion of sorts, with players asking, "How you doin'? Where you been?

How's your shoulder?" As we waited in line, Lonny told me that the men in suits at the far tables were the executives and that the pudgy guy with the round glasses and greased-back hair was the owner—Walter O'Malley. There was another table of managers and scouts and another table of newspaper reporters and administrators. I was looking right and left and taking in the excitement of the room.

We got our eggs, ham, toast, hash browns, and coffee and sat down at a long table with other players. People were coming and going, and knives and forks and cups were banging off the tables. The whole place was very dynamic. Lonny told me what to expect. He said, "They'll check us in and assign us to a field. Then we'll play a game in the morning and a game in the afternoon. Free agents like us will be assigned to a minor-league team for the day. Depending on how you do, you'll move up or down or out."

After breakfast, we went to the front desk, and they sent us to the Free Agent desk to get uniforms. They sent us to the supply room, and they weighed us and measured us and gave us a white hat and our special jerseys. These special jerseys had eight-inch-tall red *FA* letters on the front and back. These big red letters marked us as outsiders. There wasn't a Dodgers logo or anything else on the jerseys. We weren't Dodgers yet.

Lonny and I went back to our room and changed into our uniforms and spiked cleats. We got our gloves and went over to the four back-to-back fields. We were easy to spot with the jerseys, and I felt like a prisoner walking out onto the fields. They might as well have put us in orange jumpsuits. We went to the check-in booth, and they assigned me to the Santa Barbara Dodgers on field 4. I had a game against the Great Fall Electrics— both Class C teams in the Dodger organization. Lonny went to field 3, where two Class D ball teams were playing. I told him good luck, and we were off.

I walked to field 4, and the game was already going. I walked up to the coach for the SB Dodgers, and he said, "Kipp—from Kansas, yeah? We'll have you pitch in innings seven through nine. Be ready. This is the third inning." It was about ten in the morning, and I had probably an hour to wait, so I watched the game for a while. The players seemed pretty good, a little better than I was used to in college or the summer leagues.

I noticed some scouts, managers, and assistant managers with clipboards sitting in the bleachers behind home plate. They were taking notes on each of the players and talking among themselves with an eye on the game. If someone got a hit or a strikeout or made an error, they'd write it down. There were quite a few errors too, and some guys got called off the field. These scorned players usually had that *FA* on their shirts. The coaches had many sheets of paper, and I later found out that each coach had a sheet for each player and that they created a dossier on each player.

I went into the bull pen outside left field and saw some of the pitchers warming up. I warmed up, and pretty soon I was on the mound. I remember throwing well and getting a few strikeouts with some changeup pitches and my knuckleball. One guy hit a single off me, and another got on base with an error, but nobody scored. In the afternoon, I went with the Santa Barbara Dodgers to play the Asheville Tourists, a Class B team. I pitched innings four and five in that game and didn't do quite so well pitching, but I got a double at bat when everyone else on our team seemed to be striking out.

That night, I went back to the room and met up with Lonny. He said he had played horribly that day and struck out three out of five times at bat and made two errors. He was down on his luck. I was glad to get the *FA* shirt off. I was anonymous now among the other players. We ate dinner and hung out, looking for some minor-league stars.

Many of the players stayed in the mess hall after dinner and broke into groups. Some played cards, while others talked about the horses at the race track. Some tables just told stories and drank coffee. I heard basketball outside. I guessed it was like an adult summer camp that I'd never attended. I was still exhausted from the long train trip and went to bed early.

The next day, they must have liked what they'd seen, because they promoted me to play with the Asheville Tourists—a Class B team. I was going to pitch innings four through six in the morning game again, and I went out to the bull pen early to meet the pitchers. That was where I met Joe Pignatano, whom I'd play with on and off for about the next seven years. Joe reminded me of Archie Specht and had great hands and could hit. He had a good arm and good legs. We played the Miami Sunsox in the morning and the Newport News Dodgers in the afternoon. Again, I felt pretty good about how I played.

When I went back to the room, Lonny was packing his bag. He explained that he wasn't playing well, and they had given him the pink slip. He said he'd catch the night train back to Ohio that night and would probably play in some town teams again. We ate dinner together, and then he was gone. I never saw him again.

The next morning, I needed to attend a meeting with a room full of minor-league players. Coaches got up and talked about being a Dodger and playing the best we could. Other managers spoke too, but the one I distinctly remember and whose words I took to heart was Tommy Holmes. Tommy was a Brooklyn native and Boston Braves All Star. He had one of the best all-time strikeout-to-at-bat ratios. He spoke with a thick New York accent and got his point across clearly. He had coached with the Dodgers and Braves for thirty years, and he was later the director for amateur baseball relations for the New York Mets.

Tommy said, "You need to be ready to play at any time. You might only get one chance to play, and you better be ready. If you aren't physically fit, or if you're injured or hung over from chasing tail all night, you might miss your chance. Get your sleep. Stretch. Run. Warm up and be ready! That's what we need from you—365 days a year—even when you're not playing baseball."

Tommy's no-nonsense advice made sense to me. I had always been a pretty straight arrow, and his words just solidified what I already thought. After his words of wisdom, I got my sleep every night. I have been an early riser my whole life, so I was usually the first on the field in the morning. I'd stretch and jog and be mentally ready when the other players arrived. After living his advice, I never missed a game due to injury or illness. I was ready, and my arm or body never kept me from pitching for the next ten years.

I pitched again with the Asheville Tourists and started eating meals with Joe Pignatano. Joe told me how he had been around a few years already and had just gotten out of the army. From 1948 through 1950, he'd played on three class D teams in the Dodger organization and got drafted in '51. I told him how I was expecting to be drafted too but had stayed out by passing a test to become an officer and an Air Force pilot. After I graduated, I was fair game for the military and would probably be drafted that fall. He showed me around Dodgertown, and I got to know some of the other Tourists, such as Ray Hathaway and Harry Shiflett.

Joe and I talked about the advantages of playing baseball right out of high school or going to college, as I had done. I was the exception to the rule, as most players didn't graduate college. Joe lamented that he didn't have a college education, but I countered that he got to play baseball and was working his way up the ladder from Class D to probably Class B this year. We talked about whether I should have gone with the Giants back in '48, but it was all speculation now.

The next day, I switched to the Miami Sunsox and played against the Mobile Bears, a Class AA team. The Bears worked me over pretty good and scored a couple of runs in two innings. I was starting to see the distinctions between the classes and to understand the system of farm teams. The table below shows how there were seventeen teams in the Dodger organization in 1953. With twenty-five or more players on each team and the free agents like me, over five hundred players went through Dodgertown every year.

The next couple of days passed in a similar fashion, and I felt pretty good about being a class B player. I was throwing shutouts against the Class C and D teams and could hold my own in Class B. I ran into trouble against the Class A and AA teams. That was my opinion, though, and that wasn't worth much. What mattered was what the coaches thought and whether one of them would sign up to take me on for the year. My time at Dodgertown was running out, and I needed to get on a team and go back to Emporia to finish my classes and graduate.

I was leaving on Friday afternoon and went to the free-agent desk on Friday morning. The scout in charge of free agents, John Carey, met me in the lobby and sat me down. He asked me how the week had been. After some casual talk, he asked me if I'd like to join the Miami Sunsox! I about jumped right out of my seat!

I was smiling ear to ear, and this guy knew that I was going to be an easy sell. I basically lost all of my bargaining power for any negotiation that year. John got me to sign for $500 right away. I'd get another $1,500 after ninety days if I stayed on any club and $200 a month after that. He had barely pulled out the pen when I signed on the dotted line. I was now property of the Dodgers.

1953 Dodger Teams

Level	City	State	League
MLB	Brooklyn Dodgers	New York	National League
AAA	Montreal Royals	Quebec	International League
AAA	Saint Paul Saints	Minnesota	American Association
AA	Fort Worth Cats	Texas	Texas League
AA	Mobile Bears	Alabama	Southern Association
A	Pueblo Dodgers	Colorado	Western League
A	Elmira Pioneers	New York	Eastern League
B	Newport News Dodgers	Virginia	Piedmont League
B	Miami Sunsox	Florida	Florida International League
B	Asheville Tourists	North Carolina	Tri-State League
C	Great Falls Electrics	Montana	Pioneer League
C	Santa Barbara Dodgers	California	California League
D	Thomasville Dodgers	Georgia	Georgia-Florida League
D	Shawnee Hawks	Oklahoma	Sooner State League
D	Sheboygan Indians	Wisconsin	Wisconsin State League
D	Hornell Dodgers	New York	Pennsylvania-Ontario-New York League
D	Union City Dodgers	Tennessee	Kentucky-Illinois-Tennessee League

Highlights

- I took forty hours of trains to get from Emporia to Vero Beach and was one of seven hundred players trying to get onto one the seventeen teams in the Dodger organization.

- I was a free agent and had to wear a big red *FA* on my jersey.

- I pitched well enough to get signed with the Miami Sunsox in the Florida International League.

4. FROM MIAMI TO MOBILE AND THE ARMY, 1953–55

Happy to be a Dodger, I took the nice long train ride back to Emporia. These long trips were a foreshadowing of my extensive travels to come in the minor leagues, winter leagues, Japan, and the big leagues. I finished my classes and graduated in May with a degree in education. The season had started, so I rushed down to Miami to play for the Sunsox. The Sunsox were in the Florida International League, but it was mainly an intrastate league with four other teams from Florida and the Havana Cubans.

I didn't pitch very well at all with Miami. It's hard for me to say why I pitched poorly with one team and then well with another. In the month I was a Sunsox, I threw for nine innings and gave up eleven hits and nine runs, giving myself a double-digit ERA! I remember pitching well in West Palm Beach one night, but I didn't do well in the other games. It was ugly, and I started wondering what I'd gotten into. I relieved in three games and didn't get to start, so relieving kind of sets the stage for failure. Relievers at that time always went in with multiple runners on base and when the momentum was against them. Relieving was in desperation in those days, and managers would try to pitch a pitcher till he "was dying out there" before they would bring in a reliever with the deck stacked.

I don't remember many particulars about Miami from the little time I was there, but the heat was already bothering me, and it was only May. The temperature was in the upper eighties or low nineties, with high humidity. The humidity probably took some off my knuckleball and other breaking pitches, but I'm not blaming my slump on that. I just couldn't find my pitching in Miami.

When the team was getting ready to drive to Tampa for a week of games, Bill Herring, the coach of the Sunsox, told me I wasn't going to be making the trip with the team. He said the head office would be contacting me and that I'd probably be heading to the Asheville Tourists—another B-league team—or the class C Santa Barbara Dodgers. I was getting pushed out after a month and possibly demoted. Bill wished me luck and said he had to go because Hurricane Alice was blowing in.

I went back up to my room and looked out the window and saw my teammates getting on the bus as the storm front moved in. The sky blackened, and palm trees were blowing around violently in the gusty winds. As the first few drops of rain splatted on the window, I heard the bus pull away and watched my ex-teammates ride the storm out. I was left alone in Miami with Hurricane Alice.

The deluge hit soon after they left, and it did not stop. I was stuck in my room all day waiting for my orders, which seemed as if they would never come. The winds picked up to gale force toward dusk, and I'd never been in a hurricane before. The rains didn't come down; they came sideways. As the windows shook and the rain pounded down, I started to wonder if I was cut out for baseball. Could I pitch at this level? Did I want to be a minor-league ballplayer and make less money than I could doing about anything else, such as teaching?

I was sequestered in my room and had nothing to do and no one to do it with. I went away from the window and found a Gideon Bible in the desk drawer. I found comfort in the Bible for a few hours, but night came, and the power went out. I went back to the window and watched the palm trees blowing violently in the wind. All night, the winds and rain lashed the windows so relentlessly that I couldn't sleep. In the morning, the streets were swamped, and no cars were out. I couldn't make any phone calls and probably couldn't afford it anyway. Nothing was moving—especially me. I can look back now and see that the storm had brought me to my dark night of the soul.

Were even the minor leagues a dream that I wouldn't achieve? Should I move back to the farm? Did I want to live the life of traveling from town to town for years on end? Did I want to be a pawn whose future depended on the whims of coaches, general managers, and owners?

Alice raged through the next two days, and I was stuck. I couldn't have gotten out if I had had my orders. I talked to the desk clerk, and word was that several people had died in Cuba in drought-breaking flooding. Lake Placid, Florida, had gotten over thirteen inches of rain. When the skies finally cleared, I got through my dark night and decided that I was going to do whatever it took to play baseball. If I didn't make it to the big leagues, that would be fine, but I was going to give it all I had and some more. I had been given a great opportunity, and I would go for it. As the saying goes, when you ain't got nothing, you ain't got nothing to lose!

The next day, my orders came through—I was going to Asheville! I was taking a lateral move to another level B league in the cool mountain air of Asheville, at about two thousand feet. Everything got better as soon as I became a Tourist. First, I rented a room in a large house with five other Tourists, including Joe Pignatano and Jasper Spears. The house was in a great location—two blocks from downtown and two blocks from the ballpark. We walked everywhere, and I always had someone to do something with—especially Joe.

The small town of Asheville and the small Tri-State League suited me well. I learned a lot that year and got to face some good competition.

Asheville was a beautiful summer vacation spot in the Blue Ridge Mountains where people came to escape the heat. This was before most people had air conditioning. The crowds of tourists who came to see us were real fun, and we had regular fans — occasionally including Reverend Billy Graham.

What I remember most about my new home in Asheville is how my pitches seemed to improve almost instantly. Instead of the hot and humid air of Florida, I was pitching in the cool mountain air of Asheville. Joe would call my knuckleball, and it was the right pitch. I flummoxed the batters, and I started winning. I won the first three games I started, and I soon became a favorite of our coach Ray Hathaway. I found my game in Asheville.

Here's what the *Asheville Times* said:

Southpaw Retires 19 Batters in Order, Belts 3 Safeties

Tourist fans have a new hero in Fred Kipp, the angular southpaw who has won three games in his first nine days as an Asheville performer. Kipp threw a two-hitter at the Rock Hill Chiefs here last night and got more than ample batting support from his teammates to win 15–0.

Only 32 Chiefs, 5 above the minimum, came to bat as Kipp fanned five, walked one and hit one batsman. During the momentous seventh, the Tourists got six hits, including a triple and single by Kipp and a triple by Gene Castiglione.

I didn't make it to Asheville until June 15, and I still started 20 games in a 134-game season. When I got there, our club was in fifth place out of six teams in the Tri-State League. "Tri-State" was a misnomer that year because we only played in the Carolinas. In some years, the Knoxville Smokies played in the league, and that was how the league had gotten its name. The map below shows how the Tourists played in a relatively small geographic area. We'd stay in one hotel while we played games in Charlotte, Gastonia, and Rock Hill. That made our travel schedule pretty light. Small things like a light travel schedule make a big difference over a season.

The Tri-State League was in the heart of the Carolinas and had some hokey aspects to it. The league didn't follow the norm, and the Anderson Rebels played "Dixie" at the start of each game instead of "The Star-Spangled Banner." Some of the fields didn't even have outfield fences! One time in Rock Hill, Joe P. hit a line drive that got through the outfield, and they had to chase it way back into this overgrown field. Joe was rounding third and on his way home before they even found the ball. Our home field in Asheville had a ten-degree uphill slope in right field. When a ball was hit to deep right field, the outfielders had to run up a hill to get to it. I remember seeing them slow down as they climbed that hill. We joked that it was a hillbilly kind of league.

The oddest thing I remember was when we were playing in our home stadium—McCormick Field. The owners always tried to entertain the spectators and have some fun. I still don't know why this was viewed as entertaining, but one night they had a local marathon runner run around the perimeter of the field for the whole game. The marathoner was a postman,

> The Asheville announcers would often mention that I was a college graduate, which was very rare in the league. In one game, a smart-aleck fan yelled out, "Put some education on that ball!"

and he must have been friends with the general manager. That postman ran nonstop around the edge of the field for over two hours! I'd be reading a signal from Joe or winding up, and this yahoo would run behind the umpire and distract me. He'd stop if the ball was hit at him and keep out of our way, but he ran nonstop. I never saw that again.

What I liked best about Asheville was that my pitching was going great! I quickly became the ace for the Tourists, and everything just clicked. I like the way the papers spun yarns in these quotes from the *Asheville Times*:

Fred Kipp Beats Smyth in Mound Duel

Lefthander Freddy Kipp and newcomer Van Smyth turned in masterpieces. Smyth's loss was a heartbreaker. Kipp's performance was nothing short of remarkable. Kipp fanned nine and walked only one. The win was Kipp's fourth in five outings.

Fred Kipp to Hurl Series Windup

Gangling Fred Kipp will put his puzzling lefthanded slants against the Rock Hill Chiefs. Kipp, the Kansas Teachers College grad who has become a great favorite here will be aiming for his sixth victory.

Kipp's Six Hitter Gives Tourists Split With Anderson

Fred Kipp, lanky southpaw, twirled six-hit ball to give the Tourists a 9–2 verdict in the abbreviated seventh inning opener.

Kipp Shines on Mound, At Bat in Victory

If by some chance, Fred Kipp should be called to the witness chair in a courtroom 30 years from now and asked "Where were you on the night of July 24th, 1953," chances are the lean Kansas would reply instantly and correctly.

"I was in Asheville, North Carolina, on that night," Fred would reply.

And why shouldn't he remember? How often does a pitcher hit a home run, drag bunt a single and pitch an important win on the same night? Those were Kipp's accomplishments at McCormick's Field last night as he led the Tourists to a 11–1 victory.

Kipp, fair-haired boy of the Tourists fans, lost his shutout in the seventh when Joe Alexy slammed a triple and scored on an outfield fly. The big lefty showed remarkable change of pace with a bat in addition to those he served up from the hummock. In the third, he opened up a rally with a drag bunt single. Asheville added five counters in the fifth on singles by Pignatano, Jeffers, Shifflett, and Thomas and Kipp's memorable homer to right which soared 330 feet.

Tourists Win 12–3, Kipp Deals 4-Hitter

It was a case of batting 'em dizzy and stealing 'em blind last night as the Asheville Tourists and Freddie Kipp downed the Gastonia Rockets, 12–3. Fred Kipp, in addition to mowing down the opposition almost at will, also led the locals at the plate with a stellar four-for-four performance. Included in those four hits was a 375-foot triple to center field.

The Ashvillians collected a total of 7 stolen bases with three of them going to catcher Joe Pignatano and two to Harry Shifflett, while pitcher Fred Kipp and rightfielder Frank Jeffers each pilfered one.

Tourists Sweep Pair; Kipp Hits 4-run Homer

Fred Kipp of Asheville pitched and batted the Tourists to a 7–1 victory over Gastonia in the opener. Kipp had no trouble subduing the Rockets in the seven-inning opener. He allowed only five hits, fanned six, walked two, and settled the game with a bases-loaded homer in the fifth inning. The victory was his 13th of the season against four losses.

Kipp and Gastonia's Jerry Press were pressed into service when umpire Weaver was hit in the chest by a batted ball and forced to retire.

The last game was very special to me. Not only did I hit a grand slam—before they even called it that—but my parents and brother, Tom, and his wife, Ellie, were there to watch me. Tom had driven them over to Charlotte, where they got a hotel next to ours. They went to three games, and I sure was glad to show them a special game with the only grand slam of my career. They also got to see me umpire my only professional game. That turned out to be good practice for when I would later umpire in my son's little-league baseball.

Asheville turned out to be a great year for me. I ended up batting .343—fourth best on the team. I had the team's second-best slugging percentage at .582. I was never known as a power hitter, but I did do pretty well that year, with four doubles, three triples, and two homers. I never was able to repeat that kind of power hitting, and I only went to bat sixty-seven times that year, but I loved giving Joe P. trouble about how I outhit him that year.

I also helped my team move up in the standings to a solid second place, as shown in the chart above. The Spartanburg Peaches were obviously in a league of their own, with their veteran player-coach Jimmy Bloodworth leading the team. The Peaches were playing closer to A-league quality, while Rock Hill was playing closer to D-league quality, with no affiliation to the majors. The Peaches were the third-ranked farm team of the Cleveland Indians, who did not have seventeen farm teams like the Dodgers. The Indians' organization was more typical of a major-league team's farm system, with only one AAA team, an A team, and two B-league teams. Meanwhile, the Dodgers had two AAA, AA, and A teams and three B-league teams. Branch Rickey had built up the Dodger farm system, and that was how the Dodgers were so good year after year. We had a great pool of players to draw from and the infrastructure to build consistent champions.

1953 Tri-State League Standings

Team	Affiliate	Wins	Losses	%
Spartanburg Peaches	Cleveland Indians	96	54	.640
Asheville Tourists	Brooklyn Dodgers	83	67	.553
Charlotte Hornets	Washington Senators	74	71	.510
Anderson Rebels	Saint Louis Browns	75	74	.503
Gastonia Rockets	None	66	81	.449
Rock Hill Chiefs	None	51	98	.342

I was really proud of my play in Asheville and felt I was playing A-league quality. I ended up with a 15–5 record for the year, and that was very satisfying. A couple of Spartanburg Peaches beat me in winning percentage, but they had a supporting cast of powerhouse hitters and could often win after giving up five or more runs. I led the league with a 2.24 ERA, if you exclude Antonio Garcia, who only pitched in nine games that year. I was voted to the All-Star team, and everything was going great until I got a letter in the mail.

Tourists Place Four on T-S All Star Club

Asheville's Fred Kipp, from the corn country of Kansas, was a master of his trade. The parent Brooklyn Dodgers had him ticketed for higher ball next year until Uncle Whiskers stepped in to call him for a two year hitch in the service, expected to start in October.

I went home at the end of the season, and everyone was really glad to see me. All my friends had me over to dinner and wanted to hear about my baseball and what it was like. I wasn't there more than a week before I got my draft notice to go into the army. I had to go to Yates Center to check in, and then I caught a bus to Fort Riley. In Fort Riley, I caught a ride on an old cargo plane to Camp Rucker in Alabama, where I went through basic training.

Life at Camp Rucker was very different from Vero Beach. I realized that Vero Beach was designed for housing officers, while I was a grunt at Fort Rucker. We stayed in large barracks that would house our whole platoon of about thirty men. We had rows and rows of bunk beds on concrete floors like in the movie *Stripes*. Sleeping was rough, as we had to listen to one another snore and cough all night. Basic training was long and hard, but I worked my way through it.

Luckily for me, the war was basically over that summer when the armistice was signed, so I didn't have to worry about going to Korea. Even though the war was winding down, they wouldn't let us out of the army. What made my time in the military easy was that I got onto the baseball team and became the ace. We had ten teams in the Forty-Seventh Division, and I led our team with a 10–0 record. The guys on my team had lost a lot of games the previous year and were getting razzed quite a bit for losing. When we started winning, my teammates were really happy. That gave my team the chance to turn the tables and razz the other players pretty hard. Winning has a way of changing attitudes.

I was in full uniform at Camp Rucker and had stood in a similar pose a few years earlier in front of my house with friends and family.

Kipp, Ritchie Major Reasons For 136 Bearcats' Success

The 136 Bearcats captured the Rucker League title this spring. Two of the major reasons for their success to date are two top hurlers—both southpaws—Fred Kipp and George Ritchie.

Kipp has been especially effective. The 6'4," 180 pound Bearcat has won eleven consecutive games, without a loss, in Rucker and Benning League competition. Only against a strong Fort McPherson nine, did Kipp falter. Former Major Leaguer Wilmer "Vinegar Bend" Mizell, won that contest. But for that game, Kipp has been nigh invincible.

Fred Kipp Hurls and Bats 136 to Tenth Straight Win

In no team sport is one man supposed to be indispensable. However, in almost every game that the 136 Bearcats play, it appears that their star pitcher, Fred Kipp, is a direct contradiction to that rule. The big strapping southpaw put on another outstanding performance last Sunday as he lead the Bearcats to an uphill, 8–6 victory over the First Student Regiment. It was the 10th straight win for the 'Cats and it marked the 14th victory for fabulous Kipp. He has yet to lose in 14 appearances since the beginning of the Infantry Center League season. It's beginning to look like he never will.

Take Sunday's game for instance. Taking the mound in the second in relief of starter Armand Horne, Kipp was confronted by this situation. The 'Cats were trailing, 5–3, there were runners on first and third with no one out. It looked black for 136. So, wha hoppen? Kipp rared back and calmly tossed nine strikes past the next three 1st SR batters. In eight innings, Kipp garnered the total of 13 strikeouts!

That's pretty good for a pitcher. But wait, let's see what Kipp did at the plate. He had one single in three plate appearances when he came up to bat in the eighth. The score was tied at six apiece. The Bearcats had runners on second and third. So what did Kipp do? You guessed it, a sharp single to center and the 'Cats scored the two runs which gave them their tenth straight victory.

I'd been saving my money in the service and decided I wanted some new wheels—preferably a convertible. I went to the Ford dealer, and they were selling their Crestline convertible six-cylinder model for $2,400 or the V8 for

$2,500. I heard that I could get a V6 for $2,241 and save the $200 delivery fee if I picked it up in Detroit myself. That was what I decided to do. I put my money in my pocket and took a few days off and hitchhiked up to Detroit. Hitching rides in those days was easy, and I made the 850 miles to Detroit in two days. It took me two days to get up and two days to drive back. Here's a picture of the type of convertible that I got.

Because of my baseball skills, I got the easy job of serving breakfast to the officers. We cleaned up the kitchen, and I got to eat the high-end leftovers from the officers' breakfasts instead of the food the infantrymen had to eat. My workday was done by 10:00 a.m., and I had all day to mess around and play ball. Others played golf or fished in our country club–like base while I practiced my curve.

I entered into the automobile era when I bought a 1954 Ford Crestline convertible. My teams traveled by bus most of the time, but I was riding in style after I hitchhiked up to Detroit to pick this car up from the Ford factory.

I helped the 136 Bearcats win the Fort Benning League and won all fourteen games that I played in the Infantry Center League that season. The only game I lost was against the major-leaguer Vinegar Bend Mizell of the St. Louis Cardinals. Old Vinegar played with the powerful Fort McPherson Macmen—the powerhouse team from Atlanta. The Macmen were handpicked by the general and boasted Roy Hartsfield of the Boston Braves and Norm Sieborn of the Yankees.

Many professional baseball players got drafted into the military around this time. The generals would sort through the conscripts and recruit the best players for their teams. They had thousands of men to choose from and got some major leaguers in the process. Having a winning team was a point of pride for the generals and helped the morale of the men.

> I got the best of Old Vinegar on the big-league mound four years later. I started against him in Busch Stadium when he was with the Cardinals, on September 5, 1958. We battled until the seventh inning, when I left the mound up 2–1. It was my final win in the majors.

Not to be outdone, the general of Fort Benning formed the Fort Benning Doughboys—an all-star team featuring Bobby Durnbaugh, Tito Francona, and Carl Bentz. Bobby was a great shortstop who could turn the double play. He played quite a bit in the minors but only got one at bat in the majors, with the Cincinnati Redlegs in '57. Tito Francona was our best outfielder, and he would go on to play fifteen seasons in the majors with multiple teams. Carl Bentz and a couple others on my team played in the minors. We had good players and quickly became a good team.

We played other military teams, such as Fort Jackson, Fort McPherson, Eglin Air Base, Fort McClellan, Camp Gordon, and Redstone. We traveled around quite a bit between the bases, and the league was an odd mixture of small-town players, minor leaguers like me, and the captive major leaguers. The first time I faced the Macmen, I threw a one-hitter, and we were really happy to get the victory. I had a no-hitter until the eighth inning.

On the way back from the game, everyone was in high spirits after beating the number-one team. Bobby was making his way around the bus and razzing the different players like he liked to do. He was always having fun and causing trouble. The manager of the team was a regular army officer and got tired of the noise that Bobby was making. The manager made some disparaging remark like, "Bobby can field, but he's not much of a hitter. If nothing else, we'll keep him here for laughs."

Bobby didn't like the manager's trash talk at all. He got really upset and decided right then that he wasn't going to play any more ball for the army. Baseball was optional for us, and we were just playing for fun. Bobby only had a few months left, so it didn't matter much for him that he became just a regular soldier after that.

I played basketball for the base team as well, but getting back to baseball was my priority. Instead of playing in the Third Army basketball tournament, I took a leave of absence and went down to Dodgertown in the spring of '55. I enjoyed getting back on the field and seeing Joe P. and some of my other old teammates from Asheville. It looked as if Joe was going to move up to the Ft. Worth Cats—an AA-league team. I pitched well and caught the eye of Clay Bryant, the manager of the Mobile Bears—another AA team. He was interested in me, but there wasn't anything he could do while I was in the Army.

The papers later said the following:

Kipp's Control Amazes the Skipper

"I thought his control was wonderful. For a lefthander, it's remarkable. You just don't find them like that—not left-handers." The speaker, as you might guess, was Clay Bryant, the wily skipper of the Mobile Bears.

We asked the skipper what he thought about Kipp. "He was very impressive," replied Bryant. Continuing his remarks with some background information on Kipp, Clay stated that "He (Kipp) was down in Spring training when we (Mobile) reported there. He was one of the first youngsters brought down to Vero Beach to that special outstanding rookie camp they held before the rest of the farm clubs reported."

Bryant explained that Kipp, the 6–4, 185-pounder, had about a two-week leave and was just able to spend his time at the Dodgers' training camp. "He was in good shape, then," continued Bryant. "He pitched against our club three or four times and had wonderful control."

I went back to Fort Benning and took a break one day to see the Mobile Bears play in Birmingham. I went over and talked to Clay, and he asked me when I was going to join the team. I told him that I was in the army until October. He told me that others were getting out early and that I should try. I realized that I was going to miss the '55 season if I didn't get out of the army early. I suddenly wanted out of the army badly, and there were a few ways to get out.

I heard about other players getting out in less than twenty-four months if they had seasonal work. I was truly a seasonal worker. Baseball was played in the summer, and I was going to miss the season if I didn't get out early. I applied to get out in July by filing a seasonal-work release form. The form worked its way through the officers, and when it came time for the officer in charge to sign, he denied my request. I think he rejected my application to keep me on his team, but I'll never know.

I was talking to other teammates, and some of them were getting out of the military early by going back to college. I heard that some of the other players in the army would get letterhead from a university and forge letters that said they had been admitted to college. Not many of the players had college degrees. I didn't want to fake any documents and already had my eye set on going to the University of Northern Colorado in Greeley to get a master's degree in education. I figured I could get a letter of admission from them. I called them and couldn't get anywhere over the phone. They said I should come in person.

I decided I'd get a three-day pass and drive my Crestline out to Greeley to get my letter. I got my pass and took off on a Sunday morning with the top of my new convertible down. I was on a mission for baseball — kinda like the Blues Brothers. I drove straight through to Piqua while sleeping on the side of the road a few times. The roads were not so good in those days, but they were paved. I could go fifty to sixty miles per hour most of the time, but it wasn't an easy ride. It took me twenty hours to get to Piqua early on Monday morning. I only had a little time to visit with my parents and get a home-cooked breakfast. After a couple hours, I was off across the Great Plains to Colorado.

I slept in the car that night and was at the admissions office when it opened on Tuesday morning. They were very accommodating, and they wrote my letter of acceptance in about an hour. I was back on the road, and I made it to Piqua on late Tuesday night. I slept a few hours at home before I got back on the road. I got lost a few times in the dark and made it back to Fort Benning in the middle of the night. I put over three thousand miles on my new car in less than four days. What a pain in the neck to get out of the army. The war was over, and they were letting people go right and left already, but they just wouldn't let me go. I laid my head down to rest before my breakfast shift with my get-out-of-the-army letter in my hand.

Highlights

- I played so poorly for the Miami Sunsox that I got let go, but the Asheville Tourists of the Tri-State League picked me up.

- I had a great time playing for the Asheville Tourists and led the league with a 2.24 ERA and won fifteen games while losing only five.

- I got drafted into the army and played for the generals and against some major-league players who were in the same boat.

5. FROM COLORADO TO VENEZUELA — 1955

I was released from my military service and headed for Colorado. I had a much more enjoyable time driving across the country since I didn't have to drive like crazy to avoid going AWOL. I stopped in Piqua and spent a couple of days with my family before getting to Greeley and enrolling in some summer courses. While attending my classes, I found myself looking out the window a lot and dreaming of playing baseball.

It was an achievable dream. I drove down the South Platte River to Kearney, Nebraska, and started pitching for the Nebraska Independent League, where I had played in the summer of '52. I pitched a couple of weekends out there in the grasslands, but the five-hour drive was quite a hassle. One interesting event during our game on July 25, 1955, got me into *Life Magazine*.

The most incongruous rhubarb of the 1955 baseball season resulted in the banishment of the disconsolate pair shown above. The dog, a German shepherd named London, is the mascot of the Kearney Irishmen in the Nebraska Independent League. London is owned by Manager Chuck Eisenmann, and his duties include retrieving foul balls and delivering gloves and jackets to the players. He takes them very seriously, and that caused all the trouble.

Recently in the fifth inning of a 1-1 game with Kearney's bitter rivals, the Minute Men from nearby Lexington, Kearney Pitcher Fred Kipp singled. London trotted out with Kipp's warmup jacket, but he got mixed up and went to the mound before winding up at first base (*right*). The crowd cheered, but the Minute Men complained that London was delaying the game. The umpires ordered dog and master off the field. Eisenmann protested and so did London (*next page*). The umpires forfeited the game to Lexington and recommended Eisenmann's suspension. But the league president later disagreed and, when the umpires threatened to quit, offered his resignation instead.

BEFORE THE GAME London proudly wears baseball cap as he sits on infield grass awaiting orders.

CAUSE OF ROW was London's delivering jacket to pitcher. For what happened next, turn the page.

CONTINUED   49

This dog got me into Life Magazine *when he failed to deliver my jacket without delay. This might have been the only time a dog got ejected from a game!*

Chuck Eisenmann, the manager of the Kearney Irishmen, had a German Shepherd mascot named London. Chuck had trained London to play pepper, fetch foul balls, and bring players their jackets or gloves. I got a hit on a chilly night, and Chuck sent London out to bring me my jacket on first base. London got a little confused and took my jacket to the pitcher's mound instead of to me at first. London finally brought it to me, and the crowd cheered! The opposing coach was a bitter rival and complained about the game delay. The umpire agreed and threw the dog and the manager out of the game!

Well, Chuck stormed out to the umpire to protest his eviction, and London got into it as well. While Chuck argued with the umpire, London jumped up and pushed the ump from behind. The crowd was following the whole fiasco and oohing and ahhing. *Life Magazine* captured most of the action and put it in their magazine — see it on www.fredkipp.com/life. The umpire ended up requesting that Eisenmann be suspended. The president of the league disagreed and offered his resignation instead, but it wasn't accepted. This just goes to show how trying to have some fun can cause a lot of trouble — sometimes for no good reason. If poor London would have just brought me my jacket, all the trouble wouldn't have ensued.

One good thing did come from the bizarre incident. Billy Martin, a New York Yankee, saw the article and contacted me about playing for his Goodland Tigers. Billy was in military service, as I had been, and was based at Fort Carson, Colorado. Being a motivated person, Billy still figured out a way to play baseball while he was in the service. He was the de facto manager of the Goodland team and recruited me pretty hard because they didn't have any good pitchers. I remember him saying, "Why don't you come out and play for us? We'll have some fun, and you can put those schoolbooks away."

I decided to pitch one game for them when they played in Limon, Colorado — only about two hours from me in Greeley. I drove down to Limon and proceeded to strike out sixteen of the Limon players. I got the job and decided to quit school and go play for Billy's Tigers. Meanwhile, I was in contact with Clay Bryant and decided to see if his offer to play for the Bears was still open.

I went back to Greeley and packed my bags and threw them in the back of my convertible and hit the road. I pitched and won one other game for Goodland before we went to the Kansas State Tournament in Wichita. The tournament had many of the teams that I played against in '50 — including my old City of Emporia team. It was good to see my old teammates, and everyone was excited to see and play against the major-league star Billy Martin.

FOUR-GAME WINNER CONGRATULATED—Pitcher Fred Kipp (second from left) is congratulated by his teammates following his fourth straight victory for the Goodland Tigers in the Kansas Semipro Baseball Tournament in Lawrence Stadium. Left to right are outfielder John Skirurski who hit a home run, Kipp, Manager Tiny Tagtmeyer and ex-New York Yankee second baseman Billy Martin. Goodland beat Council Grove 6-0 on Kipp's four-hit hurling to enter the championship round.

I had a good time playing with Billy Martin and being a ringer in the western Kansas tournament.

Billy was already famous for his role in beating the Dodgers in the seventh game of the 1952 World Series. Billy made the unbelievable infield pop-fly catch after the ball got lost in the wind and the sun. The catch was hailed as one of the turning points in the Series, and the Yankees never forgot that catch and how Billy was a great competitor.

At the start of the tournament, we faced the Wichita Boeing Bombers, the defending champions from '54. The Boeing Bombers could really hit, and they were favored again this year, since we were basically unknown. I pitched relief, and we played well enough to beat them in the first round. Next, we faced Council Grove, and I threw a four-hitter against them for a victory. The picture above shows how happy I was after that game. Billy did know how to take control and lead the team and have some fun!

Piqua's Fred Kipp Hurls Goodland After State Title

Associated Press

Goodland held the favorite's spot today as the Kansas State Semipro Baseball Tournament moved into the semifinal round. Goodland, undefeated in tournament play, blanked Council Grove 6–0 last night behind the four-hit pitching of Fred Kipp. Kipp, a lefthander, struck out ten and walked only two. He always has been a good hitter and last night had two hits.

How Far, Fred Kipp?

Iola Register Sports Page

The chances that Fred Kipp of Piqua will some day get a trial in the major leagues are better than even. If advancement to the top transpires, imagine what a thrill it could be for the folks of Piqua. They have battled the baseball problems for years and developed a strong community feeling for the pastime.

Putting a native son in the big leagues would be more reward than they ever expected. There are really concrete reasons for thinking Fred can make it. The ex–Iola High basketball stalwart has never had anything but success since he started in Piqua baseball at 14. Progress has been steady.

He is a lefthander with exceptional control. He is big. He is smart. He is young, and athletic all the way.

During the tournament, I got word from Clay Bryant that I could join the Class AA Mobile Bears that next week in Birmingham if I could get over there. If I was going to make it to Birmingham, I had to leave right away and leave Billy high and dry without a portside pitcher. Billy wanted me to start against the Boeing Bombers for the championship, so I was torn between abandoning the team in the championship or going to play AA professional ball. I remember telling Billy, "I'm torn in two, Billy. I want to play for you, but this might be my big chance to get in good with the Dodger organization."

Billy looked at me and smiled. "We all want to go and play for the big leagues, buddy. Don't worry about it. Go down to Birmingham and give them hell!" Then he leaned in and said, "Don't tell anyone, but I'm in talks with the Yankees to get back with them later in the season." Sure enough, Billy did get back with the Yankees that fall and played twenty games before going on to the World Series against the Dodgers.

I made my way down to Mobile and joined the team with only seven weeks to go in the season. We were in sixth place at 55–55 for the season, and they asked me to start against the first-place Birmingham Barons. The Barons were 67–46 and two games ahead of the Memphis Chickasaws in the Southern Association. I was on a roll and really happy with my pitching. We crushed them 9–0.

Here's what Dennis Smithermen of the *Mobile Press* wrote:

Newcomer Kipp Spins Superb 1-Hitter!

Mobile Bears backed into fifth place in the Southern Assn. standings Thursday night—thanks to the brilliant debut pitching of southpaw Fred Kipp. Kipp, just recently arrived from the armed forces, southpawed the Birmingham Barons into submission on one lone base hit in chalking up a 9–0 verdict.

Kipp walked only one batter, hit one and whiffed five in his very impressive debut. In four of the seven frames he faced a minimum of three batters and he retired the last 11 Barons in a row. Kipp faced only 26 batters over the seven-inning distance. Kipp drove in two of the runs.

Throws Real Good Knuckler'!

Bryant stated that "Kipp has a good knuckleball, a real good knuckler. When it comes in it spells trouble." The Skipper, still offering his opinion on the youngster's deliveries, stated that "his fast ball was alive. He can improve his curve some, but he has an assortment. And that control, it's just remarkable for a left-hander," emphasized Bryant once more, who was evidently finding it hard to convince himself that southpaws do have control like that exhibited by Kipp in his sensational debut.

In fact, Kipp's one-hit shutout in a starting appearance against the Barons—and don't forget they're the league-leaders—was probably one of the most impressive debuts by a twirler in the Southern's long history. The Iowa native, it might also be added, is noted as a fine hitter, and drove in two runs with two singles.

I played out of my sox! What a way to come back after my military vacation. One pitch after another was going right where I wanted it. I won my second game too and only allowed one run to score. The team was definitely rallying toward the end of the season, and a couple of other late arrivers, Jim Baxes and Chris Kitsos, were playing well and batting strong. Jim would later play with the LA Dodgers, and Chris had played one major-league game for the Cubs the year before and was then traded to the Dodgers. Ralph Mauriello was the mainstay pitcher for us in '55, and he'd win eighteen games for us. Jim Gentile was our first baseman and a Catholic whom I'd go to church with on Sundays before the game. Thirteen of our players would eventually have big-league experience. We played well together and were a solid AA ball team.

1955 Southern Association Standings

Team	Affiliate	Wins	Losses	W-L %
Memphis Chickasaws	Chicago White Sox	90	63	.588
Birmingham Barons	New York Yankees	88	65	.575
Chattanooga Lookouts	Washington Senators	80	74	.519

Mobile Bears	Brooklyn Dodgers	79	75	.513
Nashville Volunteers	Cincinnati Redlegs	77	74	.510
New Orleans Pelicans	Pittsburgh Pirates	76	75	.503
Atlanta Crackers	Milwaukee Braves	70	84	.455
Little Rock Travelers	Detroit Tigers	52	102	.338

As the standings above show, we still didn't win that many games even though we were playing well. We seemed to split every doubleheader we played. It took us to the last game of the season to make the playoffs with the fourth-place seed. If I had missed a game or two by staying to play with Billy's team, we might not have made the playoffs.

We rallied in the playoffs and won the Southern Association title by beating the Birmingham Barons in the final series, four games to two. I pitched two four-hitters in the series against the Barons. Sometimes a pitcher lines up well against another team, and I seemed to have Birmingham's number. In this case, the Barons had seven left-handed batters, and I was the only southpaw slinger for the Bruins.

It was especially nice to beat the Barons because they were affiliated with the Yankees—our parent team's nemesis. Everything was lining up for the Dodgers and Yankees to have another faceoff in the World Series that year. The Barons had over a dozen players who would go on to make the majors. One young Baron whom I later became good friends with was Ralph Terry. Ralph came from Oklahoma and was just nineteen years old that season. I never faced him that year, but he did face our team. He had a mean fastball and excellent control. I'll talk more about my off-field antics with him later.

Three of Kipp's Six Wins Low-Hit Efforts vs. Barons

Fred Kipp, Mobile southpaw, posted only six victories during the Southern Association pennant race and playoffs, but three of them were low-hit efforts at the expense of Birmingham to help lift the Bears into the Dixie Series. Kipp, only southpaw on the Mobile staff, failed to draw a start in the semi-final playoffs, but in the finals he worked against Birmingham twice, tossing a pair of four-hit performances.

Mobile's Greatest Ball Club!

Dennis Smitherman—*Mobile Press*—September 22, 1955

Astounding! Incredible! Fabulous! Amazing!

Yes, those descriptions—and any others like 'em that you can think of—
fit the 1955 Mobile Bears.

This current Mobile team is every bit the Cinderella team. The comeback
of the Bears represents one of the greatest garrison finishes in Southern
Assn. annals, and likely has few parallels in organized baseball. The
Bruins, who swept into the play-offs on the final day of the regular
season and then went on to become the Southern's play-off champions,
stand as the minor league equals of the "Miracle Braves" of 1914.

The Bears, who had defeated the Nos. 1 and 2 teams of the circuit—
Memphis and Birmingham—now stand ready to take on the Texas
League's play-off champions in the Dixie Series, a truly amazing feat for
a Bear team that even in the waning days of July was just beginning to
shake itself loose from the No. 7 berth, which it had occupied for the
greater part of the season until that time.

Double-A baseball, as exemplified by the Bears, has seen no peer. Long
live the Bears—kingpins of the Southern Assn in 1955. May they now
make their "greatest story ever told" even greater by riding herd on the
Texas loop's titlists to become the Dixie Series Champions.

Pretty high hopes were written there, but we lived up to expectations. The
Shreveport Sports, the champions of the Texas League, were in our sights. I
pitched in one of the games but didn't do very well, and they pulled me in
the early innings. Our team was hot, though, and we swept them in four
straight. This was one of my favorite championships, and I got a nice Dixie
Series gold ring to mark the occasion. The season was over, and people were
talking about going home or going to play winter ball in the Caribbean
leagues.

Clay Bryant told me how he coached down in Caracas, Venezuela, and that
they would pay $1,000 a month plus expenses. Clay said that my arm could

take me all over the world and that this was a good offer. That sounded sweet to me, so I asked him to pass the word up to management that I was interested. I drove home and was there a few days before I got a telegram from the Dodgers. They said they'd like to have me and that I'd have to go to Brooklyn to get a visa processed. I'd have to leave the next day to make the charter flight. No rest for the weary.

Champion Bears Await Results Of Texas Loop Play-Offs

—Press Staff Photo

BEARS' 'BIG THREE'

Bob Walz, left, Ralph Mauriello, center, and Fred Kipp, were the backbone of Mobile's mound corps during the rough going. Mauriello, the big winner with an 18-8 regular season mark, is the expected choice to open the Dixie Series with southpaw Fred Kipp to follow. Walz, who pitched almost every day during the Bruins' last-minute rush to reach the Southern Assn.'s first division, stands ready to jump in and bail the Bears' starters out of trouble.

The Mobile Bears, Southern Assn. play-off champions, were taking things easy Thursday awaiting the outcome of the Texas League finals.

Shreveport prolonged the Bruins' resting period with an 8-2 triumph over Houston on Wednesday night. The Sports and Buffs will meet Thursday night in the deciding seventh game.

Mgr. Clay Bryant said the Bears would hold a light workout Thursday afternoon at 4 o'clock at Hartwell Field.

The Dixie Series will begin one day after the Texas League play-offs end unless Houston wins Thursday night. If the series opens in Houston there will be no game Saturday night because of the conflicting Alabama-Rice football tilt.

If Shreveport wins, however, the series will open Saturday night in the Louisiana city. The first two games will be played in the Texas League team's home park, the next three in Mobile, and, if necessary, the teams will move back to the Southwest to finish.

BRYANT HOPEFUL

Bryant is hoping his "team named desire" can keep the winning fever through the Dixie Series.

"No one really thought we'd win," the patient, determined Bryant said Wednesday on the team's arrival from Birmingham. "But here we are. Everybody wanted to win and that was the big difference."

"This is a good team, one which has never quit—and won't. I don't know anything about these Texas teams but I do know this club and its going to be awful tough to beat after going this far."

—Press Staff Photo

MOBILE'S CRACK INFIELD

Mobile's "inner defense" was outstanding in the final days of the season and during the Southern Assn. play-offs. The infielders are: (l. to r.) Jim Gentile, first base, Jim Baxes, third base, Dick Young, second base, and Chris Kitsos, shortstop. Gentile tied for the league leadership in runs-batted-in with 109. Young clouted five home runs in the play-offs to lead the club in that department. Baxes and Kitsos both joined the club in midseason and were instrumental in the Bruins' stirring home stretch drive.

This newspaper article gave me a chance to wear my new suit. They took this picture in front of the plane that delivered us to the playoffs. We took planes, trains, and buses to get to our games.

I'd never been out the country before and had to get my passport and my visa. They told me what I needed, and I complied. I got to New York on Tuesday, October 4, 1955—a day that Brooklyn Dodger fans will never forget. Johnny Podres had just pitched a shutout in Yankee Stadium in game seven to win Brooklyn's first World Series. After losing in 1941, 1947, 1949, 1952, and 1953, the Bums got to bring home World Series rings.

I'd get to know Johnny the next spring, and he said, "They told me to throw it down the middle, but I hit all the corners." Of course, you want to hit the corners, but that's easier said than done. He was telling me that everything just went right for him that night, and it resulted in the biggest win of his life. It's amazing when things come together for you and your team, and that was the ultimate night when the Bums finally closed the deal.

I hadn't spent any time in New York before that, so it was quite exciting to be there on the night that Brooklyn walked away with the crown. I was staying in the Bossert Hotel in Brooklyn, where the Dodger guests stayed and Walter O'Malley had regular luncheon meetings. Everyone who drove by the hotel that night honked their horns and yelled all night. The town was on fire! What an introduction to New York.

After a couple of days in Brooklyn, I went down to the New York International Airport, which locals called "Idlewild Airport" — it was later renamed after JFK. I had a direct flight to Caracas. On the flight, I met several of my teammates, such as Jimmy Williams, Stan Jok, and Buddy York. I'd play with Jimmy over the next couple of seasons in Montreal. Stan turned out to be our third baseman and had been playing for the Rochester Red Wings in the International League as part of the St. Louis Cardinals system. He told me how he'd been playing in Cuba and wanted to play there this winter but had ended up in Venezuela because they needed a third baseman. We talked a long time on the longest flight I'd ever been on.

We made it up to Caracas, and it was a beautiful city nestled among seven mountains. Caracas looked a little like Asheville, but it wasn't anything like it. Everything seemed a little off. Of course, I didn't speak Spanish, and I had trouble getting used to the food and the people. I had just turned twenty-four, and I had not been exposed to many foreign foods and cultures yet.

Things just didn't go right down there. From the beds to the food, everything was disorienting to me. I'd see people peeing in the streets and homeless kids begging for money. Things weren't as nice as they were in America. I couldn't drink the water and didn't like many dishes I tried down there. I was a meat-and-potatoes kind of guy and still basically am. The worst food down there were these hardtack rolls that they served at every meal. The outside of the roll was hard and dry, and the inside was doughy and chewy. I didn't like the feel of that in my mouth and just couldn't eat them. Other players were getting sick and had to go back to the

States to get better. Living there felt like being on a bad date where the chemistry just wasn't working.

My pitching wasn't going well either. My catcher, Early Batty, was great and had gotten to the majors for the Chicago White Sox that year. He would later win three Golden Glove awards with the Washington Senators and Minnesota Twins. The problem was that he had to relay the call for the pitch from our Venezuelan manager. The manager didn't know my pitching style and would call the wrong pitch all the time. I was a low-level minor leaguer still and didn't know how to stand up to the coach to let Earl and me call the right pitch. It just wasn't working out, and I was losing games.

I only played a few games before they asked me to leave. I just wasn't able to adapt to the changes there, so it was time to move on. There were no hard feelings. I was glad to go home for Christmas, since I'd missed the last two due to military service. It was a long flight home, and the song that was stuck in my head was "I'll Be Home for Christmas"!

Highlights
- I got into *Life Magazine* when a dog failed to deliver my jacket on time.

- Billy Martin recruited me to play for the Goodland Tigers, but I left them to play for the Mobile Bears.

- I joined the Mobile Bears late in the season and threw a one-hitter in my debut and many more low-hit games.

- I helped the Bears rally to win the Southern League playoffs and the Dixie Series.

- I was in New York getting my passport when the Dodgers finally won a World Series.

- I flew to Venezuela to pitch in the winter leagues, but it didn't work out, and I left after a month.

6. FROM MIAMI TO MONTREAL — 1956

I took another long flight back to New York from Venezuela and then took trains from New York to Iola. My parents picked me up in Iola and were surprised at how tan I was at the start of December. In Venezuela, we had quite a bit of time to lounge around the pool, since we only played Wednesdays, Saturdays, and Sundays. After all the excitement of traveling internationally for the first time, Piqua was extremely sedate and a little too quiet for me.

After a week or two of catching up with my old friends who had moved on with their lives, I moved up to Kansas City for the winter to spend some time with my brother, Tom, and his wife, Ellie. They lived in the Raytown area of Kansas City, Missouri, and I got a job working in the post office for the Christmas rush. That put a little cash in my pocket, and we had a nice Christmas. Tom was teaching and coaching and working for the Kansas City Athletics in the summer. We had a great time going around Kansas City that winter.

I kept in shape during the off season so that I'd be ready for spring training. I remembered Tommy Holmes's advice, so I worked out regularly, playing basketball, running, and pitching. I'd seen other players show up to spring training out of shape and get injured. If that happened to me, I might miss the season or more. I wasn't going to do that if I could help it.

Right before spring training, I went back to Mobile to visit some friends. The Mobile Bears weren't in the Dodger organization anymore and had shifted to the Cleveland Indians. I pitched to a high school kid every day for a week to keep in shape. Little did I know that I would soon be pitching to Roy Campanella and Rube Walker for the Dodgers.

Dodgertown was alive and kicking that spring, with over seven hundred players in camp. Spirits were high from being World Series champs, and I got to see the stars for the first time in the mess hall and occasionally on the field. It seemed that even more press was with us in '56, and they did a lot of promotional photos and filmed the team. In camp, I found out that the Asheville Tourists and the Tri-State League were no more. The three teams I had played with in the minors were no longer associated with the Dodgers. The minor leagues were very transient and changed all the time.

I started pitching with the Fort Worth Cats, where Joe P. would end up, but I played so well that they moved me up with the Montreal Royals—the Dodgers' top AAA team. I did a lot of pitching for the Royals and remember pitching a whole game, which was unusual for spring training. They were watching me closely, and pretty soon I was asked to go to Miami and play an exhibition game with the Brooklyn Dodgers. I had a shot at the majors!

While this picture was taken in 1951, these were the Dodger stars in 1956—Duke Snider in center field, Gil Hodges on first, Jackie Robinson at second, Pee Wee Reese at short, and Roy Campanella at home.

I caught up with the Dodgers, and it was surreal to be in the locker room with Jackie Robinson, Pee Wee Reese, and the others. I tried on the Dodger uniform for the first time, and I liked it! The first team we played against was the Yankees. The rematch of the World Series brought over ten thousand fans out to the exhibition game on March 24. Before the game, I saw Billy Martin by the batting cages and went over to say hi. Billy looked good in his pinstripes, and I remember him saying, "That Dodger uniform looks good on you. Are you going to leave them at the altar and come and play for us?" He was referring to my departure the previous fall to play with the Bears. I told him that I liked the Dodger Blue just fine.

Carl Erskine started for us, and I got to see Mickey Mantle blast a four-hundred-foot homer over the tall center-field barrier. Locals said it was the first time that anyone had hit a homer over that wall.

I got called up in the seventh inning. When I walked out to the mound, I looked around at the world champions on the field. Roy Campanella was behind home plate. Gil Hodges manned first, Jim Gilliam second, Chico Hernandez short, and Jackie Robinson third. Sandy Amoros was out in left, Duke Snyder in center, and Carl Furillo in right! I was so excited to be on the field with these guys. I'd never been a hero-worshipping kind of guy, but my spine was tingling by the time I made it out to the mound.

The inning didn't go very well. Don Larsen was the first up, and he hit a single on me. Yogi Berra came up later and hit Don in for an RBI. I remember the pitch being low and outside, where I wanted it, but Yogi reached out and hit it as if I had given him an easy strike. Yogi had a way of making things look easy.

Yanks Beat Dodgers, 4–2; Mantle Poles 2-Run Homer

New York Times, John Drebinger, March 24

By way of serving notice on their arch foes, the Dodgers, that this is a new year, the Yankees tonight subdued their 1955 World Series conquerors, 4 to 2.

Fred Kippe, a rookie southpaw, gave the fourth Yankee tally in the seventh.

Those New Yorkers couldn't even spell my four-letter name right!

On April 2, I got the start against the Boston Red Sox. Before the game, I walked onto the field and saw a bunch of people gathered around the Red Sox batting cage. I went over to see what was going on, and there was Ted Williams cracking balls all over the field. He was making perfect contact, and line drives shot off his bat one after another. Crack! Crack! Crack! I'll never forget the sound of those balls getting pounded into submission. I felt sorry for them and in awe of Ted.

The players were not only gathered around to watch him hit but also to hear him cuss. Ted was a player's player and liked to talk about the best way to bat with colorful language. He said something about "these World champs going to eat some leather today." Of course everyone was all ears, and my jaw dropped when I heard him cuss like a sailor. I won't repeat the worst words here, but he kept talking and hitting and sent a couple of 'em out of the park.

Ted Williams loved talking about hitting and decided at a young age that he would be the best hitter in the world. He was second to Stan Musial in my mind.

Then he hit one into the screen that the batting-practice pitcher stood behind and said, "Throw that damn ball faster! Them Dodgers ain't gonna throw me any of these pussy throws like you're doing. Throw them HARDER!" Everyone just cracked up and looked around in amazement at the legend.

This was spring training, so they were giving all kinds of players the look over and a chance to play. The lineup was almost completely different, with Dick Williams on first, Charlie Neal on second, Pee Wee at short, and Randy

Jackson on third. Jim Gilliam was in left, Gino Cimoli in center, and Carl Furillo in right, and I was the starter.

I warmed up with Rube Walker, who was the regular backup to Roy. Jim Piersall was first up and got a hit off me. He would go five for five that night. I got a few good pitches in against Frank Malzone and got him out. Then who walks up to the plate but Ted Williams! Those tingles in my spine were gone, and now they were in my stomach.

I didn't have a protective cage like the warmup pitcher, and I was a little afraid that he'd hit one right back at me. Rube called for my knuckleball, and I fidgeted with the ball in my glove. I grabbed the ball with my fingernails and looked down the lane at Rube and tried to block Ted out of my mind with virtual blinders. I went through my stretch and unleashed one of the best knuckleballs I had ever thrown. The ball moved like a hummingbird and snapped into Rube's mitt. Ted just watched it go by.

"Ball one!" the umpire called out.

I couldn't believe it. Rube looked back at the umpire, and the umpire just stared straight ahead. We knew it was a strike. Next, I threw a curve ball, and he swung and missed. I threw an outside fastball and then a couple more strikes that were called balls, and Ted started walking to first. The crowd booed me as if I had just intentionally walked one of the greatest hitters in the history of baseball.

Now I knew what I had heard was true: "If Ted didn't swing at it, then it wasn't a strike." The umpires wouldn't go against Ted. If Ted let it pass, then it was a ball whether it was or not. A few years later, in 1960, I was playing in Richmond with Johnny James, who had faced Ted numerous times. He summed up the situation when he said, "For Christ's sake! I threw him five strikes and walked him!" I was lucky to never have to face Ted again.

With Ted on first and other sluggers lined up, I was in a bad situation and wasn't able to rise to the occasion. I was flustered, and I gave up six hits and five runs in the inning. I got the loss, and it showed that I wasn't quite ready for the majors.

Red Sox Sweep Series with Dodgers

New York Times, Roscoe McGowen, April 2

Fred Kipp, a rookie southpaw not long out of military service, started for Brooklyn and was knocked out during the American League four-run third inning. Charged with five runs and six hits, Kipp also issued three passes.

After these lackluster performances, I was told that I'd be going with the Montreal Royals. A nice advancement for me to AAA ball, but a little short of my ultimate goal. Butch Boussard, the president of the Montreal Royals, said that he'd drive me in his Cadillac up to meet the Royals in Virginia. I didn't know what a hockey legend Butch was until I got up to Montreal later. He had just retired after winning his fourth Stanley Cup. He was captain of the Canadiens for eight years and eventually elected into the Hockey Hall of Fame. Butch was out of hockey now and running the Royals organization for the Dodgers.

Butch was a big, muscular guy and was known for being a very physical defender who brutally body checked opponents into the boards. Even though he was raised in Montreal, he spoke good English with a subtle French accent. We cruised his Cadillac up the Florida coast, having fun in the spring air. We drove over eight hundred miles and stopped in nice southern towns such as St. Augustine, Savannah, and Charleston. Life was good.

We got to Richmond, and I met my teammates for what I thought would be the year. The Royals and the Saint Paul Saints were the top farm teams of the Dodgers, so most of the players had been in the majors or would eventually get called up. Some players were in the twilight of their careers, such as Dixie Howell at thirty-six, Chuck Diering at thirty-three, and George Shuba at thirty-one. A few of the standouts on my team were Rocky Nelson, George "Sparky" Anderson, John Roseboro, and Chico Fernandez.

Rocky was our power hitter. He was the star, since he had hit thirty-seven homers in '55 and was getting paid major-league money—I heard over $20,000. That sounded pretty good to me, compared to the $600 a month, or about $3,000 a season, that I was making. Rocky was thirty-one and wasn't slowing down. He'd been in the majors since 1949 and had hopped around Saint Louis, Pittsburg, Chicago, Brooklyn, and Cleveland and was now back in the Dodger organization. He was like a hot potato and had played for three major-league teams in one year—1951. He excelled in the minors but had trouble sticking in the majors, like so many players—including me.

Rocky got his nickname because he liked to verbally fight with other players. He'd get angry if he'd strike out and took the game real personal. One time he hit a weak grounder to first after he chased a pitch from Lynn Lovenguth of the Toronto Maple Leafs. As he jogged to first base for the easy out, he said, "Get that shit over the plate. I can't hit any crap like that. You don't even give me a chance!"

Lynn was a wily veteran and snapped back, "OK, Babe Ruth."

Sparky Anderson was known as George back then, and he was red hot at the start of the season. He was batting .400 by June 1, and the press was all over him. They asked him if he could keep that .400 up through the season. He said, "I might be able to," and immediately went into a slump. He ended up batting .298 that season but never got close to that .400 mark again. Asking a batter to think about his hitting is the ultimate jinx. Sparky was a fidgety type and chewed his nails down to nubs. He had gray hair by twenty-two. He played only one year in the majors, for Philadelphia in '59, but he turned out to be a very successful Hall of Fame coach and the first manager to win World Series in both leagues.

John Roseboro was another great catcher I got to throw to. I played with John for a number of years, and he was a solid catcher who was strong, quick, and smart. He was the best blocker of home plate I've ever seen. Challenging him at the plate was a mistake I saw many guys make. He was like the proverbial unmovable object.

Chico Fernandez was another teammate worth mentioning. Chico was Cuban and would always show us around Havana when we played down there. He got called up to the majors that year when Pee Wee got injured. One night we were playing the Miami Marlins, and Chico went to bat against Don Cardwell. Don was throwing amazingly powerful fastballs that night, and Chico struck out in three straight pitches. Chico came back into the dugout, set his bat down, sat down, and looked straight forward as if he'd seen a ghost. All he said was "Smoke." We all laughed, and it kind of broke him out of his trance.

Cleo Moore threw out an opening pitch while promoting her last movie — Hit and Run. *After growing up in Louisiana and marrying Huey "Kingfish" Long's son, the blond bombshell died tragically young, at forty-eight.*

Living in Montreal in the summer was a great experience. Several of the players and I lived on the McGill University campus and enjoyed the collegiate lifestyle. We took streetcars around town and to the ballpark. I didn't learn any French, but the food was delicious. I particularly enjoyed the meat-and-potatoes-type places like Chick 'N' Coop, with rotisserie chicken and corn fritters. Before Saturday-afternoon games, Billy Harrison and I would eat a nice fat ribeye steak and a baked potato that they served on a cutting board for $1.35. They say Montreal is one of the most European cities in North America, and I liked it.

I was the only lefty pitcher on the team, so they told me that I was going to see quite a bit of action. I started out well and was the first five-game winner in the league on May 29. If you start doing really well in AAA, it's your ticket to the big leagues. Minor-league teams are plagued with morale problems when the big leagues come and harvest the hottest players. As soon as a player gets hot, he gets taken away. It's great for the person getting called up but hard on the morale of the team left behind.

On June 5, the papers said that I was being called up to the majors with Rocky Nelson. This was huge news in Piqua, and Bud from the *Iola Register* wrote the following:

> The familiar sports term, "sleeper," might be applied to Fred Kipp of Piqua and his swift rise to the lofty heights of the National League, in fact the lofty place of the very champions of the baseball world, the Brooklyn Dodgers.
>
> A "sleeper" is a fellow who has more hidden promise and prospects than the sideline public may be aware of. For one thing, Brooklyn moved so rapidly in calling up Fred. The Dodgers may even have surprised themselves. And certainly it must have surprised the pride of Piqua. He could hardly be expected to calm down by the first time he faces Eddie Matthews, or Stan Musial or Willie Mays — or Dale Long — if he does.
>
> Just Kipp's sudden jump from Montreal to Brooklyn shows, baseball is full of the unexpected, so whether the hero ever faces those murderous batters, or some of the others in the big time, still cannot be certain. In two weeks, he may be back at Montreal. The game is unpredictable.

I guess Bud couldn't even see how unpredictable the majors were. After this article and several others mentioning that Rocky and I were moving on up, they only took Rocky. I never left the team. I don't know what really happened there in Brooklyn, but I just kept playing for the Royals nonstop. We played well, and I made the All-Star team and was 13–3 by July 19. On July 20, the papers again started talking about me moving up, and this came from the top.

Alston Seeks Starter, Eyes Kipp

International News Service

CHICAGO—Walter Alston, manager of Brooklyn's third place Dodgers, reported that he is calling up a pitcher from the Montreal farm club "to bolster the hard-pressed staff." The Dodger manager, who had his team in Chicago to play the Cubs, said that he will probably send for youthful Southpaw Fred Kipp, a knuckleball throwing hurler who just got out of service.

In Rochester, where the Royals are playing a series with the Red Wings, Montreal Manager Mulleavy told the Herald that he hadn't heard anything about the Dodgers calling Kipp. Mulleavy commented that he didn't think Kipp was quite ready yet for the jump to the big leagues, although he could be called should the Brooks find themselves in desperate straits.

The papers wasted a lot of ink talking about me going to the majors, but nothing came of it for the second time. If my coach didn't hear about it, you can be assured that I didn't either. Sometimes coaches such as Alston talked about changes to the lineup to light a fire under the players. I might have been that motivational tool.

Meanwhile, the season kept moving on, and I was hitting and pitching well. Going into the homestretch of the season, I was batting well over .300 and leading the team in batting average after Rocky moved up. I did lose a few games pitching, but my record was 17–7 when Lynn Lovenguth of the Toronto Maple Leafs won his twentieth game of the year for a 20–10 record. The talk around the league was that I was in the running for the most valuable pitcher, which was a battle between Lynn, Satchel Paige of the Miami Marlins, and me.

At this point in the season, the winning-percentage leader, at .786 (11–3), was the storied veteran Paige. Satchel was forty-nine years old and in his thirtieth year playing professional ball, having started in '26 in the Negro Southern League—five years before I was born! There's no doubt that he'll always hold the record for being the oldest rookie in the majors by starting for the Cleveland Indians at age forty-two. He had mellowed by the time I saw him, but I still heard stories about how he'd tell his teammates to sit down in the field because he knew the batter wasn't even going to get a hit!

He always had a smile on his face, and players would always gather around the old codger to hear him tell stories before the game. The fans loved him too and came in droves. 1956 was the first year for the Marlins, and their Hall of Fame owner Bill Veeck, known as "Short Shirt Bill," was a great promoter of the team and Satchel. Bill liked to surprise the fans, so on opening day, he had Satchel Paige delivered to the game via helicopter.

Before the start of the game, the two-man bubble helicopter slowly descended right behind the pitching mound and blew up an amazing dust storm. The players had to run from the field, and the fans in the best front-row seats got a face full of dirt and grass. The fans scrambled to get away from the brown cloud before the helicopter finally landed. Nobody, not even the players, knew what was going on as the blades slowly rotated to a stop.

Then out of the helicopter stepped this thin scarecrow of an old guy. That was Satchel Paige's reintroduction to baseball after a couple of years in retirement. Nobody thought he could come back at such an age, but there he was, and he could still pitch—sparingly. I pitched against him and the Marlins for the next couple of years, and he continued to pitch into the 1960s—but mainly as a celebrity. He even pitched for the Kansas City Athletics again in 1965, long after I'd retired.

Satch knew how to move a ball and work the batter. He was known for his control, and I want to share one more story about Satchel that Whitey Herzog told me. Whitey, Satchel, and I all lived in Kansas City in the sixties, and I refereed high school and some college basketball with Whitey in the winters. Whitey liked to tell the story about playing with Satchel and his Marlin teammates against the Columbus Jets in '57. I played in that quirky Jets Stadium for five seasons, and they had a hole in the right-field wall that faced slightly away from home plate, toward third base. For a gimmick, some company said they'd pay a ballplayer $100,000 if he could hit the ball through that hole—a nearly impossible feat and an ongoing joke.

Whitey taunted Satchel and asked him if he could throw the ball through that hole. Satchel said, "Sure I can. You bet ya." The players gathered around, and Satchel got in short center field about a hundred feet away and aimed at that hole, which was about twelve feet off the ground. It's odd for a pitcher to aim at a target twelve feet up in the air, but Satchel wasn't deterred.

Satchel played for the New York Black Yankees in 1941 for a little while but mainly played for the Kansas City Monarchs in the Negro American League. He became the oldest rookie to ever start in the Majors when he joined Cleveland in 1948 at forty-two years old.

Satchel wound up and threw the ball, and it sailed right at that hole. The ball hit the edge of the hole, chugged around in the hole, and fell out. The players said, "Augh, good try. That's not an easy one to get." Not to be put off, Satchel got another ball, backed up to about 150 feet, and threw it again. This time the ball flew right through that hole. That Satchel had some great accuracy — even at a hole 12 feet up a wall!

When I faced Satchel at the plate, it took me back to my Piqua days when some of the old farmers would come out and play. The difference was that Satchel was still one of the greats. I remember the one time I went up against him and he threw a low-breaking ball. I chased it and hit a grounder to second. I couldn't get the best of him. He had a way of staying a little ahead of batters so that they were always guessing about what they were trying to hit. Every pitcher tried to do it, but Satchel did it from the 1920s to the 1960s.

The little rivalry between Satchel, Lynn, and myself was heating up in the homestretch of the season. We each played about forty games that year, and Lynn led the league with twenty-four victories. His low ERA and 153 strikeouts made him the most valuable pitcher for the year for the first-place powerhouse Maple Leafs. Satchel led the league with an ERA of 1.86 — truly amazing!

1956 International League Pitching

Pitcher	Age	W–L	Winning Percentage	ERA	SOs	Innings Pitched
Fred Kipp	24	20–7	.741	3.33	99	254
Lynn Lovenguth	33	24–12	.667	2.68	153	279
Satchel Paige	49	11–4	.733	1.86	79	111

I ended up winning my final three games to end the season with a 20–7 record. It was nice to get that twentieth win, and it gave me the second-highest number of wins and winning percentage in the league, at .741, for pitchers with more than ten wins (Bob Spicer was 12–4). Satchel's and Lynn's ERAs were much better than mine, and I was glad to be compared with them in my rookie year. Because of my age, they made me Rookie of the Year in the International League.

We finished in fourth place in the league and were the fourth seed in the Governor's Cup. We faced the Toronto Maple Leafs in the first round, and I started the first game for us. They beat us up pretty good in the series: 4–1. After that loss, I got called up to Brooklyn. The third time was the charm. This time I was getting called up for real when the Dodgers could expand their roster to forty players after September 1. The Dodgers were caught in a tight race for the pennant, and I was going back to New York!

Drysdale Named Top Brook Rookie

The *New York Times*, December 27, 1956

Don Drysdale was named yesterday the top Dodgers outstanding rookie of 1956 by the Brooklyn Chapter of the Baseball Writers Association of America.

Two of the Brooks' finest prospects come from opposite corners of the baseball map. One is Fred Kipp, a knuckle-ball, southpaw pitcher, who completed a 20–7 record for Montreal. He had an earned run average of 3.33 and was voted the International League rookie of the year. The other is Rene Valdez, who was a twenty-two-game winner for Portland in the Pacific Coast League. Valdes tossed eighteen complete games and eight shutouts.

Sports News and Views — *Iola Register*

In due time, Fred Kipp certainly can be expected to be a Dodger regular. To close observers, it has seemed as definite as anything ever in the sports. It isn't because friends here have stood on the sidelines for years and watched Freddie wheel over 15 or 20 strikeouts in kid games, then boys' games, then adult games.

The confidence in turn comes because Fred is a steady sort. He isn't the kind, as some are, who could pitch about as well at 19 as they'll ever pitch. He is the type who would get better every game, year by year. There are other reasons why friends think he is so likely to succeed, and apparently that includes the Dodger management. He is tall, he is strong, he is left handed, he can bat as well as pitch, he is studious, smart, likeable, ambitious, healthy and clean living.

Most of that is all accounted for by the fact that he came from among good people in a good rural community. His arrival at the top may not be a bit premature after all.

Highlights

- I returned to Dodgertown with the world-champion Dodgers.

- I pitched well enough to start for the champs in exhibition games against the New York Yankees and Boston Red Sox.

- I pitched against Don Larsen, Yogi Berra, and Ted Williams, and it didn't go well, so they pushed me to the Montreal Royals to work on my pitching.

- In Montreal, I won Rookie of the Year and got twenty wins and seven losses.

7. TO BROOKLYN FOR THE PENNANT RACE—1956

I got down to New York on the night of September 17, when the Dodgers were in first place and one game ahead of the Milwaukee Braves. The Braves had led the National League for over 120 days in the season, so the world-champion Bums weren't used to being on top this year. The Dodgers had just won four games in a row, though, and were hot. The New York Yankees had already wrapped up the American League and were just waiting for the Braves or Dodgers, or even the Reds if we both caved.

The Yankees played great all year, and Mickey Mantle wrote the book *My Favorite Summer 1956* about that year. The Yanks wanted to reclaim the Crown from the Dodgers, who had taken it for the first time in '55. The '56 World Series was two weeks away, and we had eleven games to play. The exciting part for me was that I was going to have better than a front-row seat. I was going to be in the dugout with the players.

I was so excited that I can still remember the first time I walked onto Ebbets Field on September 18. We faced old Vinegar Bend, whom I hadn't seen since the service. He was back pitching for the St. Louis Cardinals and had just thrown two shutouts, including a two-hitter against the third-place Reds. The night was cool, and the smell of beer was in the air. I walked toward the dugout and looked around at the noisy crowd.

Ebbets Field had a moderate crowd of about fourteen thousand fans who wanted to "beat them birds." The fans called out to players in those thick Brooklyn accents and wished us luck. One fat Bum with a beer and a few days' stubble called out to me and asked who I was. I told him I just got called down from Montreal. He said, "Yeah, you that rookie of the year up in Montreeall, ain't ya? Good ta have ya here, son."

I walked into the dugout and took a seat on the far end of the bench. Even with our regulars in the field, the dugout was still full, with thirty-one players watching. I sat away from Walter and the coaches. The view was better than any seat in the house, since we were looking out at about the level of the grass. The dugout smelled of chewing tobacco, and the bench was well worn.

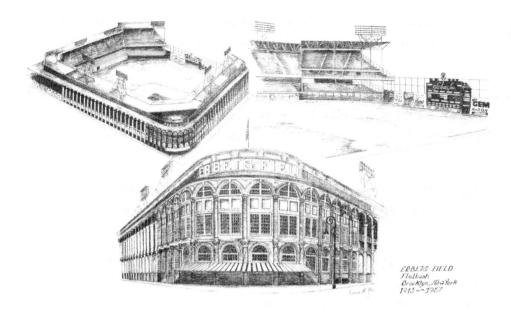

 EBBETS FIELD
Flatbush
Brooklyn, New York
1913—1957

Ebbets Field was an old-time stadium because they squeezed it into a small city block. The fans were up close and personal, and many were feisty.

Roger Craig got off to a bad start in the first inning when Walley Moon hit a triple with Musial and Blasingame on base. Moon got hit in as well, and it was 3–0 after the first inning. A somber mood came over the dugout when the players came off the field. Jackie Robinson paced in the dugout with his pigeon-toed gait and was really agitated. He had fire in his eyes and was rallying the troops in his nasally voice. "We're in the pennant race, men. We don't have another game to lose. Every play counts out there. We got to hit 'em with all we got! Every pitch. Every swing. Every throw." I was enthralled and watched him walk back and forth until he had to bat. The intensity was definitely higher with the Dodgers than anything I'd ever seen.

Jackie changed the mood in the dugout, but we still couldn't get anything going on the field. Stan the Man hit a home run in the top of the third to make it 4–0. A hush fell over the bench when all the starters were in the field. A twenty-one-year-old Don Demeter was sitting next to me and was a tall, thin guy like me. He yelled out, "Don't worry, men! We're gonna come back. Hang in there!" He looked at me and quietly said, "We ain't going nowhere at this rate." He shook his head and looked back out at the field with his big eyes. Don had just been called up, like me, and he would turn into a good friend over the years. He'd end up playing for the first time that day.

In the bottom of the third, they pinch hit Don, and it was unfortunate that he struck out the first time at bat. When he came back and sat next to me, he was panting really hard, and I could see how emotionally worked up he was. I told him, "You'll get him next time."

He said, "Will there be a next time? I hear about guys who only get one chance, and this could have been mine. This could be my only cup of coffee."

I said, "Well, if you keep striking out, they won't keep you around. Just hang tough. It'll work out." I patted him on the back, and we laughed. He felt better when Jim Gilliam got a hit right after him. Vinegar started falling to pieces after that and loaded the bases with a couple walks. Jackie came up to bat and hit a line drive to left field and scored two runs. The intensity in the dugout grew with the runs.

Vinegar walked Gil Hodges next to load the bases again. That was the end of Vinegar, with the score 4–2. Herm Wehmeier replaced him and managed to get out of the inning with no more scores. Our batters kept up the onslaught in the sixth when Sandy Amoros hit a single to drive in Charlie Neal. In the seventh, Gil cracked a homer to left center with Jackie on base to give us the lead at 5–4.

Everyone jumped up and patted Gil on the back or butt as he walked through the dugout. I told Don D., "I knew we could do it." Gil's homer really got the fans going too. The Sym-PHONY was making a racket, and I couldn't believe how excited all these grown men were about our lead. Pee Wee Reese was giving high fives as he walked back and forth in the dugout. This was how I wanted to watch games!

We were still up 5–4 in the top of the ninth when Stan came up and hit a solid line-drive single to right field. He had gotten his nickname "the Man" in Brooklyn, and he was playing the part. We got a couple of outs on fly balls, but Stan got into scoring position on second when Ken Boyer came up. Boyer was batting over .300 and hadn't gotten a hit that day. Boyer was due, and he walloped a two-run homer to put the Cards up for good with a 6–5 victory. The team fell from our high spirits on Gil's homer to a new low when we couldn't get a run in the ninth.

With our loss and the Braves' win that day, we fell into a tie with the Braves. We didn't have long to wait and were back the next day. The Cards again started off with a homer, off Newcombe. Newk fought back and led the team with home runs of his own in the second and third innings. Sandy Amoros hit a home run as well, and Don Demeter got his first hit in the majors and made it count as a home run. He was so excited to add to our lead and sat next to me afterward. I congratulated him, and he said, "When it rains, it pours!" He was right, as we piled on to a 17–2 victory. That was a lot of fun beating up on the Cards after they got us the day before in such a good game.

The Braves lost on September 20 to put us a game up again. This up and down in the standings was nerve wracking. We took the night train to Pittsburgh for our last series away from home, against the hapless Pirates, who were twenty-four games back. Regardless of how we played, this would be the last road trip of the season, since the Series would be played in New York if we got that far.

Sal Maglie, "the Barber," pitched the next game, and he had the Pirates' number. He'd beaten the Pirates six straight times and had beaten them twenty-five of the twenty-nine times he had pitched against them over the years — mainly with the Giants. Sal was new to the Dodgers that year, but our players knew him from his years playing against us for the Giants and Indians. That night, he pitched most of the game amazingly well and only gave up two hits until the seventh inning, when the wheels fell off. In the seventh, he gave up a hit and then a two-run homer to Frank Thomas. After another hit, Alston took him out. The Barber looked great until the seventh, when he started getting tired and gave up those runs. Sal was thirty-nine years old, but Rube Walker said he was pitching as well as he'd ever seen him.

The Pirates' low position in the league didn't keep them from beating us that day or three times out of four in that series in Pittsburgh. Things were looking down as we were going into the last week of the season. We were only a half game back, but we weren't playing well at all. If we couldn't beat the sixth-place Pirates, we didn't deserve the pennant.

We flew back to LaGuardia and had a night on the twenty-fifth against the Phillies. It was a rather chilly night, and I decided to watch it from the bull pen to see how the pitchers warmed up and talked about the game. I sat next to Clem Labine and Rube Walker. The pitching coach Joe Becker was talking to the veteran Dixie Howell, and Don Bessent sat on the end, alone. Sal Maglie was up pitching again—four days after his six-inning shutout that ended in a loss. A light breeze blew through the bull pen, and the wool uniforms weren't quite warm enough to fight off the cold. I wished we had French bouillon soup to warm up with, as they did in Montreal. All I could do in Brooklyn was sit on my hands.

Clem asked me who I was, and I told him. He said, "Weren't you supposed to come up with Rocky in the season?" I told him it was only in the press. He started talking about the cold too and wondered if he should pitch just to stay warm. Don said that he wished he were Sal and out there pitching. He said, "Sal pitched in the Canadian leagues in '44, during the war. Sal said it snowed for the entire game in a nasty storm, and they couldn't see the foul line by the fifth inning. They should have called the game but didn't. Sal said he would be fine tonight. This little chill won't bother him while he's pitchin'."

The game started out as a pitchers' duel, with no hits until the bottom of the second. Jackie came up and hit a double to left field to break the standoff. They intentionally walked Gil, and that got Jackie excited. Jackie started dancing off second and distracted Jack Meyer, the Phillies' pitcher. Jackie had a way of getting the pitcher's attention and holding it. Jack turned around and threw to second to pick Jackie off. But he made a bad throw, and the ball sailed into the outfield. Many thought Jackie would run home, but they held him at third, and Gil went to second. Jackie kept up his distractions and started dancing off third now. When Carl Furillo hit a grounder to Roy Smalley at short, Jackie scored to set us on a course to victory. I'd never seen anyone work so hard for a run. His efforts paid off.

Next up was Roy Campanella, who was having a rough season. Catchers' gloves back then weren't padded as well as they are today, and he had the most crooked and beat-up hands I'd ever seen. In the clubhouse,

Everyone called Sal Maglie "the Barber" because he brushed batters back so often that he gave them a close shave.

he'd hold up his catching hand, and each finger pointed in a different direction. His right thumb was so swollen by that time in the season that it looked like a sausage. He said his right hand felt "like it's coming off." He had to use a thick-handled bat because he couldn't grasp the thin one he liked to use. He was a trooper and went right up there and hit a homer to give us a 3–0 lead in the bottom of the second. Watching that ball fly out of the park warmed my heart, and everyone was up and yelling in the bull pen.

Sal was pitching well, and Dixie said that he'd never seen such control and determination. We scored a couple more runs on an error in the third, and Sal wasn't giving them any slack. The innings kept adding up, and no hits were tallied for the Phillies through the fifth. I looked over at the corner of the bull pen and saw Don Bessent sleeping in the corner. Clem told me that Don would nap in the dugout and it never seemed to affect his play. "We can wake him up, and he'll be ready to pitch in about five minutes."

During the seventh-inning stretch, Don woke up when they sang "Take Me Out to the Ball Game." He looked over at the scoreboard and said, "Is Sal really doing that? They don't have a hit on him yet?"

Rube said, "Yeah, he's doing fine. You can go back to sleep."

Don said, "You just wake me up if I'm needed. I think Sal is going to do all right. He likes this cold weather."

The night continued to get colder, and we all just sat on the bench rubbing our palms to stay warm. Pee Wee would go out to the mound and rub the ball to warm it up for Sal. Sal gave up a walk in the eighth, and Beckers got a call from Alston. Becker called out, "Clem, get warmed up. We might need you."

Clem jumped up, and Rube did too, just to get out of that chilly bull pen. They were warming up right in front of us when Elmer Valo came up to bat. Elmer was an established veteran at thirty-five and had over a thousand hits in his career. He was batting a solid .285, but that wasn't as good as the previous year, when he hit .364. The two veterans went at it, and Sal fell behind in the count at 2–1.

Dixie called out, "Come on, Sal. Strike old Elmer Fudd out." We laughed and were on the edges of our seats for every pitch as the tension grew. I was getting a kink in my neck from looking left at the pitching. The bull pen faced out to center field, so we had to lean forward and look left to see the action. Elmer fouled a couple off and then watched a ball to take it to a full count. The pitches were adding up, and we were worried about Sal's arm. On the seventh pitch to Elmer — the ninety-sixth pitch of the game — Elmer popped up to Pee Wee, who made the routine catch. On the next pitch, Solly Hemus grounded to first, and Gil and Pee Wee made a sweet double play to end the inning.

I looked over at Dixie and said, "Sal's three outs from a no-hitter! I can't believe this."

Don, who was awake now, looked over at me and said, "Don't talk like that. You're going to jinx it. You rookies come up here and don't know how much pressure Sal is under. You might ruin everything."

I was taken aback and leaned back and away from Don.

Clem and Rube came back to the bull pen, and Clem sat next to me and said, "They aren't going to need me now. Sal will finish this off for sure." He leaned over toward me and looked at Don, who was napping again, and back at me. He put his thumb to his mouth and raised his pinky to symbolize Don's drinking. He smiled and whispered, "Don't worry about Don. He's a little superstitious and thinks someone ruined his no-hitter once by talking about it. You definitely don't want to talk to Sal about it, but how can you avoid talking about a no-hitter out here? Old Sal is going to be fine either way."

Nothing much happened in the bottom of the eighth, and Sal got the first out in the top of the ninth with a fly ball. Two outs to go for a no-hitter. The Phillies were at the bottom of their order, so Mayo Smith sent the lefty Frankie Baumholtz to bat to ruin Sal's streak. Sal didn't care, though, and pitched a curve ball for the first strike. On the second pitch, Frankie popped one up toward the Dodger dugout.

We all jumped out of the bull pen to see Campy running to get the ball. The ball took Roy all the way to the dugout, and the wind kept carrying it out.

Campy just looked up and stepped right into the dugout and started to fall down into it. Roy was battered and bruised, but there was nothing that was going to stop him from helping Sal get a no-hitter and catching that ball. As

Roy Campanella was always on his toes and ready for action.

Campy started to fall into the dugout, Charlie Neal, another rookie, jumped up and held Roy under the arms as the ball came down. From the fans' point of view, it looked as if Campy was floating in midair as he caught the ball. The crowd went wild. The myth of that catch grew, and people started saying that he defied gravity to make that catch. They couldn't see Charlie holding him up.

We went back in the bull pen and took our seats, talking about how Roy risked it all and made plays happen. That was the kind of clutch player Campy was.

Mayo decided to pinch hit Harvey "Chicken" Haddox. Chicken was another lefty, and Sal later told me that he didn't know what to pitch to Chicken because he'd only pitched to him once before. He went with a few curves, and it was enough. After a couple of foul balls, Chicken struck out with a weak swing on the fifth pitch. One out to go for Sal's first no-hitter.

The Phillies were at the top of their order, and their left-hitting center fielder, Richie Ashburn, came to the plate. Richie was their best hitter, batting .302. Clem leaned forward. "Sal's not going to like this. You see Richie crowding the plate? Ohhh…you don't do that to Sal. You watch— he'll brush him back." On the first pitch, Sal zipped one high and inside, and Richie fell backward and into the dirt. Richie got back up and dusted himself off. Sal had shaken him with that hard ball, and Richie backed up in the batter's box. Now that Sal had the plate back, he threw a nice curve-ball strike to even up the count. The next pitch looked like a fastball, and Richie fouled it down the third baseline.

I noticed something odd and asked, "Why are Sal's hands so black?"

Clem said, "That Sal. He wants to get a good grip on the ball. He keeps a towel in his back pocket that is black with pine tar, shoe polish, and rosin. He likes his hand to stick to the ball, so he rubs his pitching hand in that combination of muck. He takes it to the extreme, though, until his hand is all black. You won't want to shake his hand. On cold nights like this, when your hands are a little tight, that rosin can make all the difference. It's sure working for him tonight."

Richie moved back in a little to home plate, and Clem said, "Don't do that, Richie. You'll only aggravate the Barber. Don't aggravate the Barber." Well, he didn't aggravate Sal too bad, because Sal threw another strike, and Richie popped it up behind the plate and out of Roy's reach. The count was 1–2 now, so Sal had some room to work. Richie didn't heed Clem's distant advice, though, and moved in to crowd the plate again. Clem said, "There is no way Sal will give up the plate like that. On a 1–2 count, there's no way he's going to let him stay in there."

Sal went into his windup and zinged another one at Richie to push him back. Richie tried to get out of the way again, but he wasn't fast enough this time. The ball hit him right above the left knee. Richie dropped the bat and fell over in pain, pulling on his leg. He had a pained grimace on his face. After a minute of wallowing in the dirt, he gave Sal a mean and dirty look.

Sal looked away, and Clem said, "I told you. That's the Barber! There's no one as territorial at the plate as Old Sal. He'll bean the batter sooner than he'll throw a strike when they get over the plate. He hates that. That plate is his, and nobody's going to take it away from him. Our hitters used to hate Sal. Sal has a way of getting in the batter's head. You ought to pay attention to that, Fred. He's one helluva pitcher, that Sal."

Dixie added, "There's no way to *not* remember getting beaned by a ball at ninety miles per hour. It hurts."

Clem said, "I've been hit twice this year already, and it changes your thoughts when you're worried about your life out there. A bad ball could end your season."

There was still one out to go in the bottom of the ninth when Marv Blaylock came up to bat. Sal later said that he threw a fastball to Marv on his 110th pitch. Marv hit a grounder to Gilliam on second, and it was all over. Sal got his first no-hitter in his twenty-first year in the majors. We all ran out on the field to congratulate Sal. I'd never seen such excitement in grown men. We were out there yelling and screaming and jumping up and down. It was total bedlam.

After what seemed like an hour, we made it into the clubhouse, and beer and champagne were flowing as if we'd just won the pennant. Alston gave Sal all the money in his pocket—several hundred dollars—and everyone was jubilant and smiling ear to ear. Some even had too much of a good time. John Griffin, the extremely overweight clubhouse manager, was drinking like crazy and wearing a blond wig when he fainted. Everyone gathered around. They had trouble reviving old Griffin, and he got sent to the hospital. He spent the next day in the hospital while we had to go back to work against the Phillies.

Everyone thought Sal's no-hitter would start a rally for us at the end of the season, but it didn't work out that way. We lost the next day to the Phillies and fell a full game back from the Braves. Don Newcombe had already won twenty-six games that year, but he couldn't win this one. I was back in the dugout for this game, and Don caused a big stink after Sandy Amoros, a star from the '55 World Series for making a great catch, made an error when he lost the ball in the sun. Don was a bear of a man and was my height at six four, but he had 50 pounds on me, weighing in at 240. He had his emotional ups and downs, and I'm sure he was frustrated with Sandy's error.

Don confronted Walt about the error and basically demanded that he replace Sandy "with somebody who can catch!" Walt knew it was a mistake to throw a great player out because of one error. Walt wasn't afraid of Newk and wouldn't take orders from one of his players. He told Don to focus on his pitching and sit down. While Sandy didn't speak much English, he knew what was going on, and it flustered him. The real impact of Newk's negativity was on the whole team. We lost our momentum and lost to the Phillies 7–3.

After the game, the clubhouse went from ultrahigh because of Sal's no-hitter the night before to subzero. On top of the internal conflicts of the team, we fell a game back from the Braves. It was hard to focus on the game when player politics were getting in the way. Instead of focusing on winning, Don tore the team apart that night. He sulked around the locker room, and no one felt good about our chances to win the pennant. We all knew that the only way to win now was to win all three of our remaining games, while the Braves had to lose two out of their three games.

We had Thursday off and went to the field on Friday in a light rain. We all sat around in the clubhouse, and the mood was still down. Some guys played bridge, but most of us just sat around talking. Roger Craig was going to start when the rain stopped, but it didn't. They called the game off, and that set us up for a doubleheader on Saturday. This lifted the mood of the team because Walt said that Sal would be able to pitch the first game in the morning after three days of rest.

Newk put a lot of pressure on himself and caused a lot of problems for the team in his later years, when he had a drinking problem.

Red-hot Sal was the king of the locker room, and we all felt good about our chances. On top of Sal pitching, the day game would help our players see Bob Friend's wicked curve. Friend had seventeen wins for the Pirates, and we knew he'd put up a big fight. Friend was famous for his strong curve ball, and Pee Wee was glad about the delay because "I can see his pitches better in the daytime."

The players all left before we found out that the Braves had lost their Friday-night fight with the Cardinals, leaving us a half game back. Our fate was in our hands again. If we won our last three games, we'd be in a playoff with the Braves for the pennant.

I was in the locker room on Saturday morning, and I remember Jackie coming in the clubhouse and proclaiming in his nasally tone, "They're waiting for us to beat 'em!" He was talking about the Braves, who were stuck watching or listening all day while we played our doubleheader. There was nothing the Braves could do but wait.

Over twenty-six thousand fans showed up to watch this critical doubleheader climax to the season. In the first inning, Frank Thomas, an up-and-coming star, smashed a two-run homer to give them a nice lead in the first. This didn't stop our guys, though. Jackie hit Junior in, and Sandy hit a two-run homer for a 3–2 lead. After the first inning, Sal brushed 'em back and beat 'em down hard. No Pirate got past first base until the ninth inning, and Sal closed them out with a 6–2 win. Sal's complete game moved us into a tie for first place. I remember the fans going wild when they lowered the Braves flag that represented first place in the division and then we hoisted the Dodger flag. It was a glorious day.

Roger Craig was set to start the second game, but Walt threw the Pirates a curve ball and shook things up by starting Clem. This was unusual, but it was a tactic that Walt used in crucial situations like this. Clem only started thirty-eight games in a twelve-year career of more than five hundred games. I knew Clem starting would be a treat to watch. After hanging out with him in the bull pen, I'd watch him in this crucial game of the regular season. An All Star that year, Clem was the Dodgers' ace in the hole and led the National League with nineteen saves.

Clem had great control and knew how to win. He pitched brilliantly and shut out the Pirates until the eighth inning and only gave up one run. Roy hit a homer for us, and Gil hit a triple that scored two runs to give us a 3–1 victory. Winning both of our games on Saturday put us a half game up over the Braves, who were taking the field in Busch Stadium that night.

The Braves were giving it all they had and started their thirty-six-year-old star Warren Spahn. Warren would go on to become the sixth-winningest pitcher in baseball, with 363 wins. Over his career, he had thirteen seasons with twenty-plus wins and is the winningest left-handed pitcher ever. Another veteran was going to the mound to fight for the pennant. It was a must win for the Braves.

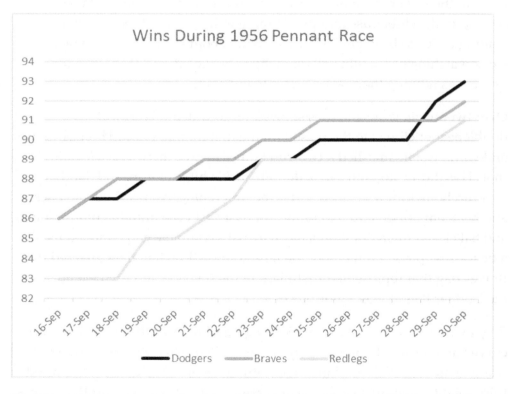

The three-way pennant race between the Braves, Dodgers, and Redlegs got hot in mid-September. The Braves couldn't get their final win and keep up with the Dodgers.

Spahn was facing Herm Wehmeier of the Cards, and it would turn out to be a classic pitchers' duel—the likes of which will never be seen in today's game because they'll pull pitchers after about one hundred pitches. After the Braves hit a homer in the first and the Cardinals tied it up in the sixth, no runs were scored until the twelfth inning. Both pitchers stayed in the whole game. In the bottom of the twelfth, Stan Musial hit a double, and Rip Repulski hit another one to score Stan for the win. It was a heartbreaking loss for the Braves and especially Warren. They said a photographer tried to take a picture of Warren crying after the tragic loss, but the Cards wouldn't let him get the shot. Warren had pitched his heart out, and it was a horrible way to end the season for him.

Warren Spahn won 363 times (sixth most in history) and had a wins above replacement (WAR) of over 100! Warren faced Stan Musial 291 times, and even he gave up ninety-five hits, fourteen homers, and a .326 batting average to the Man.

One team's loss is another team's salvation. Our doubleheader victories and their twin losses put us a game up. The only way we could lose the pennant now was to lose to the Pirates, and the Boys of Summer weren't about to let that happen.

Almost thirty-two thousand fans came to Ebbets Field that Sunday hoping to see the world champions win the pennant. Walt put Newk back on the mound, and the Pirate pitcher, Vern Law, couldn't make it out of the first inning before Duke hit a three-run homer to score the first three men up to the plate. This game turned into a slugfest, and Jackie hit a homer in the third before Duke hit his forty-third homer of the year in the fifth. Sandy piled on with another homer in the sixth to give us a nice fat 7–2 lead.

Everything was going our way, and it looked as if Newk might get his big win. Newk had high hopes, and he wanted a complete game where he got carried off the field. I was in the dugout with Don B., Rube, Dixie, and others. When the bases got loaded in the top of the sixth, Dixie said, "This doesn't look good. Newk looks tired and is losing his control. We better get warmed up, Don."

Next thing we knew, Bill Verdon hit a double with the bases loaded to score three runs. Walt made the call, and Don Bessent and Rube scrambled to warm up. Newk rallied, though, and got out of the seventh. He was tired, though, and the end came in the eighth when Lee Walls popped a homer. Newk huffed off the field and was really down on himself for giving up four runs in the clutch. It wasn't his best pitching performance, but we still had the lead.

Bessent came in and shut the Pirates out after that. Roy later told us in the locker room, "All I was calling was fastball after fastball. That's what Don wants. My hand was killing me from catching those fastballs, but they work!" When Bessent threw his last fastball for a strikeout, he started jumping up and down for joy. Roy ran out and caught him while he was in midair. We had won the pennant!

I started to run out of the bull pen, and Becker stopped me and said, "Hold on to your glove and hat, or those bums will steal it from you." I said thanks and put my glove on and put my hat in it and ran into maelstrom. I only made it a few steps when some guy from the stands came up and hugged me. I wasn't used to hugging in my family, but it seemed appropriate at the time. I made it out to the mob of players, and we were in a strange jumping-up-and-down group hug. It was pure chaos, and I didn't really know whom I was hugging and who was patting me on the back. Someone ripped the back pants pocket off my pants and almost pulled my pants down. It was chaos in the best way!

After a few minutes of that, we made our way to the clubhouse, and all kinds of people were in there. This party put Sal's no-hitter party to shame. This time, they let lots of fans in—including the Sym-Phony. The Sym-Phony added their colorful music to the bizarre atmosphere, and Walt was making his way around and shaking everyone's hand. Duke poured champagne over Newk's head, and Newk danced with a dwarf who was part of the Sym-Phony. Newk kept calling out, "We're the champs! We're the champs!"

National League Leaders

	1949	1950	1951	1952	1953	1954	1955	1956
1st	Dodgers 97–57	Phillies 91–63	Giants 98–59	Dodgers 98–57	Dodgers 105–49	Giants 97–57	Dodgers 98–55	Dodgers 93–61
2nd	Cardinals-1	Dodgers-2	Dodgers-1	Giants-4.5	Braves-13	Dodgers-5	Braves-13	Braves-1
3rd	Phillies	Giants	Cardinals	Cardinals	Phillies	Braves	Giants	Reds
4th	Braves	Braves	Braves	Phillies	Cardinals	Phillies	Phillies	Cardinals
5th	Giants	Cardinals	Phillies	Cubs	Giants	Reds	Reds	Phillies
6th	Pirates	Reds	Reds	Reds	Reds	Cardinals	Cubs	Giants
7th	Reds	Cubs	Pirates	Braves	Cubs	Cubs	Cardinals	Pirates
8th	Cubs	Pirates	Cubs	Pirates	Pirates	Pirates	Pirates	Cubs

The Dodgers were the perennial leaders in the National League and in first or second place for the eight years before I joined the team.

The party went on for what seemed like hours, and the room was packed to the gills. Reporters were asking everyone for quotes, and Vin Scully was drinking with all of us. Everyone seemed happy for the first couple of hours, until Newk had a few too many drinks. Newk started getting down on himself, and the papers quoted him as saying, "I can't get a big game. Can't hold a five-run lead. Had a chance to be carried off the field. That's a great thing, but I couldn't do it." Newk got his twenty-seventh win of the season that day and would win the first Cy Young award for his success, but that wasn't good enough for Don. He wanted to be the hero and fell a little short of his own dreams.

Looking back on that now, I still can't believe how everyone was so excited about the pennant after they'd won it so many times. The table above shows how the Dodgers had won five of the last eight pennants and had been in second place the other three years. The Braves thought it was their year finally, but we proved them wrong. The Dodgers were always in the race, and I was starting to see how hard it was to just get that pennant. I also started to realize that you need to celebrate these victories when they come along, because they might not last.

The emotional roller coaster that the team was on was breathtaking. The up-and-down ride started in the first game against the Cardinals. We were way up and ended down by losing our first-place lead in one day. Then we felt the exuberance of Sal's no-hitter and then the doldrums of Don's loss. Finally, we ended with a three-game winning streak to win the pennant. We only had two days off before we'd start the next and biggest ride in baseball—the World Series against those damn Yankees.

Highlights

- I met up with the Dodgers during the pennant race with the Milwaukee Braves.

- I got to watch the games in the dugout and the bull pen and was having the time of my life just watching the games with them and celebrating wins and mourning losses.

- I saw Sal Maglie's no-hitter, which energized us toward the pennant.

- Don Newcombe won his twenty-seventh game and won the first Cy Young Award, but he was struggling with his demons and hurt the team's spirit.

8. THE NEW YORK SERIES — 1956

The next day, I turned twenty-five, and Walt gave us the day off before the World Series drama started. I was going to pitch batting practice through the Series, so I got to stay with the team. My birthday usually coincided with the end of the baseball season, when the final statistics for the season came out, so I went downstairs to the lobby of the Bossert Hotel and picked up a *New York Herald Tribune*.

They called the Bossert "the Waldorf Astoria of Brooklyn," and it had a grand exterior with lots of pillars, arches, and balconies. The Bossert was designed as an apartment hotel, and several of the players stayed there with me, including Don Demeter, Clem Labine, and Don Bessent. The hotel was bustling with out-of-town press and fans for the Series. The Bossert was where the Dodgers had celebrated the '55 World Series victory. I really enjoyed staying in that historic and grand hotel, which stands to this day.

For my birthday breakfast, I went up to the Marine Room on the fourteenth floor, at the top. I didn't usually eat up there and was impressed with the clear panoramic view of Manhattan from Brooklyn Heights. I saw Don Demeter at a table by the window, and I joined him for breakfast. He had a copy of the *New York Times*, and we had a lot to talk about over coffee. The newspaper had all the end-of-year stories about the season, records set, and the upcoming series.

The biggest story of the year was that Mickey Mantle had won the triple crown by hitting .353 with 52 homers and 130 RBIs. The Mick was heading his battleship at us now. Mickey was the first Yankee to turn the triple trick since Lou Gehrig had done it in 1934. Mick was the first and only player to hold the triple crown with over fifty homers — that showed how he could hit and hit with power. Don and I wondered how our pitchers could stop him and the rest of the Yankees.

Of the eighteen American League players who hit over .300, four of them were from the Yankees. Yogi Berra was nineteenth at .298 and had pounded thirty out of the park. Of the ten National Leaguers who hit over .300, the only Dodger was Jim Gilliam, and Duke was our next-best hitter, at .292.

The Yankees were coming off a hot season, and they wanted revenge for last year's defeat in game seven. There's nothing more motivating for a good team than losing.

The Yankees set a lot of records that year and many more over their glory years. They set an American League record by hitting 190 homers and a bad record of leaving twenty men on base in one game. They had to have a lot of hitting power to get that many people on base in one game. The Yankees had won sixteen of the twenty-two World Series they'd played, while the Dodgers had won only one in six — with all five losses going to the Yankees. Everyone wanted to see the rematch.

The stats weren't in our favor, but we had the home-field advantage. We'd have the first two games at home, three away, and two more at home — if needed. We had needed all seven games in the '47, '52, and '55 series. In '55, the Series started at Yankee Stadium, and the home team won every game until game seven, when Johnny Podres turned Brooklyn upside down and shut the Yanks out at home for the win.

This year, Podres was serving in the Navy, so we knew we were going to miss him. We had Sal, though, and he was set to start against Whitey Ford, their strong portsider. Whitey had set a record that year, pitching six shutouts. That's not easy to do. Whitey still has the most wins, innings, and strikeouts in World Series history. Sal hadn't won a World Series game yet.

Over breakfast, Don told me how he wasn't eligible for the Series but was going to Japan with me when it ended. Don told me how he played for the Fort Worth Cats that summer and had popped out forty-one homers. We spent the day together and walked over the Brooklyn Bridge to Manhattan. He was six four and 190 pounds, like me. Neither of us had seen the big city, so this Okie-and-Kansan pair had a swell time that beautiful fall day. We walked around the bustle on Wall Street and into Battery Park. Women were everywhere in their long skirts and bobby socks. Don said he would be around the field tomorrow, so we should go together.

The next day, we caught the trolley down to Ebbets Field. When we got there, the clubhouse was a madhouse. Besides the extra players such as Don and me, reporters were everywhere with their papers and pens, and they all wanted to get their story. I suited up and went out on the field, and even more reporters were there.

After I warmed up, Joe Becker sent me to the mound, where several buckets of balls were waiting for me behind the protective screen. I warmed up with a few throws to Rube, and Jackie came up to the plate. The reporters gathered around home plate when Jackie stepped into the batting box. He looked intimidating to me even during practice, with those determined eyes. I threw him some easy pitches at about 90 percent, and he made perfect contact with every one of them. He sent line drive after line drive out to the field like a machine gun. He started down the third baseline and worked his way around to first. He even hit a few out of the park — that got the reporters scribbling.

Pitching batting practice was hard because there was no messing around. No looking around the bases or getting signs. I'd throw the pitch, and Crack! went the bat. I reached down, grabbed another ball, threw the pitch, and *Crack* again. Rinse and repeat. I was throwing a pitch about every ten to fifteen seconds. I worked up a sweat real quick like this.

Next up was Pee Wee. The reporters loved Pee Wee, and he stopped to answer their questions. They asked him about how he was going to beat the Yankees without Podres. He talked about Sal and Newk and Drysdal and Clem and all the others. Pee Wee was facing the Yankees for his seventh time — more than any Dodger ever. He was a sophomore in '41, when he faced the Yankees the first time, and he was the only remaining player from that venerable team. The questions kept coming, and Pee Wee kept talking. I liked the break.

When Alston saw that Pee Wee wasn't getting his hitting practice in, he said, "You guys let my men hit. Kipp, throw the ball in here, and keep 'em comin'." I resumed, and Pee Wee hit the ball solid. Pee Wee had an air about him, and I knew I could count on him.

Next up was Duke Snider. Man, could he pound that ball! He pulled two in a row out onto Bedford Avenue. Roy and Junior came up as well, and I worked up a good sweat before Chuck Templeton came to relieve me. Sandy Koufax and Ken Lehman were also lined up to get the batters used to lefties as much as we could. I figure that if I was pitching once every fifteen

WORLD 1956 SERIES

*This was the last World Series at Ebbets Field, and this program promoted the
stature of the two managers – Casey Stengel and Walter Alston.*

seconds for twenty-five minutes, I got in a hundred pitches. Now I understood why Newk had complained about pitching batting practice. It was like pitching a whole game without a break.

Coach Becker came over to me and thanked me for pitching, and I thanked him for having me there. I told him how excited I was and that I was having the time of my life. He said that they were going to have a pitcher's strategy meeting in the bull pen if I wanted to join. I said sure and walked across the field with him.

All the pitchers who weren't in batting practice were in the bull pen, and Joe wanted to work out some new signals. I sat down with Sal on my right and Clem on my left. Don Drysdale was standing tall outside in the sun. Stealing signs had a long history, and Becker had a new strategy worked out so no one could figure out the signs—even if they saw them. He said he'd been working on it with Roy and Dixie, and it was the time to reveal it to the whole pitching staff. Roy went out and squatted in front of us with his glove on.

Joe started explaining that the glove position would be the indicator, and the throwing hand would call the pitch. Roy said that the catcher would show multiple signs, and if the glove was pointed up, then the pitcher would throw the first hand sign. If the glove was on his left leg, then it'd be the third sign. If the glove pointed down as if he were going to catch a pop fly, then the pitcher would take the second sign. If the glove was on the right leg, then we would throw the same pitch as last time regardless of what he signed.

Joe explained the signals. "Showing one finger is a fastball, and pitch it inside or outside based on the opposite direction of the lean of the finger. Two's a curve. Three's a slider. Four is a knuckle. A pinky up is a screwball. A finger down is a brushback."

Roy said, "I thought the pinky was the brushback."

Dixie said, "No, the pinky is a screwball."

Joe butted in, and they were discussing the signal strategy while all the pitchers were looking at one another and shaking their heads in disbelief.

After another minute or two of squabbling between them, I could feel Sal getting frustrated. He leaned forward and said, "Wait a minute. Wait a minute. Hold evvveryyything! There's no way I'm going to remember all this horse shit. I'm an old dog, and I don't want any new tricks — especially not with this circus going on all around us. Roy, you show me a one, and it's a fastball, and two is a curve. It's that simple." All the pitchers nodded and yepped in agreement.

Sal continued. "Our signs have been working great all year, so I don't think it's time to change. If they're looking at the signal, I'll make them forget all about it with a brushback. I've done this my whole career, so I don't see any reason to change, especially since they haven't played me since '51. OK?"

Joe and Roy agreed. We'd just keep it simple and effective. We all knew that Sal had the control and power to make it happen. We started talking about each hitter and how Yogi seemed to be able to hit anything. Keep it high and tight on Mantle but low and away on McDougald. We kept going through the roster and discussed which hitters would take the first pitch and which ones would swing.

Joe talked about how to stay ahead in the count and not to worry about this or that. Sal was looking down at his glove and didn't seem to pay much attention. He'd heard it all before and knew what to do. I looked around, and the others were intently nodding away and trying to remember everything. We concluded the meeting, and I hit the showers before heading back to the Bossert.

I was so excited for the Series that night that I hardly slept. I got up early the next morning and went out on the field at about eight thirty in the morning, before anyone else but the ground crew. Today was going to be the day I watched my first World Series game. I'd never even seen one on TV before. I walked up onto the mound and just looked around at the field and stands that held so much history.

The Ebbets Field outfield walls were at about four different angles around the scoreboard. The high scoreboard in right field was a foreshadowing of the China Wall in the LA Coliseum in years to come. The beer advertisements on the outfield wall are permanently etched in my mind. My favorite had to be the hole in the right-field wall that offered a free suit to anyone who could hit the ball in the hole. No one could ever hit that hole when Carl Furillo was defending it.

Carl got a lot of credit for fielding the sharply angled right-field wall like a champion. When a reporter asked him how he got so good at it, Carl looked hard at the reporter and said, "I worked f***ing hard at it!" The reporters couldn't print that, so they weren't very happy with the reply. They wouldn't selectively quote a player.

While Carl got to work or practice in Ebbets Field, visiting outfielders didn't get the same opportunity. The right-field wall was a focus for our batters because of this difference. During the little time I was at Ebbets, I saw my team hit two inside-the-park home runs. The walls weren't padded, so the ball would shoot off the wall. Sandy Amoros hit a fly ball, and it hit the bottom of the wall, which was made of concrete. The ball ricocheted off the wall and rolled across the whole field behind third base, where nobody was ready. Sandy just churned around the bases and scored easily.

Carl knew how to intercept the ball and then unleash his second weapon—his arm. Carl was known as the Reading Rifle and could throw home without a relay man. The Ebbets Field crowd definitely focused on Skoonj—our name for Carl—when the ball went to right field.

I walked back into the clubhouse and heard that fans had started lining up outside at about nine in the morning. The gates opened at eleven. Some people had camped out to get tickets, and a few standing tickets were still available up to game time. They'd set up special seats wherever they could fit them for games like this. It was going to be packed.

I pitched batting practice again, and everybody hit a lot less and was just getting warmed up. I still worked up a sweat and hit the showers and got back into my civilian clothes. I wasn't allowed to sit in the dugout, so I decided to watch the game in the clubhouse. The clubhouse was all concrete and rather damp from the showers and all. I felt as if I were watching the game from a bomb shelter.

When I heard the Fourteenth Regiment band play "Hail to the Chief," I had to go see the president. I walked down the tunnel and stood in the dugout while all the players were out on the field. Dwight D. Eisenhower was running for reelection and was driven into the stadium in his bubble-top limousine. He was waving to all of the possible voters as they drove him behind home plate. He got out and shook all the players' hands. There were lots of photo ops with the managers, the commissioners, the governor, the mayor, and even the Duke of Windsor. It went on for quite some time before Eisenhower finally threw out the opening pitch. I went back down the long hallway to the clubhouse before the game finally started at one o'clock.

The Yankees were eight-to-five favorites to win the Series but only six-to-five favorites to win the opening game against Sal. The papers talked about how Ebbets was a graveyard for lefties such as Whitey and me. Right field was just over a hundred yards away because the field had to stop short of Bedford Avenue. Homers over the thirty-five-foot scoreboard wall often flew into the used-car lot across the street and shattered windshields.

Mickey Mantle was a switch hitter and had one of the most powerful swings in the game. His powerful legs, back, and arms uncoiled to deliver devastating blows.

Watching the game on TV in the clubhouse wasn't nearly as exciting as watching it from the dugout and bull pen. John Griffin, the guy who passed out at the pennant party, was in there with me and wasn't looking too good. I wondered if I would have to call another ambulance for him. I wandered up to the dugout and stood in the doorway a few times at key moments in the game, but I couldn't stay there for long.

The game started as expected, with Mickey hitting a home run in the first. Our guys weren't put off, and Jackie hit one of his line drives out of the park in the second inning. Gil Hodges followed with a three-run homer in the third, so Casey took Whitey out of the game. That three-run homer pretty much made the difference in the game and extended Gil's dominance of the Yanks. Gil had hit in the only two runs of game seven of '55. He was our offensive stalwart.

After the win, it was exciting seeing all the players file into the clubhouse. Sal, of course, was the other hero of the game and was swarmed by the press. People thought that he had been interviewed more than Eisenhower over the last couple weeks. Sal said, "This was my greatest thrill. Yes, even more of a thrill than my no-hitter."

Sal was now the hero of Brooklyn after he'd been the Dodger nemesis for so many years. Sal was primarily hated for brushing back our hitters and for how he pitched for the Giants in the third game of the '51 playoffs. Sal pitched until the ninth inning in that game before his teammate Bobby Thompson hit his walk-off homer that became known as the "shot heard 'round the world." Because of that game, Sal needed to rest during the first games of the World Series and didn't get to pitch until the fourth game. Sal lost that game against the Yanks, but he finally got his World Series victory.

Sports of the Times, Splashes from Ebbets Field

Arthur Daley, *New York Times*, October 5, 1956

Fresco Thompson, the Dodger vice president in charge of the farm system, stepped into the dressing room. His eyes glistened at the sight of the Barber. "My one regret," said Fresco, "is that every young pitcher in our organization couldn't have been here to watch Maglie work. There was the artist supreme. Mantle had tagged him for a terrific homer and old Sal wasn't going to let that happen again. So the next time up he teases Mantle until Mickey begins to spot the target he's gonna reach next, that apartment house three blocks beyond Bedford Avenue. Then Maglie slips him that nickel slider to strike him out. What a job!"

I went to Ebbets Field again on the morning of Thursday, October 4, in a slight rain. We all gathered in the clubhouse, and I was suited up for batting practice when commissioner Ford C. Frick called the game at 11:00 a.m. Half the players were dressed, and half weren't, so everyone but Don Newcombe got back into our civilian clothes. Newk said he didn't like the delay and was going to run on the field to keep in shape. The rain wasn't stopping Newk. He always had a good workout routine—rain or shine.

Whitey Ford was the most consistent pitcher on the Yankees.

The skies cleared on Friday the fifth, and we got in the same routine. I pitched batting practice, and as I was going off the field, I saw Billy Martin in the Yankee dugout. I walked over to him and said, "Nice job on the homer in game one."

Billy nodded his head with a smile and said, "Thanks! You aren't getting any playing time here, are ya? You should come and play for us."

"Like I'd get more of a shot here with Whitey, Sturdivant, McDermott, and your lefty relievers." I said.

"We do have a lot of lefties, but you never know. We're going for it today. We don't want to fall two games back."

"We're going for it too. Good luck out there," I said.

I went back to the clubhouse and showered and stayed in there again until the opening pitch. I watched from the dugout again when Adlai Stevenson, Eisenhower's Democratic rival, threw out the opening pitch. Adlai didn't get any of the pageantry of Ike. Ike had driven around the field after the third inning in his limo too, but Adlai just stayed in his seat. It must be good to be president.

We called this game the "Battle of the Big Dons" because big Don Newcombe was battling big Don Larsen. Both men were six four like me, but they both had forty to fifty pounds on me. It was interesting how many tall Dons were on the teams. Don Demeter was also my height, and then Don Drysdale was six five. I'm not sure how that happened, but I can't remember being anyplace else except my family reunions where I could stand up and look so many men straight in the eye. The Dodgers liked them big, and Roger Craig was right up there too.

The game didn't start out well for Newk. He'd been talking about winning the big game for so long, but he wasn't going to get it today. The Yanks scored one in the first, and then Don Larsen hit Billy in before Newk let the bases get loaded with a walk and a hit. Then, Newk's nemesis came to the plate. Yogi Berra always had Newk's number. This encounter ended in a grand slam, and it finished Newk off for the day. The Yanks were up 6–0, and things were looking down.

Newk stormed into the clubhouse slamming lockers and sulking around. He hit the showers, put on his clothes, and left. A player isn't supposed to leave in the middle of the game. Newk was fighting his demons and just couldn't control himself. Right after he left, he punched some smart-alecky parking-lot attendant in the gut and almost got arrested for it. Newk was on a downward spiral, and no one seemed to be able to help him.

The Dodgers could help themselves, though. They were in the World Series for a reason, and their resilience was one of their strongest suits. In the bottom of the second, Roy came up with the bases loaded and hit a sacrifice fly to score the first run. When Larsen walked Jim Gilliam to load the bases again, Casey pulled him.

Roy Campanella runs to first while Yogi Berra directs the fielding. These were the two best catchers I ever played with.

Johnny Kucks was his replacement, and Pee Wee came up and hit a single to score two more. Casey didn't like the way Johnny lined up against the Duke, so he put in Tommy Byrne. Casey was burning through his dugout faster than a forest fire. With two men on base, the Duke hit a homer to even the score at 6–6 in the bottom of the second. That's how Dodgers get up after they've been hit down!

In the third, Alston put in Don Bessent, and Casey put in Tom Sturdivant. Sturdivant couldn't get out of the inning before another Dodger score, so Casey put in Tom Morgan. In the fifth, Gil hit a couple of guys in, so Casey put in Bob Turley. In the sixth, Casey put in Mickey McDermott. After a couple more scores, Casey basically threw in the towel and stuck with McDermott. Casey worked through seven of his ten pitchers, and we won 13–8.

The hero of the game turned out to be another Don—Don Bessent. Bessent gave up only six hits, which were scattered over seven innings. Gil continued his streak against the Yanks with four RBIs, and Duke had three. Our hitting really came through for us with thirteen runs. The Dodgers were up two games now, and the locker room was upbeat but reserved. It was always hard to go into legendary Yankee Stadium, and that was where we were headed. More times than not, the Dodgers left there with heads down.

On Saturday the sixth, I paid my first visit to Yankee Stadium. I suited up and walked out to the mound. The stadium was so much roomier than Ebbets Field. Center field was 461 feet, compared to Brooklyn's farthest distance of 393 feet. That 70-foot difference could lead to a lot of pop flies instead of home runs. One odd feature of Yankee Stadium was that it was only 296 feet down right-field line—one foot closer than Ebbets. But the home-run wall in the stadium quickly falls back to 344 feet, while Ebbets's right-field wall dropped away slowly. I knew it would be fun to play in this monster stadium, which seated over twice as many fans as Ebbets—seventy-four thousand to thirty-six thousand.

I wasn't able to stay in the locker room for the games at Yankee Stadium. My batting-practice work earned me a seat right behind one of the support girders. I could see the pitcher, but I had to lean forward and to the right to see the batter hit. I don't have a lot to say about this game except that Whitey Ford was on his home turf that day, and the Yankees were due. Roger Craig pitched pretty well for us until Enos Slaughter, whom they called Old Forty because of his age, hit a three-run homer. Just as in game one, that homer made the difference, and Enos was the hero. Billy Martin also hit his second homer of the Series. We played well, just not good enough to beat the Yankees at home.

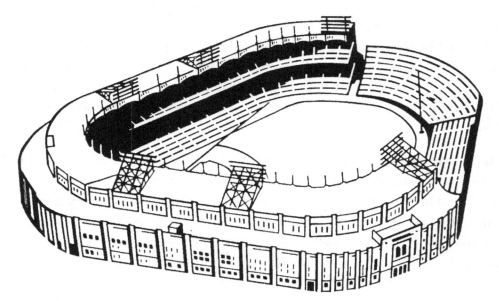

Yankee Stadium, New York——First Game Played April 18, 1923

We called Yankee Stadium the Roman Coliseum because of its overwhelming stature. The stadium was laid out well, but the right field flag pole was only 296' away while center field was a distant 461'!

Monday was game four, and this time Yankee Okie Tom Sturdivant went the distance and gave up only six hits. Mickey Mantle hit his second homer of the Series, and Hank Bauer slashed one as well. Carl Erskine started for us but let in a couple of runs and got pinch hit out of the game. It was nice to see the rookie Don Drysdale get in a couple of innings. He was only nineteen, but I could tell that he was going to be a strong pitcher for us. The Yanks thus tied the Series up at 2–2, and we were headed into the crucial game five before we headed back to Ebbets.

Monday, October 8, 1956, turned out to be a perfect day for Don Larsen. For only the fifth time since the turn of the century, Don kept the Dodgers from ever getting on base. From the scoreboard perspective, it's a string of zeros all the way across. No one had thrown a perfect game in the majors in thirty-four years! No one had ever even thrown a no-hitter in a World Series before that day. Larsen was one of the key pitchers for the Yankees that year and had thrown four four-hitters, but this was still beyond anybody's dream of what he could achieve.

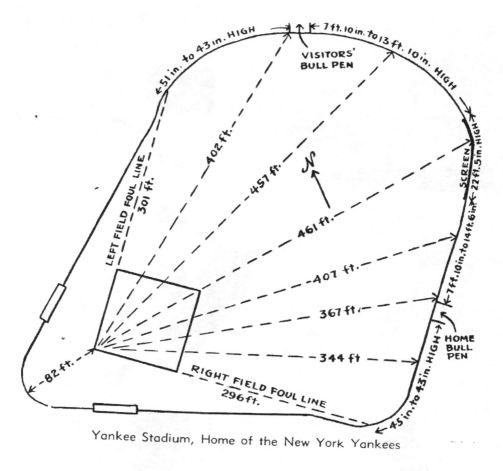

Yankee Stadium, Home of the New York Yankees

Yankee Stadium was only about three hundred feet down the foul lines but went deep in left and center field to four hundred and sixty feet.

Casey had always been a fan of the big righty and often said, "He can be one of baseball's great pitchers anytime he puts his mind to it." Larsen was known as a partier and didn't have the best work ethic. A few years later, when I was talking to Don about the game, he said, "I tried to throw down the middle, but I hit all the corners." A perfect game is also a team effort because no one can have an error, and the Yanks had to make some great plays to get us out. His pitching was still over the top. With twenty-seven batters, only once did Don ever get a batter to three balls and flirt with a walk. Sometimes you're hot, and sometimes you're smoking hot. Just a perfect day.

Don Larsen was a big man and had twenty pounds on me. Every pitch came together for him on that perfect day.

I've watched a lot of baseball games in my time, but I've never felt anything close to the tension in the air in the ninth inning of this perfect game. It was an odd game to watch, too, because of how Don threw without a windup—something he'd started only a month earlier. Don would just stand there looking at home plate until he let it rip without the windup. As the game progressed, everyone held their breath while he stood there on the mound. Everyone was mesmerized and didn't want to miss a pitch—that one pitch that would ruin his perfect game.

After each pitch, the whole crowd would look around and whisper about what was going to happen. The whole stadium hung on every pitch. It wasn't until Yogi Berra caught the last strike that the stadium erupted. Yogi ran out and jumped in Don's arms, and the Yankees swarmed them. Total chaos.

What many people forget about the game was that Don was going up against our hot pitcher—Old Sal. Who's going to talk about the great five-hitter that Sal pitched when your opponent throws perfect? Sal gave it all he had, but it just wasn't good enough on this Monday. Sal matched Don for the first eleven batters, until the Mick clobbered one into the lower right stands. Sal even struck out the last three batters he faced in the eighth, but it just wasn't good enough on that day.

The talk in the clubhouse, particularly from Sal, was that if we had been playing in Ebbets field, the result would have been different. For starters, Mick's line-drive homer would have bounced off the high right-field wall in Ebbets. It was a homer here because of the low walls of Yankee Stadium. The second observation was that Gil's long hit to left center would have been a homer in Ebbets. I found this talk rather useless, though, because the pitcher and hitter work differently in each stadium. Talking about these odd possibilities is just wasted talk about parallel universes.

The week was rolling by at a harried pace, since the only traveling either team needed to do was to catch a bus across town. With only one rain delay, the games came on fast, one day after another. The Series had played out the exact opposite of '55. We were back in Brooklyn now, and Walt decided to pitch Clem Labine again, since he had only relieved for two innings so far. We hoped for a repeat of his last start against the Pirates.

On Tuesday, October 9, Clem faced off against the 215-pound right hander Bob Turley. Bullet Bob had come to the Yankees the year before with Don Larsen in a massive eighteen-player trade with the Orioles. Bob and Clem both gave up hits in the first inning, but no runs. They both held their opponents scoreless until the tenth inning.

Some fans don't like pitching duels like this with no major hits or homers, but I was enthralled and watched every pitch from the clubhouse. I was amazed by Clem's sharp sinker, which kept causing grounders. Turley was even throwing harder and better and set a team series record of striking out eleven. He only gave up four hits. He excelled all afternoon until it hurt the most in the bottom of the tenth. Jackie hit a line drive to left field to score Gilliam for the only run of the game. This was only the second World Series game in which the pitchers kept a shutout going into extra innings—1914 was the first one. It came down to game seven, and the tension rose to a crescendo.

For the final game, Walt gave Newk one more chance to win the World Series. This was definitely the big game that Don was looking for. Hank Bauer was the first up, and he hit a single to left field. Then he struck out Billy and Mickey in three pitches each. Don looked good, but the next player up was his old nemesis—Berra. Yogi laid into a pitch and put the ball into the cheap seats to put the Yanks up 2–0 in the first. In the third, Yogi came up again, and Billy was on first this time. Newk got a couple strikes on Yogi and a foul tip before Yogi clobbered another one into the stands. Unbelievable!

Yogi had set the record that year for the most career home runs by a catcher, at 238, and he just kept adding to that total. Yogi set all kinds of World Series records, including most games played and singles. He hit homers in nine different World Series and hit and scored at least one run in twelve. He played thirty games without errors. And the list goes on. It is likely that no one will ever surpass his records unless a team becomes as dominant as the Yankees were in the 1950s.

Walt still had faith in Newk and kept him in after Yogi's homer, but he had to pull him in the top of the fourth when Elston Howard hit the third homer off him. I was in the clubhouse again when Newk came in. I could just feel his anger. I saw Irving Rudd, a press agent for the Dodgers, follow Don into the showers. He was trying to keep Newk from leaving, but nothing was going to stop Newk from leaving. Newk was inconsolable and put on his street clothes and walked out. He ended up wandering through the streets all night.

Back to the game. While we had bounced back in game two from a 6–0 deficit, there would be no comebacks on this day. The twenty-three-year-old Tommy Kucks threw an impressive four-hitter, and it was Alston's turn to go through the pitching ranks. Don Bessent lasted a few innings. Then Roger Craig got pummeled for a grand slam off Elston Howard and didn't even get anyone out. Ed and Carl came in to relieve as well, but there was no stopping the Yanks.

The Series was the exact opposite of '55, when we beat the Yanks in game seven in Yankee Stadium. This time we got beat with four homers and a grand slam. There's not a lot to talk about after you lose the final game by nine runs without getting a score. The score for a forfeit is 9–0, and that is what it was like. Some said this was the day the Bums died. The next day was going to be the start of a long set of flights to Japan for our goodwill tour.

Highlights

- I pitched batting practice for the Dodgers, but I couldn't wear the uniform or be in the dugout or bull pen for the games.

- I joined the team in celebrating Sal's game-one victory in the clubhouse.

- I saw one of the most famous games in World Series history when Don Larsen threw his perfect game against Sal Maglie in Yankee Stadium.

- The Series went to seven games, and I saw Don Newcombe and the Dodgers go down to the Yankees in their fifth World Series defeat to the Yankees out of six tries.

9. THE GOODWILL TOUR OF JAPAN — 1956

On the morning after losing the World Series, we had our World Series party in the Bossert. A gloom hung in the air, and it wasn't much fun talking about how we had lost. We weren't the world champs now. We were the Bums again. If we counted the two losses by the Brooklyn Robins, Brooklyn had lost eight of the nine World Series we'd been in. We were the chumps of New York.

The drama of the day was about Newk again. He didn't show up at the party, so everyone was talking about whether he'd make the tour. Buzzie Bavasi, our general manager, was saying that we'd have to fine him if he didn't make the Japan tour. The party ended before noon, and we headed out to Idlewild for our Pan American Airways charter flight on a DC-7 to Los Angeles.

When we got to the airport, a slew of reporters were waiting for us. We took many photos, and when we started boarding, Newk showed up in dark sunglasses. It turned out that he had been in court that morning for punching the parking-lot attendant after game two. The court had delayed the hearing until after the Japan tour, which would keep us away for over a month. He had dodged reporters all night, so they gathered around him and hounded him.

Fifty-one people got on the plane that day, including the National League president, Warren C. Giles. Additional people for the Dodgers included our announcer Vin Scully. Walter O'Malley brought his wife; his son, Peter; and his daughter, Terry. Alston brought his wife and daughter, and several players brought their wives, including Randy Jackson's wife, who had been Miss Georgia. They had some Japanese stewardesses on board, who gave us robes and other gifts.

After we got seated, the piston-powered engines on the DC-7 revved up, and the whole plane shook. The four-prop plane rolled down the runway and took off to start a bumpy ride. I was sitting with Don Demeter, and Newk and Campy were sitting a few rows in front of us. Across the aisle from us were Walt and his wife. Alston's daughter and some other couples were behind us. Someone had brought a bottle of whiskey, and they were passing it around. We had about a seven-hour flight, and the guys were getting pretty loud after a couple of hours of drowning their sorrows.

After a lot of laughter, yelling, and jacking around, Walt finally got tired of their noise and told them to keep it down. They quieted down for a little while, but they were just having too much fun and were blowing off steam. I could see Walt repeatedly apologizing to his wife about the ruckus.

A few minutes later, Newk lumbered down the aisle toward us, bumping into the chairs in a drunken state. Walt looked really pissed and stood up and blocked his way. Walt wasn't afraid of anybody and was man enough to take Big Don on if he needed to. Walt got in his face and said, "Don, you go back and sit down. I've heard enough out of you for the day."

Newk looked really upset and confused and just stood there for a few seconds, wobbling and trying to figure out what to do. Then he looked at Walt and said, "Get out of my way, Walt, or I'm going to piss on you!"

I could see Walt was about ready to explode. His wife and daughter were sitting right there watching. Walt was in a pickle. We were just a few hours into a month-long trip, and tempers were already boiling over. Walt looked up at Newk and said, "You go to the head, and then you get back in your seat and shut up!" Walt took his seat and let Newk go to the bathroom.

Everyone started talking in hushed tones, and Walt was again apologizing to his wife for their behavior. The players weren't usually in such tight quarters with the wives and families, so it was quite the controversy. Don Demeter looked over to me and said, "Fasten your seat belt. It's going to be a bumpy ride!" I started cracking up, and when I stopped, I saw Walt looking over at us and giving us the stink eye. I immediately turned on a frown, and Walt went back to consoling his wife. Newk walked back after a few minutes, and nothing much happened after that.

Everyone was very exhausted, and none more so than our announcer Vin Scully. Vin had been fighting bronchitis and had not slept much for a couple nights. He'd just announced one of the most famous games of his illustrious career—Don Larsen's perfect game. When Vin got on the plane, he fell into a deep sleep, and Walter O'Malley thought it would be funny to draw a unibrow across his forehead and a beard on his announcing prodigy. The result of O'Malley's work is shown in the picture below. I knew this would be an unusual trip.

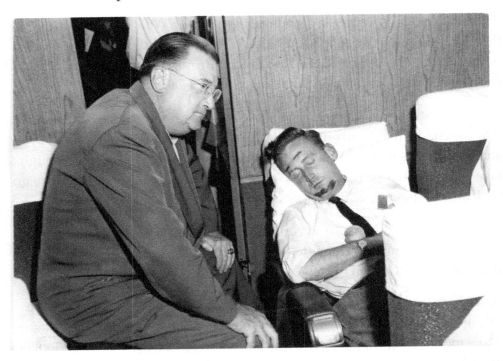

Walter O'Malley thought it would be funny to draw a unibrow and beard on Vin Scully when he slept deeply after fighting bronchitis, jet lag, and a long season.

We had a layover for the night in Los Angeles, and none of the players knew that Walter O'Malley was talking with city councilmen and women about moving to LA. We took off the next day for another long leg of the multileg journey. Next stop—Kahului, Maui, Hawaii. We played an exhibition game there in a little farm field. It took me back to the small-town games in Piqua, but these locals were playing the National League pennant–winning Dodgers! We had a good time playing them, and we joked around a lot.

The next day, we flew to Honolulu, where we had a big reception at the airport. Thousands of people came out to see us. We got big, fragrant leis put around our necks. It was a beautiful day, and I remember the hula girls dancing and lots of hullaballoo to welcome us.

A few special guests met me in Honolulu. Three of my old college colleagues from Emporia State came to greet me — Robert Ikehara, Bill Akana, and Morris Yonamine. I had played baseball and basketball with them at Emporia State, and they were great athletes and good friends. They gave me the shirt shown in this picture.

They had a funny story about how they had gotten to Kansas from Hawaii. When they were seniors in high school, they put a map of the United States on the wall and threw a dart at it to see where they'd go to college. Just like in the movie *Doctor Doolittle*, the dart landed in the middle of the map and next to nowhere. When they went closer, they saw that it had landed on Emporia, Kansas. That was when they decided to go to little College of Emporia. They later transferred to Emporia State, where we became teammates and good friends.

I met up with my old college teammates in Honolulu — Robert Ikehara, me, Bill Akana, and Morris Yonamine.

We played two exhibition games in Honolulu. We won the first game against the Honolulu All Stars 19–0, but the second game, against the Oahu

Red Sox, went into extra innings. We ended up winning 7–3 in the tenth inning off a grand slam. We had a big luau and a lot of fun in Hawaii. We had one day off in Honolulu and went to Pearl Harbor to visit the historic site. We also went to Waikiki beach, where I saw surfers for the first time. Few people had heard of surfing then, and I don't remember any of our players going out in the waves.

After our one-day break, it was back on a long flight to Wake Island. We had some tire problems there and were stuck in the airport for five hours. Wake Island was just a speck of an island with an airstrip out in the middle of the ocean. When the islanders heard about the delay, they declared a national holiday, and the whole island seemed show up at the airport to see us. We signed a bunch of autographs and talked with the locals.

We had time to kill and were just waiting around the airport. It was hot, so Pee Wee decided to go for a swim and put his trunks on. He went out there as everyone watched. After he came back, someone told him there was a shark problem in the bay. Pee Wee's face turned white, and he shook with fear and said, "Why didn't you tell me that before I went out there?"

After the repairs were finished, we got on the final leg of the journey to Tokyo. The flight was long and rough. Our plane, the *Clipper Fortuna*, got thrown around like rag doll in the wind. Don Demeter was sitting next to me, and we were both throwing up. After hours of turbulence that slowed the flight down, we hit a smooth spot, and several of us got up and congregated in the galley. Don Drysdale, Campy, Newk, and others came in and out to stretch our legs. The stewardesses were very accommodating, and we had a good laugh at Pee Wee's swimming misadventure. I really enjoyed hanging out with the guys.

When the plane finally got to Japan after nine thousand miles and about thirty hours of flying, we were treated to a grand parade from Haneda Airport to the Imperial Hotel. We got in a bunch of Cadillacs and paraded through the streets of Tokyo. They had expected five hundred thousand people to show up for the parade, but because of the rain and our delay, only about one hundred thousand people watched us enter the city. When we got to the Imperial Hotel, the Japanese showered us with more flowers than I'd ever seen. Forty beautiful actresses from Daiei Studios gave us big wreaths of flowers and silk robes and headbands. They served us a never-ending stream of crab cocktails and sparkling wine.

Travel Time to Japan

Departure	Destination	Mileage	Flight Time
New York	Los Angeles	2,475	8 hours
Los Angeles	Maui	2,490	8 hours
Honolulu	Wake Island	2,298	7 hours
Wake Island	Tokyo	1,991	6 hours
Total		9,254	29 hours

We had a planeload of people lined up for one of the many photo ops. I'm below the black arrow. I identify many of the people on my website at www.fredkipp.com/Japan, where I have many more pictures of the trip.

Dignitaries were everywhere in the hotel. From American military personnel and ambassadors to Japanese politicians and baseball legends, everyone was at the hotel shaking hands and greeting others. Matsutaro Shoriki, the father of Japanese baseball, was prominent, and other Japanese were always bowing to him. Most of this trip would turn into these big photo ops.

We were only the fifth major-league baseball team to tour Japan. The first two tours were in the 1930s and featured an all-star team of Babe Ruth, Lou Gehrig, and Jimmie Foxx. Professional baseball started in Japan after the Babe Ruth tour of 1934. The legend goes that Sotaro Suzuki of the Yomiuri Group tracked down Babe Ruth in New York City and found him in a barbershop while getting a shave. While the Babe got cleaned up, Sotaro persuaded him to come to Japan for the tour.

Sotaro was a prominent businessman in the Yomiuri Group, which is still the largest media company in Japan. The Yomiuri Group still owns the *Yomiuri News*, or *Shimbun*, the newspaper with the largest circulation in the world. They also owned the Yomiuri Giants baseball team and organized the whole goodwill tour. Other goodwill tours included the New York Giants' in 1953 and the Yankees' tour in 1955. Sotaro Suzuki had arranged all five tours and was instrumental in the Dodgers-Japanese relationship, which continues to this day.

Suzuki corresponded with Walter O'Malley and arranged the nineteen-game tour. The tour would start in Tokyo and go from the far northern island of Sapporo to the southern island of Kyushu. The Dodgers would play a mixture of all-star teams and regular teams, and I would end up pitching.

The Dodgers' relationship with Japanese baseball increased after 1956. The Dodgers traveled to Japan and played more exhibition games in 1966 and 1993. In 1957 and nine other spring trainings after that, Japanese players and coaches trained at Vero Beach with the Dodgers. Peter O'Malley was on the goodwill tour and was instrumental in signing Japanese pitcher Hideo Nomo, who became rookie of the year in 1995 and the source of Nomomania in Japan. The Dodgers continued by signing Kazuhisa Ishii in 2002. All of these Dodgers-Japanese relations started back in 1956.

Actresses from Daiei Studios gave us large bouquets of flowers in the first of many glamorous receptions. The white arrow points at me in the background, and Walter O'Malley was the first in line.

Iola Register Sports Editorial

The Dodgers — and the Japanese — may look at Fred Kipp quite a bit on the National League Champions' tour of the Orient. In Japan, 500,000 persons are expected to greet the Dodgers Wednesday on their eight-mile motor ride from the Tokyo International Airport to their headquarters in the Imperial Hotel. The Japanese hero-worship the players much more than Americans do, so Freddy may be looked upon by them as one of Uncle Sam's greatest citizens.

The Yomiuri Giants were our first competitor on the tour, and we faced them the day after our arrival. Don Drysdale started and gave up a couple of homers before he was replaced by Don Bessent, who gave up a couple more.

We got beat that first game by the Giants, and people wrote it off as jet lag. We won the next day but then got beat again by an all-star team. O'Malley was fed up with the losses and tried to rally us by telling us to "remember Pearl Harbor." We won the next game in Sapporo, and then they decided to give me a chance.

On October 24 in Miyagi Stadium in Sendai, Japan, I pitched a shutout for seven innings before Ralph Branca relieved me. Ralph finished off the shutout, and I got the win as we pulled ahead in the series for the first time, 3–2. This win started a rally for us, and we didn't lose the next eight games and had only one tie when the game was called because of darkness.

Kansan with Dodgers Beats Japs, Wins Praise

Associated Press — October 25th

Big Fred Kipp, formerly with Brooklyn's farm team in Montreal, faced 23 batters in seven innings Wednesday, fanned six and gave up four hits and one pass. He blanked an All-Star Japanese team in Sendai, Northern Japan before 30,000 fans. The Japanese team was composed of top players from the Tokyo-Yokohama-Nagoya area.

Nobuyasu Nizuhara, pilot of the Yomuiri Giants said, "Japanese batters are able to handle the fast ball but we're still helpless against curves and change of pace such as those so flawlessly demonstrated by Fred Kipp."

Kansan Kipp Hogties Japs

Third sacker Atsushi Hadoka shook his head and said, "Kipp is a hard pitcher to get to. I couldn't hit any of his inside balls. They cut the corners sharp. They were puzzlers and I still don't know if they were a knuckleball or a palm ball."

Japanese players are calling Kipp a "knuckleball artist." Kipp admits he threw at least two dozen knuckleballs in the Sendai game. High praise also came from Manager Walter Alston and Kipp's teammates. Alston told Japanese reporters it was Kipp's second starting assignment before a packed stadium and said he was excellent.

Dodger's batting coach, Joe Becker, said "Kipp's a fine boy and has some good stuff on the ball. He's sure to figure in our hopes for next season."

Catcher Roy Campanella said: "Too bad we didn't use him in the World Series."

Those last three comments really felt good to hear. Joe was the pitching coach, not the batting coach, as the papers incorrectly said, so it was good to hear that Alston and Joe thought so highly of my performance. Having Roy say that I could have helped them in the World Series just made me ecstatic. My plan to play with the Dodgers seemed to be going just how I wanted it.

I was really glad that I had written a letter to O'Malley to request that I join them on the Japan tour. I'd heard about the tour and dictated a letter to a secretary in a Columbus, Ohio, hotel during the season so that I could get a chance to play on the tour. Besides playing with the Dodgers and giving Walter a chance to see me pitch, I was getting $2,000 for the six-week tour. That was a professional-league salary and over three times what I was making in Montreal at about $600 a month.

After that Sendai performance, I got to relieve in another game, and then I started again against the All-Japan team in Shimonoseki Stadium in southern Japan on Halloween. Maybe there was something to the Japanese saying they couldn't hit my knuckleball and changeups, because I threw a two-hitter and shut out the All Stars.

The next day was All Saints Day, and I went to church with the O'Malleys in the morning with some of the other Catholics. After that, we went to the Hiroshima Atomic Memorial, which is now known as the Hiroshima Peace Memorial Park. We went to pay our respects to those who had died just a little over eleven years earlier from the first atomic bomb that struck a city. It was a somber occasion. Later in the day, we dedicated a plaque at the Hiroshima Stadium that read, "We dedicate this visit in memory of those baseball fans and others who died by atomic action on August 6, 1945." It was signed by O'Malley, Alston, and several of the players.

Later in the day, we played the Kansai All Stars, and I had the day off to watch the game. One story I want to tell you about is Jackie Robinson's competitiveness. During the tour, he stole home base for the last time. We didn't know it then, but this tour would be his last games in professional baseball. Jackie would be traded to the Giants in the off season, and he would retire instead of playing for the hated Giants. He was thirty-seven on the tour, and his best years were behind him, but he was still a hero.

Don and I practiced our chopsticks at one of the many events that the Japanese put on for us.

Even in these exhibition games, Jackie was intense and would tell everyone what he thought. When the sixteen-year veteran umpire Jocko Conlan called a runner safe at second, Jackie started hollering and told Jocko that he was "out of position." Jocko wasn't going to put up with his antics and threw him out of the game. Jackie's competitive attitude really set the tone for the team.

I started another game on November 4, in front of forty-five thousand fans in Nishinomiya Stadium in Osaka. Don Demeter, my roommate during the tour, hit his fifth home run in the game to put us in the lead. Don was in a home run duel with Duke. Duke wouldn't let that stand and hit his sixth homer of the series to tie the game in the ninth inning. Many of these games were coming down to the ninth. With the bases loaded, Tetsuji Kawakami of the All-Japan team blooped a single toward Don to score the winning run on Clem Labine. We led the series 9–3–1.

People always say that Roger Craig and I look alike. This Japanese program put pictures of me pitching with a big picture of Roger. I guess we do look alike!

A funny story happened on the express Swallow train to Gifu, a city in central Japan. Our translator had told us that the train was very punctual and that we'd only have one minute to get off the train when it arrived at Gifu. Rain was pouring down when we got into the station, and thirty of us had to get off with all our gear. Most of us had big duffel bags with all of our clothes, jerseys, cleats, and gloves. People were fussing about getting out in the rain and gathering all their stuff, and our translator started yelling, "Get off the train! The train won't wait!"

We kept piling off the train into the rain, but a line of people was still waiting when the whistle blew to signal that it was departing. To get off the train fast, some players decided to improvise a door. I stepped off the train just in time to see Carl Erskine and a couple others throwing their bags out the window. The train started rolling, and the next thing I knew, Oisk and others were climbing out the window and falling without grace onto the platform. We were laughing like crazy in the rain as Oisk and the others rolled around on the platform as the train took off. Everybody got off the train in time, but the game was rained out, so we had the afternoon off.

We walked around Gifu and other parts of Japan, and women and kids seemed to be everywhere. Japan had a large population explosion after World War II, so kids five to ten years old were everywhere in the streets. I saw them playing baseball from dawn to dusk in little baseball parks we'd see around the cities. In the bars and clubs, beautiful women were lined up along the walls and were ready to dance with the players. We noticed how many of the women were well educated and in their thirties. We guessed that was because so many of the men of their age had been killed in World War II. About two million military personnel were killed in World War II, and the majority were men, so that left a lot of single women.

We'd also go on shopping excursions to places such as the Canon factory. Here's a picture of Don Drysdale and Campy with me, looking at lenses and cameras. We also shopped for china, and I bought a set of nice Noritaki china for my mother and shipped it home. It took about a month to get there, but she cherished that beautiful set for the rest of her life. We had a fair amount of time to wander around the towns and eat sushi and drink beers. I was amazed at how many people were in Japan—on bicycles or walking around. It was such a far cry from the countryside of Kansas where I had grown up.

Another funny story from Japan was Gil Hodge's clown act. Gil was not known for being a clown in Ebbets Field, but he put on little skits for the fawning Japanese. He was put out in left field to give Jim Gentile some time on first base. I guess it was the casual atmosphere of the goodwill tour that gave Gil the freedom to have some fun.

In between plays, Gil kept pantomiming the other players and gave some good impressions of Campy catching or Roger pitching. When Pee Wee made an error and kicked the ball in a game in Nagoya, Gil glowered and pointed his finger at Pee Wee in disapproval. Gil would make his legs quiver or shake a fist at an opposing player who got a hit. We were all watching him from the dugout, and he was quite the comedian when he'd swing his arms or stomp the ground. He'd frown at bad plays or smile real big at good ones—things he would never do back home. Back home, they'd skin him alive if he did that and made an error.

朝早く、東京を出発したドジャースは、十時半、元気に甲府駅に姿を現わした。ホームでは甲府市のブラスバンドが、「アメリカ「国歌」」を吹奏して出迎えた

Don Demeter, Pee Wee, and I were at attention while they butchered the national anthem on a bugle. This picture is from a Japanese magazine about the tour.

I was a regular pitcher on the tour now and getting a start every fourth day. On November 8, I started against the All-Japan team in Kusanagi Stadium in Shizuoka, in front of twenty thousand fans. Satoru Sugiyama hit a two-run homer off me in the second. In the fifth inning, I hit an RBI double to score Herb Olson and then scored on an infield error to tie the game at 2–2. We stayed tied into the ninth inning when Kohei Sugiyama got a single to start the inning off. On the next play, I couldn't chase down a bunt in time to throw out Sugiyama at second. With runners on first and second, they brought in Don Bessent, who gave up

The November 8 game was rebroadcast on November 23 on WRCA AM 660. The *New York Times* said, "The fans seemed decorous and no epithet in any way related to 'dem bums' was audible. Vin Scully and Billy McCord helped make the sports program into a breezy and educational cultural affair by their descriptions and interviews."

the winning run. I was just a few outs from finishing the game.

Campy, Don Drysdale, and I were into our cameras at the Canon factory. Don Demeter and Randy Jackson are in the background.

On November 13, I started the last game of the tour—a makeup game in Fukuoka's Heiwadai Stadium of a rainout on October 30. I pitched the whole game and gave up only six hits. My roomy hit in the last run to give us a 3–1 win over the All-Japan team. By the end of the series, I had pitched forty-three innings and only gave up six runs. I also had the most strikeouts on the team, at twenty-six. I had a good hitting streak and was one of seven Dodgers who hit over .300 for the series. I couldn't have asked for much more success on the tour.

After this series, the Dodgers had played in 218 games—probably more than any other season. They played 35 in spring training, 154 regular season (I played that many in Montreal too), 7 in the World Series, 3 in Hawaii, and 19 in Japan. What a whirlwind of a season.

Freddie Kipp Home; His Work Cheers NL Champions on Tour

Iola Register

The recently lost Fred Kipp, on the way home from a Japanese tour with the National League champion Brooklyn Dodgers and spending some time in Honolulu with former Emporia State College friends, was in the home haunts of Piqua and Iola during the weekend.

The big former Iola High basketball star, now quite a mature man and apparently a pretty mature major-league pitcher already, continued on to Kansas City Monday evening. Fred's mother, Mrs. Charles Kipp, has been there recently helping introduce people to a new grandson, the son of Tom Kipp, brother of Fred who is basketball coach at Southwest High School in Kansas City.

Fred plans to hold down a Christmas season postal job in Kansas City, as he did last year. By February, however, he is due in Vero Beach, Fla., to work in the Dodgers early spring camp for the rookie hopefuls.

Dodgers Found New Hurler in Japan—On Own Roster

The *Sporting News*, November 28, 1956

"Fred Kipp looks like he could help our pitching," Alston said.

Fresco was especially eager to talk about Fred Kipp, the tall southpaw pitcher. "We think Kipp is real good and that he will be a big help to the club," he said. "Fred needs a little improvement in control. Not that he walks many batters, but he gets behind on 'em. He's pitching entirely too much on a three-two or three-one count."

"He doesn't throw too many knuckleballs," Thompson said. "The knuckleball is a threat, but his best stuff is different. He has a good fast ball, faster, it seemed to me, than I remembered him having before."

Highlights

- The Bums, with their families, flew a grueling twenty-nine hours to Japan with stops in Los Angeles, Hawaii, and Wake Island. The players blew off some steam on the flight, and some took it a little too far.

- The Yomiuri Shimbum opened the doors to Japan for us on our nineteen-city tour across the island, where we visited dignitaries and military leaders.

- With many of the players exhausted from the long season, World Series, and travel, I pitched more than anyone and confused them with my knuckleball and changeup to deliver a 1.26 ERA.

- I got to know many of the players, and many great pictures were taken throughout the tour.

10. MY CUP OF COFFEE WITH BROOKLYN—1957

On the way home from Japan, I stopped in Honolulu for a week and visited my college friends from Emporia again. I returned home to Kansas in time to see my family and friends and saw my brother Tom in Kansas City. He had a new baby and was working for the Kansas City Athletics on the side. He had such a different life than I was living. He was a basketball coach and high school teacher and living a busy family life. Meanwhile, I was traveling all over the world and playing baseball.

By February, I was back at Vero Beach, and it was so much fun. I knew a lot of people now from my years with the organization. I hung around more with the younger players such as Don Demeter and Joe Pignatano, but many of the big leaguers were asking me how I was doing, and I was playing with them on the field. The Japan tour had made me one of the guys. Things were looking up, and most of the talk in the papers said I was going to make it to the big leagues this year.

Kipp Proves Big Hit at Vero Beach Camp

International News Service

"All of our lefthanders—Johnny Podres, Karl Spooner, Sandy Koufax, Chuck Templeton, Ken Lehman and Fred Kipp—are potential winners," Alston enthused. "I'm sure at least one or two of this group can figure into our starting rotation and that our bullpen will have southpaw strength."

In the early going, Kipp, a 25-year-old, has been very impressive. The young man from Piqua, Kansas fashioned a brilliant 20–7 record in Montreal last season and has been sought in trade talks with many National clubs.

Kipp came into camp described as a lefthanded knuckleball artist. But he has been the hit of the base with his variety of stuff. "Maybe 10 per cent of my pitches in a game are knuckler." The rookie insisted. "I have found it a good strikeout pitch, effective after I have two strikes on the hitter."

Joe Becker, Dodger pitching coach thinks highly of the rookie lefthander. "He has them all." Becker says, "fast ball, curve, change up and knuckler."

Kipp impressed Alston on the Dodger tour of Japan. He was the best Dodger pitcher on the tour with an earned-run-average of 1.26 in 43 innings.

Kipp in First Dodger Warmup

Associated Press — March 6

The Pitlers blanked the Hermans 4–0 in six innings in the first intra-squad game of the season for the Brooklyn Dodgers. Fred Kipp gave a two-hit shutout performance as the losers' starter, but Roger Craig and Charlie Templeton yielded runs.

Dodgertown was a unique experience, from what I had heard. Bringing the Dodgers' extensive farm system of minor- and major-league teams together for training was a unique experience. I thought this quote from Fresco Thompson, a vice president in charge of the minor-league teams, summed up the effect of Dodgertown on the organization. This quote is from the excellent website www.walteromalley.com, about Dodgertown and the Japan tour.

> "One of the main advantages of a central training camp is fraternization," wrote Thompson. "The players with all clubs become acquainted with one another; firm friendships develop. During the season if a player should be transferred from one club to another, or when the Dodgers cut down to their active limit of twenty-five, he goes to a club where he is not a stranger to the players or the manager."

The problem I was facing was that Alston wasn't going to have six lefthanders on the twenty-five-man roster. With eight other positions and seven backups, that left room for about ten pitchers. In '56, only three lefties pitched at all, and they only played in forty-seven games combined. The

Dodgers' shortcomings with lefties was well known, but the lefty Johnny Podres was back from the service and ready to pitch. We had so many strong pitchers that it was going to be hard to make the roster. I was the new kid on the block, and I had to effectively knock one of the field-tested players off the bench to get a spot. I was pleased that they were giving me a chance in our exhibition games.

Kipp Victor in First Brook Start

Associated Press — March 9

The Braves go only four hits off the pitching of Don Drysdale, Sandy Koufax and Fred Kipp, a rookie southpaw up from Montreal. Both of the run came off Drysdale in the third inning.

Athletics Homer Tops Dodgers 6–5

New York Times, Roscoe McGowen, March 20

John Groth, the first man to face Fred Kipp in the tenth inning, drove a home run over the left-field wall to beat the Brooks 6–5. Kipp, who had shut out the Athletics from the seventh inning on, had nearly put the Dodgers ahead in the top of the tenth. Fred's sinking liner to left field went for a double when Gus Serial missed a shoestring catch. Gino Cimoli followed with a long single to right on which it appeared Kipp would score. But Manager Walt Alston held him at third base.

Then followed complete frustration for the Brooks. Carl Duser, a southpaw replaced Tom Gorman and stopped the Dodgers cold. Sandy Amoros grounded to Curt Roberts and Kipp was nailed between third and home, Cimoli reached third and Amoros second on the rundown.

Alston had basically screwed up. Instead of having me score an easy run on Gino's double, I got tagged out in a rundown. I could run, but I wasn't a Jackie Robinson on the bases. My hitting almost put us in the lead in extra innings, but instead of being a possible hero and scoring a tenth-inning run, I was held up on third. Then I gave up the walk-off homer. That hurt.

My pitching still felt good, and I was in the rotation. The next game was the big one in Miami — a rematch with the Yankees. Everyone liked the rematches of the World Series. Games against those damn Yankees always meant a lot more than when we played the other teams. Ford and Maglie started, as they had the first game of the '56 series. I got my chance later in the game.

Dodgers set back Yanks in 9th, 3–2

New York Times, John Drebinger, March 23

Single Decides for Kipp of Brooks Before 11,047 at Night Game in Miami

The Dodgers, who have been doing a deal of brooding since last October when they blew the seventh game of the 1956 World Series to the Yankees, got a measure of revenge tonight. For Alston, the victory provided a filip. For in the top half of the ninth the Brooklyn skipper had deftly out-slickered Casey Stengel, which is no simple trick in or out of season.

Kipp Commits Balk

In this inning, the Yanks worked a runner around to third with two out. Joe Collins walked, advanced to second on a balk by Fred Kipp, a young lefthander, and went to third on a sacrifice. After an infield out left the position unchanged, Stengel sent Mickey Mantle up to bat for Bob Martyn. But Alston, noting that Grim was the next batter and that Stengel had no other pitcher warmed up, directed Kipp to walk Mantle intentionally. Grim then ended the threat as expected by grounding into a force play at second base.

Roger Craig blanked the Yanks in the sixth and seventh and Kipp did the same in the final two innings.

It felt good to close the game out in victory against the Yankees. I pitched well and wanted to pitch to Mickey, but I didn't have a choice. Our first game was about three weeks away, and Alston had to start making some hard choices. I wasn't sure I'd make the cut.

White Sox Pound Drysdale, Kipp for 7-to-1 Triumph over Brooks

New York Times, Roscoe McGowen, March 31

The time has come for Manager Walt Alston to begin separating the men from the boys, and on the basis of today's doings, some separations are imminent. Fred Kipp, a southpaw whom high hopes had been placed, was tagged with four runs in the next inning and five hits, a pass and a sacrifice bunt. Drysdale and Kipp lacked control and were otherwise unsteady.

Four separations came this morning. Karl Spooner, Don Demeter, Jim Gentile and Dick Gray were sent to Vero Beach "for assignment."

Don and Jim, the other two rookies who had toured Japan with me, got sent down to the minors. The pitcher Karl Spooner had hurt his arm and only recovered enough to make it to the Macon Dodgers in the South Atlantic A League. He never made it back to the big leagues after such an incredible start, when he struck out fifteen players in his first game. He hurt his arm in '55 after not warming up well and basically never recovered. He was a fastball pitcher, and he lost that pitch after the injury. He was a classic example of how one injury, especially to your shoulder, could end your career. I was ready, though, and in good shape.

After I let go of those four runs in one inning against the Sox, I didn't think I'd make the team. To make the team as a rookie, I really needed to shine—enough to knock a veteran off the roster. One bad performance like that could cost me my season. I only played one more game, on April 8, and pitched fine. Our first game was on April 16, and I still wasn't sure if I'd make the team. When the final cuts came, I wasn't on the list! I was so excited to make the team. This was going to be my breakout year. All my hard work was paying off—or so I thought.

The season started well, and we were off to a good start. We were flying to games in the new Convair 440 Metropolitan. The Dodgers were the first team to have their own plane, and it cost a pretty penny at $734,000. We flew to exhibition games in Florida on the new plane and from Florida to Brooklyn.

Based on my success in Japan, I was a regular in spring training and participated in group pictures like the one on the lower left with the pitching staff.

Unfortunately, I wasn't getting a chance to pitch, though, so I was in a no-man's-land. I didn't do anything for them to keep me on the team or to send me away. Another rookie, Rene Valdez, started getting to pitch. Rene was a Cuban rookie and was quite a character. He had a mean curve ball and liked to hot dog on the field. One time after a guy hit a triple off him, Rene walked over to third and chatted with him awhile. He was about my height but twenty pounds lighter than I was. We always joked that he looked like a scarecrow on the mound. He was strong and quick, though, and could pounce on grounders like a cat catching a mouse. He'd won twenty-two games in the Pacific League in '56, so we were basically fighting for the last pitching spot on the team. One or both of us would be sent down when a player came off injured reserve or when they had to cut the roster to twenty-five players.

The games kept rolling by, and I never got off the bench. On the twenty-second of April, we played in Roosevelt Park in Jersey City, and we were 5–

1. Playing outside of Brooklyn got a lot of people talking and fans wondering if we were going to stay in Brooklyn. We kept winning, and Walt would put Clem in to relieve, and he didn't seem to have room for me. On the twenty-fourth of April, they let Rene start, and he got the win.

On April 27, they finally announced that I was being sent down to Montreal. I didn't even get a cup of coffee—a short relief stint for an inning. Walt had basically chosen Rene over me. It was disheartening to have to get on the train and go back up to Montreal. I only wished he'd given me a chance on the field. I had to wonder if that one bad inning had made the difference. Decisions on players are often made on less information than that.

Back in Montreal, everything was different. Only seven of the players from last year were on this year's team. The completely different team was totally disconcerting, and we were losing badly. One thing that was the same was that John Roseboro was still catching for me, but he moved up into the majors in June. My old friend Joe Pignatano was on the team now, after he had spent '56 with the Saint Paul Saints.

We were not playing well, and that included me. I lost the first few games, and the pain just kept coming. It's always hard to say why things aren't working out when they aren't, but I was in the middle of a downturn like I'd never seen. My team or I couldn't pull out of the dive. I was facing my sophomore slump, and it was hard. The newspapers were hard to read.

Royals Hit But Errors Costly

Al Parsley, Columbus, OH

Kipp, tagged with his seventh straight loss was sailing along with a 5–2 lead and things looked cozy until the roof fell in.

Montreal—The inability of Southpaw Fred Kipp, a 20-game winner last year, to get started is also hurting the Royals. When Columbus shelled him out during an eight-run inning on June 4, he went down to his seventh straight defeat, 10 to 8. Kipp had yet to win and had a stratospheric ERA of around 7.50. Kipp turned in one of his best efforts of the campaign, May 31, when he held Toronto to six hits in seven innings, but he again came out on the short end 2 to 1.

Kipp Flashes Form of Old

Fred Kipp turned in an excellent pitching performance as he showed signs of regaining his old form that made him one of the top pitchers of the International League last year. Kipp, of Piqua, went the whole distance, allowing only four hits and one base on balls while striking out three batters. That upped his record to 3–9.

1957 was basically a lost season. We ended up in last place in the International League with a 68–86 record. I ended up 8–17, with the most losses in the International League and an ERA of 4.09. Maybe it was a character-building season, but I just couldn't get the wins. If my pitching was good, my team couldn't score. When my pitching was bad, we just couldn't score enough. One strong note was that I hit .318 for the season and was only one of two players who hit over .300 for the Royals that year. I was almost surprised when the Dodgers called me up at the end of the season to play for the team.

I thought it might be a repeat of last year, when I got called up to the big leagues to watch the games, but this year was different. To start, the Dodgers weren't in first or second place, for the first time since 1948. The Braves had a great season, and we were eight games back with no real hope. On September 10, we arrived in Chicago to face the Cubs. The hapless Cubs were over thirty games behind the Braves, and only 3,489 fans showed up at Wrigley that late summer day.

Sandy Koufax started the game and gave up three runs in the first and never got back in the game. This game turned out to be the last start of the season for Sandy, and he still didn't have Walt's confidence. Don Bessent relieved in the second, and when he gave up a homer to Ernie Banks in the third, they had me warm up. After another single, Walt called me in. In front of a meager yet excited crowd, I walked onto the mound for my first foray into the majors!

With a runner on first, I threw a few warmup pitches to Roy. He signaled me to throw it harder and keep it coming. Dale Long, the Cubbie first baseman, came up to bat. On the first pitch, Dale shifted into bunting position and dribbled it down the third baseline. I was typically a good

146

fielder and charged the ball. Campy got to it first, though, and I ducked out of the way as he threw a line to Charlie Neal at second for the first out. Dale was now on first with one out.

Next up was Bobby Morgan, their second baseman. Campy came out and told me that Bobby didn't like swinging at the first pitch, so I threw a nice curve that he watched go by for the first strike. On the second pitch, Campy called a knuckler. The ball dropped nicely, and Bobby swung at air for the second strike. I had him right where I wanted him, with an 0–2 count. Next, we tried to tempt him with an outside curve ball, but he didn't bite. Next up was my fastball. I threw all the heat I could muster, but Bobby saw it coming and hit it out of the park. Welcome to the big leagues!

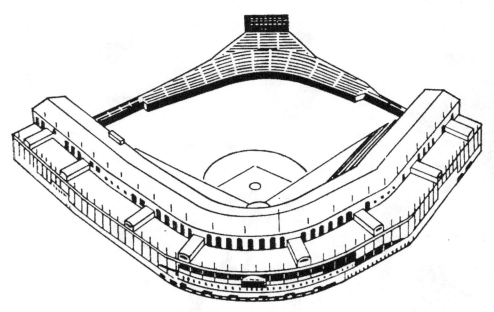

Wrigley Field, Chicago—First N. L. Game Played April 20, 1916

Wrigley Field is the second oldest stadium in modern baseball after Fenway Park. Dodgers Stadium is the third oldest and opened in 1962.

The next batter got a hit, but then they hit into a double play to end the inning with us down 6–0. I was glad to get out of the inning, and when I sat down on the bench, I noticed my heart was pumping as if I'd just run a mile. Campy told me to relax and focus on each hitter. He told me the top of the order was coming up, so I'd better get ready for Ernie Banks—Mr. Cub. He said, "Keep it high and tight on him, and you should be all right." Our conversation was interrupted when Roy went up to bat. I was on deck and watched Dick Drott bring his heat. Dick had already won thirteen games that year and had shut us out so far.

Roy fouled a couple balls off and struck out swinging on the third pitch. Roy was shaking his head as he walked off the field, and I walked up to bat for the first time. I got in a couple of good practice swings, and the adrenaline was pumping. Drott was looking intently at his catcher, oblivious to me, whom he didn't know. He threw a fastball right down the middle, and I swung and made perfect contact. I sent a line drive right to Ernie Banks at short. I barely took a step before the ball was in Ernie's glove. It was nice to make contact, but I needed to hit the gap.

Roy wasn't afraid to guard the plate, and Billy Martin wasn't afraid of going for it.

That was the inning, so I ran back and got my glove. Walt was usually quiet, but he encouraged me with a "Show me what you got, Kipp." Their third baseman, Bobby Adams, was up first, and he went for the first pitch and grounded to short. Next up was Lee Walls, and he watched the first strike go by. My control felt pretty good, and I was throwing strikes when I wanted to. On the third pitch, he hit a sharp grounder to Pee Wee at third. Pee Wee was usually at short, but he played more at third base in '57 while Randy Jackson was nursing an injury. Reese usually made the routine play, but he bobbled the ball and didn't even make the throw. Now I had a runner to contend with.

Walt "Moose" Moryn, their right fielder, came up, and he looked more like a bull to me. Walt had come up through the Dodger organization, so I knew him from spring training. He had a good eye, and I threw him an outside pitch that he watched go by for ball one. Then I threw a screwball, and he pulled a foul ball down the third baseline and into the stands. We traded off another ball and foul, and then Roy called for my knuckleball—my go-to pitch for strikeouts. I held my knuckleball on my fingertips instead of my knuckles, as most pitchers did. My knuckleball had good action that day, and I saw it rise sharply as it got to the plate. Moose swung and missed for the third strike. I got my first strikeout, and it felt good!

The only problem now was that Ernie Banks came up to the plate. Ernie was their star and would eventually get into the Hall of Fame with 2,583 hits and 512 homers. I threw it high and tight—maybe a little too tight, though, as they called it a ball. I got behind in the count with Ernie before he hit a couple foul balls, and I had him at 2–2. Roy called for a fastball, and I delivered a slow one that Ernie drove into left field. Gino made the easy stop and held them to first and second.

Now I had two runners to worry about. Jim "Dutch" Bolger came up to bat. We traded fouls and balls until the count was 2–2 again. Roy called for a screwball, and I wound up and released a tight curve over the plate. Jim swung and slugged it to deep center. I turned around and watched Duke back up to the warning track. He kept going back and had to jump a little to make the catch. Three outs, and I let out a big sigh of relief. It had been only a few yards from a three-run homer. I was glad to get out of the inning and to the bottom of the order.

In the fifth, I went three up and three down with another strikeout. In the sixth, I struck out Drott, and then the top of the order came up again. I got Adams out with a fly ball, so we had two outs. Just one more out to break up the top of the order and get out of the inning. It's important to scatter hits across the innings and not let them pile up in one inning. I still had quite a bit to learn, it seemed, because Walls and Moryn both singled to left field before Ernie came back up to the plate.

Ernie Banks was quick out of the gates. Look at how he's already on the way to first with the ball still in the picture frame.

I threw Banks a couple balls to fall behind in the count, and then Roy called for another fastball. I didn't bring much heat, and Ernie popped it long and far for a three-run homer. Watching three players run around the bases and hearing just a few fans scream their heads off was disheartening. Bolger came up next. He hit a line drive to Pee Wee at third, and he made the third out. I got out of the inning with the score 9–1. They pulled me after that bad inning, and that was all the action I saw in '57. At least I'd had my cup of coffee, but it didn't taste very good to give up four runs and six hits in four innings.

The season wasn't over, and I worked hard and practiced every day after that. I continued touring with the team, and I remember our final game at Ebbets Field. Charlie "the Brow" DiGiovanni, our bat boy, put out a big spread of food and drinks, and we were happy because we had beat the Pirates. We usually were happy if we got a couple of beers to drink, so having some food after the game was nice. When we started digging in, Buzzie Bavasi came in and didn't like what he saw. He got all over Charlie for spending so much money. Buzzie ruined the meal by saying, "You'd think we just won the pennant!" Most of us left after that because the food just didn't taste good anymore.

The Dodgers arranged for me to play winter ball in the Dominican Republic to work on my control. I had until mid-October to get down to the DR, so I took the train home to see my family after the long season. It sure was good to see my family and get some of my mother's home cooking.

There will never be another stadium like Ebbets Field.

I stopped in at the *Iola Register* to talk with Bud. It turned out to be a momentous day for the Dodgers.

Piqua's Brooklyn Dodger Suddenly an L.A. Dodger

Bud Roberts, *Iola Register*, 10-10-57

It was just the dutiful annual call suggested by *The Register*, but the visit Tuesday afternoon turned out somewhat memorable at that, for Fred Kipp of the Brooklyn Dodgers and Piqua.

The bell tingled a "bulletin" signal on the Associated Press teletype and this message followed:

"BULLETIN

"NEW YORK AP—The Brooklyn Dodgers will move to Los Angeles in 1958, President Walter O'Malley announced today."

That was it. The official word that Kipp and the rest of the Dodgers are no longer the Brooklyn Dodgers. Big Fred showed not much more outer concern about the news than others in the office who bent over the teletype machine to look.

There is not much any Dodger could say, and the Piqua resident, usually on the quiet side, would be the one to say the least perhaps. So Fred Kipp took it in stride, or attempted to do so, more than the ardent fan who enjoys saying his piece, one way or another.

Reading about the move from the teletype machine was interesting. I knew about it sooner than most of my teammates because I was in the newspaper room when the word got sent out. Brooklyn was crying, but everybody knew it was coming. After hearing about the move, nostalgia for the final game in Brooklyn grew in me. It was a significant night and the end of an era. I can still hear the organist Gladys Goodding playing a lot of odd songs on that last day and finishing with "Auld Lang Syne." We knew our time in Brooklyn was over, but now it was in writing.

After another week visiting family and friends, I went down to Miami and caught a flight to a new country—the Dominican Republic. We called it the

152

DR. They put us up in a nice hotel off the beach but still in the middle of the capital city, which was called Cuidad Trujillo, after the military dictator Rafael Trujillo. The people were very friendly, and I had a few days to rest on the beach to work off my baseball tan. The beaches of the DR were quite different from the mountains of Venezuela, and lots of beautiful women were on the beach. Without speaking Spanish, I was facing a big disconnect between me and the people. That was about to change.

Highlights

- I had a great spring training and joined the team for the first two weeks of the season, but I got sent back to Montreal without a chance to pitch.

- My sophomore slump didn't go well, and I accumulated an ugly 8–17 record and a 4.09 ERA.

- After pitching many exhibition games for the Dodgers, I finally got my cup of coffee against the Chicago Cubs in Wrigley.

- I rode the pine during the final game at Ebbets Field.

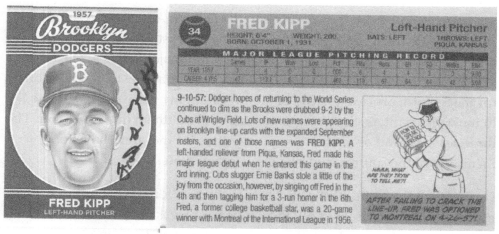

This commemorative card for the one game I played in 1957 was released in 2011 by Ronnie Joyner.

11. THE DOMINICAN WINTERS — 1957–60

My fortunes in the Dominican Republic (DR) changed when Rudy Hernandez arrived and became my roommate. Rudy was my age and born in the DR, but he had been raised in New York. Rudy played many years in the minor leagues like me and later pitched for the Washington Senators. He was a regular in the DR winter league and knew how to bridge the gap between the DR and the United States. Rudy was our ringleader and took me and other players along for the ride.

Rudy was built about like me, at six three and 185 pounds. He was very handsome and a ladies' man, and his fluency in Spanish got him into places regular gringos wouldn't find. He was a hit with the ladies, and he always had beautiful women around. He knew where to get the best paella, when to eat pizza on the beach, and which nightclubs to go to. If the electricity went out or the plumbing needed fixing, Rudy would have a few players sign a baseball and would get the problem fixed in a jiffy. Rudy made all the difference for me in the DR and made it worth my time to come back over the next three winters.

My memories of those three winters in the DR (1957–58, 1958–59, and 1959–60) are a little fuzzy, and I don't have all the game stats and newspaper articles to fall back on, as I do for the minor and major leagues. The *Iola Register* in rural Kansas didn't have connections or a translation department for the Spanish articles. Instead of talking about my three seasons in the DR in multiple chapters, I'm going to reminisce about them in this chapter. The three seasons kind of melt into one crazy time for me, and I have fond memories of the country and playing baseball there.

I want to set the scene a little bit, because it was a foreign country to me and my fellow teammates. First off, the temperature was not too hot in the day and very nice at night. The fall humidity was high but not oppressive, as it would be in the summer. The climate was excellent from October to February. Instead of shoveling snow and scraping ice in Kansas City, I would spend my winter days at the hotel pool and my evenings on the field.

East Coasters might know the experience of getting out of the cold and flying down to Miami for the winter, but it was even warmer in the DR.

The DR felt like vacation, and I only pitched about once a week and got paid more in the DR than in the minor leagues—about $1,000 a month. We only played three or four nights a week, and I'd pitch about every three or four games, since I was on rotation. The tropical pace seeped into my pores, and the nights were long. After the games ended about nine o'clock, the city was just getting going. Instead of restaurants closing, they were opening. We could go out and eat dinner after the game for a pittance, and Rudy always knew where to go.

I can remember walking into many restaurants and bars in Rudy's entourage. When Stan Williams at six foot five, Frank Howard at six foot seven, and I walked in with Rudy, it was as if the basketball team had showed up. Everyone in the restaurant would stop eating and look up at us while Rudy would greet the owner with a big "Como esta?" We'd get the best table in the place and have excellent service.

Our hometown was the main city of Cuidad Trujillo, or Santa Domingo today. Cuidad Trujillo was the cultural, political, industrial, and financial center of the DR. It is the oldest city in the Americas and was founded by Christopher Columbus's younger brother Bartholomew in 1496. While Cuidad Trujillo wasn't as lively as Havana in those days, the city could hold its own and knew how to have a good time. They had casinos and race tracks and some of the best food I ever ate. The simple chicken-and-rice dish was always my favorite, and paella and seafood were plentiful, fresh, and delicious. We had it good down there, and we knew it.

I played for the Escogido Lions (Leones del Escogido), which means "Lions of the Chosen One." The chosen one during our time was the dictator Rafael Leonidas Trujillo Molina. Trujillo had ruled for thirty years and excelled at getting his way. We didn't know about the corruption and violence because he controlled the press. Even the locals, like Juan Marichal, didn't know about the abuses. Trujillo ruled with an iron fist and was omnipotent throughout the country. The backs of our jerseys even said "El Benefactor" to show that we were the playing for Trujillo.

Many of the best Dominican players were on my team. Rudy had been playing in the minors since '54 and was working his way up through the Giants' farm clubs. The first Dominican to reach the majors, Ozzie Virgil, played for us, and his son Ozzie also made it to the big leagues. Ozzie had just finished his first full season for the Giants, and he was famous in the DR. Manny Mota, a future Dodger pinch hitter and coach for thirty-four years, was young and strong at nineteen and had just played D League for the Michigan City White Caps. Most Leones were young, and I was fortunate to play with some future major leaguers before they made it big and even into the Hall of Fame.

Juan Marichal had just turned twenty and was still throwing sidearm when I arrived. That first winter season, Juan didn't pitch with the high kicks that he was later famous for. He didn't know his way around the mound that first year, but in the summer of '58, he went north and played for Michigan City in the D-Level Midwest League. When he came back in the winter of 1958–59, he was a polished pitcher. His coach, Buddy Kerr, was a fatherly figure to Juan. Buddy was concerned that Juan was going to hurt his arm throwing sidearm and suggested that he throw overhand. Juan had pitched sidearm since his grade-school hero Bombo Ramos pitched that way.

When Juan tried to throw overhand, he felt odd in his delivery unless he kicked his leg exaggeratedly high over his head. I've still never seen anyone pitch like that. YouTube videos show how he kicks his foot about a foot over his head. This exaggerated motion gave him great power, and it confused batters, who couldn't see what he was throwing until the ball was flying at them.

Juan had five pitches—fastball, curve ball, slider, screwball, and changeup. When he combined those five pitches with his sidearm, three quarters, and high overhead delivery, he came at batters with fifteen different pitches. His strikeout pitch was often delivered sidearm, and that threw batters off when they'd been getting overhand throws. I noted how he changed his delivery from nine o'clock to twelve o'clock, and I used those three deliveries myself to confuse batters. I didn't have the crazy kick that he had for his overhead pitch and never mastered my control to the extent that Juan did. Juan's control was what set him apart. He delivered pinpoint accuracy with a variety of pitches and deliveries.

Juan Marichal was known for his high kick, but he only threw sidearm when I first played with him in the DR.

Juan was strong from his days growing up on a farm, like me. He had to be strong to kick his leg up like that over eighteen seasons and in the winter leagues. He started playing for the Giants in 1960 and didn't stop until 1975 and made it all the way to the Hall of Fame. He would win 471 major-league games and became the first Dominican to get inducted into the Hall of Fame. He won more games in the 1960s than any other pitcher. He won over twenty games in six seasons with the Giants. He even played for my

Dodgers in 1975. I got to see him young and see how he learned quickly and never forgot.

One crazy coincidence with Juan was that he was childhood friends with the Alou brothers. The Alou brothers were a big draw for the Leones. Before the three brothers, Felipe, Matty, and Jesus, played on the field at the same time for the Giants, they were playing with me in the DR. They were always running around the field, teaching one another, and having fun.

Felipe was the oldest and had been working his way up in the minors through the New York Giants organization. He just finished his first season playing AAA ball for the Minneapolis Millers in the American Association and became a regular San Francisco Giant the next year. He had great baseball instincts and hit the ball hard. Felipe ended up getting over 2,100 hits in the majors and was the groundbreaker for his brothers.

Matty was eighteen when I met him and had just finished his first year in the American minors. He was working his way up the minors as well and made it to the majors in '61. Jesus was just fifteen that first year but was playing regularly by the time I left the DR. The three brothers were naturals and knew how to play ball. They are first, second, and third place for many Leone team records such as home runs, hits, at bats, and several other categories.

All three Alou brothers, Jesus, Matty, and Felipe, eventually made it into the majors and set a record of batting three in a row for the San Francisco Giants in September of 1963.

Besides the locals, we had about six northern teammates, who were mainly a mixture of Giants and Dodgers. The league limited the number of gringos on a team to about six a season. While we were enemies in the States during the regular season, we were teammates down on the island.

From the Dodger organization, I pitched a lot with my old friend Joe Pignatano, as well as Norm Sherry. It was always good to pitch to Joe and Norm. Ron Negray pitched on our team and played in the International League with me. George "Sparky" Anderson also played for us and must have been studying our coach Salty Parker's managerial style. George only played one year in the majors but went on to the Hall of Fame as a coach.

From the Giants organization, I played with future hall-of-famer Willie McCovey before he became the stalwart of the team. Willie Kirkland and Bill Wilson played outfield for us and challenged the Alou brothers. One exception to the Dodgers-Giants rule was Ken Aspromonte of the Boston Red Sox, who played infield for us. Playing with a mixture of natives and "gringos," as they would often call us, was an interesting mix that led to some great baseball.

We played in Trujillo Stadium (Estadio Trujillo), which is now known as Estadio Quisqueya Juan Marichal. The stadium was opened in 1955 and was pretty new when I played there. I had déjà vu playing there because it was an almost exact copy of the Bobby Maduro Miami Stadium, where the Dodgers played exhibition games during spring training. One addition to the stadium that Miami didn't have was a jail underneath the stands to hold unruly fans!

We shared the stadium with our archrivals, the Licey Tigers (Tigres del Licey). We were the red team, while the Tigers were the blue team. Because the two teams played in the same stadium, locals could go to games almost every night of the week. The fifties were known as the golden era for the DR winter leagues because of the fierce competition within the league and the gringos like me who came in to add some variety. Their best players were infiltrating the minors and majors, but they still came home and played the winter season.

The stadium was usually full, and the fans were fanatic. They loved us, and we were very successful over the three years I was there. We were in the championship all three years, and we won twice. On special occasions such as New Year's, they'd throw cherry bombs out onto the field—sometimes behind our players to scare them. Luckily, I was on the mound and far from the fans when they did that.

The fans would taunt opposing players too. When Rudy would come up to bat, they would taunt him with an effeminate "Rooodeee, Rooodeee"—implying that he was gay. I mentioned how Rudy was a pretty boy, but he had a lot of beautiful women in those days. He'd write letters to girls in different towns, and when he showed up, he was set. Those fans tried to get under our skin, but we wouldn't let them. Another funny thing they'd do was shake their hankies at us when they didn't like what we did. They ended up shaking a lot of hankies at me when I struck their batters out and won a lot of games

The games were like the wild west with dodgy umpires. Many things happened there that wouldn't happen in the United States. One great story was the mighty Frank Howard getting into a scuffle with an umpire. I've heard many different versions of this story, but this is what I remember. This Dominican story has grown to mythical proportions because it was hard to believe what Frank could do. Frank was a cartoonish character at six eight and 275 pounds of pure muscle. He was one of the few players who lifted weights at that time. His dedication to lifting turned him into a Popeye-like character with a thirty-four-inch waist and a fifty-two-inch sport coat!

We called him Hondo, after John Wayne, and he would later be called the Capital Punisher and Washington Monument when he played for the Senators. His size and strength were awe inspiring. Frank was the strongest man I ever played with, and I saw him hit home runs farther than anyone else—over six hundred feet!

He was in his early twenties at the time, and he ate like no one I've ever seen. He would eat three to five times as much as any of the other players. For breakfast, he would order a dozen eggs, a pound of bacon, a few sausages, and some hash browns, and then he'd wash it down with some OJ and a pot of coffee. You didn't want to get between this dog and his food. We always talked about Hondo because he was such a freak of nature.

One night, Frank was on first base with the bases loaded. We were playing the dreaded Tigers, and we were losing. Matty Alou came up to bat and hit a line drive down the third baseline, and it hit right on the chalk. The local umpire called it fair, and we scored three runs, with Frank being the last to score. We were all excited to start a rally, and Frank and the others made it into the dugout with us.

Then there was a delay in the game. The Tiger players surrounded the local third-base umpire who had made the fair call and started yelling at him. The next thing we knew, the umpire yelled, "No! Foul ball!" We were all shocked at this scam, but the players made it back to the bases except for Frank. Frank refused to go back to first base and act as if the hit had never happened. The umpires got the other runners to return to their bases, but Frank refused.

Frank wouldn't budge from the bench. He just sat there and shook his head. The first-base umpire, Bill Sneathen, wasn't going to stand for this disrespect of the shady third-base umpire. Bill was a lug of a man himself at about 250 pounds, but he was stocky, at about only five nine. Bill was supposed to be a wrestler and had an ego of his own. Sneathen started yelling at Frank to get on first base, and Frank started beating his chest and yelling back. The tempers just escalated from there—two big egos going at it. With adrenaline pumping, Frank stormed out of the dugout and picked up 250-pound Bill. People swear to this day that he lifted him over a foot off the ground to Frank's eye level!

While holding him in the air, Frank started shaking this burly umpire, who was squirming and kicking his feet in the air. Bill's shirt ripped right down the middle of the back, and everybody ran out of the dugout to try to keep Frank from killing Bill. Bill was no lightweight fighter and managed to wiggle free and upend Frank in some kind of wrestling move. That was when we reached them, and we all piled on and started pulling at the arms and legs of these kicking and screaming Goliaths.

We were lucky no one got hurt. It took quite a while for the dust to settle and for order to be regained. Of course Frank got thrown out of the game, but now he was freaking out in the dugout. Frank was pacing back and forth and throwing bats and coolers around. No one could calm him down. He was the proverbial bull in the china closet, and we were all scared.

Frank Howard was a powerful hitter and one of the few players who lifted weights back in the day.

He finally went to the door to the locker room, and it was locked. Frank was in no mood to ask for a key, so he reared back and kicked the door down.

The door just shattered into little pieces, and he walked through it. I remember walking through that door after the end of the game, and it looked as if a hurricane had blown it down. It was Hurricane Hondo!

That was a night I'll never forget. Frank was quite a character and lived life to the hilt. His wife, Carol, was a great contrast to him at only five two and a hundred pounds. I actually have about the same height differential with my wife, Lorraine, who comes in at four ten. Frank had been an All-American in baseball and basketball in high school and college. He'd been drafted for basketball by the Philadelphia Warriors but signed with the Dodgers, who offered him a $108,000 signing bonus. That $108,000 was a lot of money in '58, and Frank did draw a lot of fans. Everyone wanted to see the Incredible Hulk on the field.

Another story from those days was about Stan Williams. Stan was quite a bit bigger than me, at six five and 230 pounds, and wilder — on and off the mound. He was a very aggressive pitcher, and he would brush people back often — sometimes intentionally and sometimes unintentionally because he threw out of control in his early years. These wild pitches and his attitude got him into trouble with some of the native players, but no one wanted to charge the mound and get beat up in front of a bunch of fans by an aggressive pitcher who weighed over 230 pounds.

One time in our hotel, he was coming out of the elevator when one of the local players from another team was going into the elevator. The native player recognized Stan and had some deep bruises from when Stan hit him in a game. The wounded opponent clenched his fists and looked up at Stan and said, "Stan, one day, I keeel you!"

Well, Stan looked this guy in the eye and said, "Let's do it right now! If you got a bone to pick with me, let's settle it right now!"

Well, the "keeeller" wasn't ready to back up his words at that moment and backed away. Stan was mean on and off the field. I could never play like that. It just wasn't who I was.

In my first year with Escogido, our team was playing great, and I was on fire. I was the first player in the league to win ten games and ended up with an 11–3 record. I was pitching well, and everything just fell into place. Joe

Pignatano and I had time to work on my pitches, and we weren't afraid to try new pitches in a game. I wouldn't typically try new pitches or techniques in games up north, but down here, everything went. I learned a lot down there through real-world experience.

Kipp Gets Fast Start With Two Wins in 3 Days

Escogido Pitcher Triumphs in Relief and on Shutout; 15,016 Fans in Inaugural

By Felix Acosta Nunez, CD. Trujillo, D. R.

Led by Gen. Hector B. Trujillo Molina, president of the Dominican Republic, who threw out the traditional first ball, a crowd of 15,061 was entertained with a sparkling show when Escogido defeated Licey in in an 11-inning game, 5 to 4, October 24th, to open the Dominican League's 1957–58 season.

Ron Negray (Saint Paul), George Sackey and Fred Kipp (Dodgers) divided the pitching for Escogido, while Gary Blaylock (Red Sox) hurled the route for Licey.

Kipp in Pitching Groove

Fred Kipp, local resident who has been pitching in the winter league of the Dominican Republic since early December, has hurled successive shutout victories for Escogido, leading team of the four team league, according to this week's Sporting News. Kipp beat Licey 1–0 and Aguilas Cibaenas 3–0. Before that, we won 4–1 on a four-hit performance.

Southpaw Fred Kipp (Dodgers) of Escogido became the circuit's first ten-game winner. Kipp hoisted his record to 10–2 by baffling Licey on seven hits to win. Southpaw Vic Rehm (Milwaukee) who had kept pace with Kipp in the victory column most of the season, failed twice in conquest of win No. 9.

There were only four teams in the league, so we had a fifty-fifty chance of making it to the final each year. My Leones made it all three years, and I started some of the deciding games. We beat the Estrellas Orientales in '58 and '60 and lost to the Licey Tigers in '59. The Alou brothers were reaching maturity, and Juan became an excellent pitcher for us after the first winter. I know I became a better pitcher by playing in the DR those winters, and it kept me in shape. Instead of shoveling snow and doing odd jobs in Kansas City, I was playing ball in the tropics for good money. Some said that I even started pitching faster down there. I'm sure it helped me in '58, when I showed up to spring training well oiled, tan, and possibly faster.

Kipp Flips Shutout in Open Finals of Dominican Playoff

CD. TRUJILLO, D. R. — The Escogido Lions, first place finishers in the regular season, go the jump in the Dominican League Playoff finals by winning two of the first three games from Licey. The set was the best-out-of-nine affair.

In the opener, February 6, Southpaw Fred Kipp (Los Angeles) blanked Licey on four hits, 5-0. The Alou brothers, Felipe (San Francisco) and Matty (Springfield) — sparked the attack as Escogido took the third game, 4–2.

Highlights

- I spent three winters with the Escogido Lions, won many games as a starter, and got to work on my pitching instead of taking odd jobs all winter.

- A great cast of characters played winter ball, and Frank Howard left his mark on the stadium.

- I loved the DR and have many fond memories of my winters there.

- Many of the local players, such as Juan Marichal, Manny Mota, Ozzie Virgil, and the Alou brothers, were just getting started in the majors.

12. FULL-TIME DODGER — 1958

When I got back to Vero Beach in February, the Dodgers were reeling from tragedy. Everyone talked about the loss of poor Roy Campanella, who was now paralyzed from the neck down. The devastating car crash on January 28, 1958, just weeks before spring training, hit the team hard. Roy was a mentor to me, and he always had a ready smile that I could even see from behind his catching mask. Campy was fun to be around and didn't have the conflict that Jackie brought with him. These two greats were vastly different, and books have been written about it. How does a team get over losing their three-time National League MVP?

It wasn't easy, but the tragedy opened the door for two of my teammates from the year before, Joe Pignatano and John Roseboro. Both played with me in Montreal in '57 and were ready to step in and fill the void. John had played in Montreal with me until June, when he was called up to give some relief to Campy and Rube. John played thirty-five games in '57 for the Dodgers and would play over a hundred games in each of the next dozen years. Joe and Rube were destined to be John's backup now.

Spring training went well for me, and things were looking good again. The biggest change may have been the status of the pitching staff instead of my improved ability. The coaches liked talking about my speed improving, but the sore arms of some of the other pitchers were having a bigger impact on my ability to make the team. The pitchers had been in good shape in '57, but Alston needed my help in '58 because Sandy and Don Drysdale were serving in the military until mid-April. I was glad to step in.

Hurlers Set for Opening Dodger Tilt
Vero Beach, FL, Frank Finch, *Los Angeles Times*, March 3, 1958
Williams and Kipp Selected by Alston to Pitch Saturday

Speed Impresses Boss

Kipp's speed has impressed the boss. "Ordinarily, pitchers don't get faster, but Kipp looks faster than last year." Alston said. "Of course, both he and Williams pitched winter ball and are farther along than the others."

Dodgers Win

Miami, FL, Charlie Park, March 11, 1958

The Dodger boss also was pleased with the relief work of Lefty Fred Kipp. "I'm convinced now that his fast ball actually is faster now than ever. And that's rare, believe me."

With the move to LA still being big news, we opened the season with six games in six days against the Giants to get the West Coast excited about baseball. The first three games were in Seals Stadium, where Joe DiMaggio got his start. Seals Stadium held only about twenty-two thousand people, but they made a lot of noise. The stadium is long gone, but it was in the Mission District at Sixteenth and Bryant. With everyone watching that first game, the Giants pounded us and shut us out for an 8–0 loss. We fought back in game two and punished them 13–1. They beat us in the third game to put us down in the series 2–1 before we got to head home to our new digs.

When we flew back to LA after the loss, the Baseball Writers' Association threw a big dinner for us in the ritzy Biltmore Bowl, which still sits off Pershing Square in downtown LA. The fans and stars came out in droves to welcome us to the city. I don't think there had ever been such a mix of glamor and baseball. Dinah Shore and Bob Hope performed at the dinner, and Art Linkletter was the MC. The baseball commissioner, Ford Frick, and the NL President, Warren Giles, were there with many politicians. Politicians from Sacramento, such as Pat Brown, the future governor and father of Jerry Brown, came down for the event. O'Malley tried to merge the entertainment world, the political world, and the baseball world in the City of Angels.

O'Malley had ulterior motives as well. He was trying to rally the city for the June 3 vote on Proposition 3 to ratify the contract with the Dodgers and grant them 352 acres of land for Dodger Stadium. In exchange for building Dodger Stadium, the city would give the Dodgers Chavez Ravine, north of downtown. O'Malley had made a very wise financial move by coming to LA. LA was ready to do about anything for him, and he wasn't going to let the opportunity pass.

The next day was opening day in LA, and the gala continued. The whole team went to city hall, and we got in a bunch of convertibles and drove through crowded streets to the Coliseum. The throngs of people reminded me of the motorcade through Tokyo in '56. All the dignitaries were in the procession too, and the mayor, Norris Poulson, threw out the opening pitch to the San Francisco mayor, who stood at bat. The governor, Goodwin Knight, was there with many Hall of Famers from the Giants and Dodgers.

Our parade through the streets of Los Angeles; two of us rode in a convertible.

Did I mention that A-list stars came to opening day? It seemed as if all the stars were there from the film, TV, and music industries. As young bucks, we were mostly interested in Zsa Zsa Gabor, Lauren Bacall, and Dinah Shore. The crowd was a who's who of Hollywood—Jimmy Stewart, Bing Crosby, Burt Lancaster, Jack Lemmon, Alfred Hitchcock, and even Groucho Marx.

By game time at 1:45 p.m., the 78,672 fans had already used their binoculars to spot the stars as well as Carl Erskine on the mound. The Coliseum supported the high attendance, which shattered many records, such as the largest regular-season crowd, largest opening-day crowd, and largest crowd in National League history. It was a historic day for LA and the team. No one was happier than Walter O'Malley. He had suffered so much scorn from Brooklyn and the press. Now he was the hero and saw the flip side of the story from LA's perspective. One city's loss was another's gain.

Opening Day, April 18, 1958, was filled with pomp and circumstance. I'm number 26 on the right and look rather tall next to one of the coaches — 55.

I remember how the press liked to overanalyze the move to LA because it was historic. Alston got pissed at a reporter for asking him a bunch of details about the move. I think it was Howard Cosell who pushed Walt to the edge. Of course, Alston had nothing to do with the move. He was in charge of the players on the field, not where we played. Alston would get mad at people, but he knew to keep his cool in front of reporters because they were the conduit to the public. He saved his ranting for the locker room after the Cosell interview. Alston stormed around yelling how stupid Cosell was after the press had left.

After all of the fanfare, the first game in the Coliseum went well for us. Because of the parade and festivities, we didn't have batting practice before the game. So when the Giants went up to bat for the first time, they always looked around the field in astonishment. The China Wall always looked enticingly close at 251 feet. Meanwhile, right center looked forbiddingly far away at 430 feet. I remember Willie Mays walking up for the first time and scanning the field like an artillery captain. I could imagine him thinking, Where should I send my bombs?

Juli Reding of horror-movie fame had Elmer Valo's and the crowd's attention.

We ended up winning the opener 6–5, but I didn't get on the mound. I did get on the mound the next night, on Saturday, April 19. It was another beatdown by the Giants. Danny McDevitt started for us and gave up a few runs in the third, and then Ron Negray gave up a couple runs before Ed Roebuck gave up three more. Then it was Larry Sherry's turn to give up another. By the time I got in, in the eighth inning, we were down 11–4. I was the last resort, and I managed to hold them to one hit and no runs in the last two innings. I was the only pitcher to not let a run score that night.

When I came into the dugout after the top of the ninth, Walt said, "Good job, Fred. We needed you out there." I guess he liked what he saw, because he decided to start me on the next Friday. I talked about my first major-league start, on April 25, in the first chapter. With the win and a solid performance,

I was regularly in the rotation after that. I don't have time to go into each of the forty games that I played that year, but here are some highlights and stories.

Kipp to Face Musial, Cards,
Los Angeles Evening Herald Express, John B. Old, April 25, 1958
Dodger Manager Walter Alston fingered the left-handed Fred Kipp (0–0) for his initial start of the campaign.

May 3. I got the start against Pittsburgh and held them to three runs in seven innings. We only scored one run and couldn't get going offensively. I had a no-hitter until the fourth inning, when I gave up two homers. When I gave up a third solo homer in the seventh and a couple singles, they pulled me before the seventh-inning stretch. That dropped my record to 1–1.

May 7. The Phillies came to town, and I held them to three runs until the seventh. I got the third out with the bases loaded in the fifth and sixth, so maybe I was getting tired and squeaked by without more runs. I gave up a couple hits in the seventh, so Walt replaced me with Clem Labine with the score tied 3–3. Then Clem gave up three runs. I got the loss because I put the losing runs on base—that's baseball!

May 13. The Giants were in first place with a 17–9 record, and we were in last place at 9–16. The Giants were hot, and they continued their reign of terror by scoring seven runs in the first two innings off Newk. I came in to relieve in the third with one out and men on first and second. I got out of the inning, but Willie Mays hit a triple on me to open the fourth. Orlando Cepeda hit Mays in on his first pitch, and they pulled me. My ERA rose to over 5 that night, and I could never get it below 4 for the rest of the season. That gave me my third loss, and things were about to get worse.

May 18. My sister, Donna, took the train to Saint Louis to see me pitch the opener of a doubleheader. She had to make a last-minute trip to come and see me because I didn't know I would pitch until the day before. She had little kids, so it was a big deal for her and me.

I walked the first batter, and then Don Blasingame hit into a double play for a quick two outs. Only one out to go in the first when my nemesis—and about every other pitcher's nemesis—came up to bat. I'd seen enough of

Stan the Man to know to avoid giving him something to hit. I kept the ball away from him and, unfortunately, out of the strike zone. I walked him, and then Del Ennis hit a single to put Stan in scoring position on third. The quick inning was turning into a challenge.

Ken Boyer ruined my day with a grand slam.

My control wasn't very good that night, and I walked Gene Green to fill the bases. Then Ken Boyer came up to the plate, and I couldn't get him to swing at a bad pitch. He fouled the third pitch and then watched the fifth pitch go by as a strike. Then he hit a series of foul balls that I'll never forget. They went to the right and to the left and behind the catcher, but not on the field. On the thirteenth pitch, I threw a changeup, and he tipped the ball into Roseboro's mitt, and it fell out. John didn't make a bad play, and I probably wouldn't remember the ninth foul if it weren't for the next pitch. On the fourteenth pitch, Boyer sent it out of the park for a grand slam.

It's a game of inches or less, and I had missed it by that much! Walt pulled me after that inning. I did throw thirty-seven pitches that inning, which was a bad sign, but I didn't get to pitch the way I wanted to for my sister. I liked it better when I hit a grand slam for my parents and brother in Asheville instead of giving one up!

My teammates came back in the top of the second, and Rube hit a three-run homer to tie the score. Because of that, I didn't get the loss even though we lost 5–6 that night. Statistics can be deceiving.

May 31. We were in Wrigley Field on a Saturday afternoon, and Carl Erskine got the start. I came in, in the fifth inning, after Ernie "Mr. Baseball" Banks hit a homer off him. I held them to three hits and no runs for the rest of the game and got the win to make my record 2–3.

DODGERS BEAT CUBS, 9–4,

Chicago Sunday Tribune, Edward Prell, June 1, 1958
KIPP YIELDS 3 HITS IN RELIEF: ENDS WRIGLEY FIELD HEROICS

Southpaw Quiets Chicago Bats, 16,324 Fans

Until a lanky left hander with the unlikely name of Fred Kipp from the Kansas town of Piqua came along in the middle of yesterday's action, the Cubs appeared to be bent on making their third colossal winning rally against the Los Angeles Dodgers.

Kipp Halts Noisemakers

Then, the 6'4" Jayhawker appeared and stopped the recently boisterous Cubs on three singles. The noise from the stands gradually subsided. [The crowds the last two days have acted like they've been taking lessons from Milwaukee.] There was nothing in Kipp's 1958 record to suggest the Dodgers finally had found a pitcher to stop the Cubs. He had lost three of four decisions and had been roughed up for 34 hits in 25 previous innings.

June 15. Don Newcombe got torn up by the Pirates in the Coliseum. In the second inning, Newk gave up a hit to Ted Kluszewski, a homer to Frank Thomas, a single to Roberto Clemente, another homer to Bill Mazeroski, and a third homer to Verne Law. Walt called me in for relief, and Newk would never return to the mound as a Dodger. After he had won the Cy Young Award and NL MVP two years earlier, Buzzie Bavasi traded him to Cincinnati.

> While Don Newcombe had drinking troubles in his younger years, he eventually became a counselor for the Dodgers and helped many players with addiction problems. I respect a man who overcomes his challenges and helps others.

The word in the locker room was that Newk missed his best friend on the team—Campy. We knew that Newk was drinking too much and that he was always moping around the clubhouse. No one knew how to cheer him up the way Roy could. Newk and Campy had had a very tight relationship since they'd played together for the Nashua Dodgers in '46, the Montreal Royals in '47, and Brooklyn for all the years after that. Their relationship came to a tragic end when that car crash took Campy away. I know it wasn't the same for Newk throwing to anyone else. Together, Campy and Newk had won four MVP awards. They were a powerful combination.

Without Roy, Newk went 0–6 in '58, and his ERA went over 8. The Dodgers would have never played anyone who was performing like that, but they respected Don's storied past and all that he'd done for the team. Some say that the Dodgers had pitched him too hard—especially in '56, when he pitched 268 innings. In '57, he had his first losing season, but now he couldn't even win a game. It was rough to see him go, but that's the here-today, gone-tomorrow world of the MLB.

Roy Campanella (sixth), Larry Doby (second), Don Newcombe (ninth), and Jackie Robinson (first) were four of the first nine African American players in the majors. The pressure and ridicule that they received was monumental and inhumane, but they opened the door for many other players.

June 22. I opened a doubleheader in Forbes Field on a beautiful Sunday afternoon. In the second inning, RC Stevens got the first hit off me. RC was a big guy, at six five and 220 pounds, and he acted as if he wanted to steal second base. I got him closer to first by throwing to Gil a couple times, but it distracted me to have him so far out there. It bothered me so much that I walked Frank Thomas, so RC got to second. RC was still leading off second—as if he was going to steal third.

I'd been talking to Don Zimmer, our shortstop, about picking a guy off at second. I told him that if I kicked the dirt behind the mound forward, I wanted him to be ready for a throw. I usually kicked dirt backward, so that was the sign. I looked at RC, and he was quite a way off second. I looked back at Joe P. at home plate and kicked the dirt forward. Without seeing Don moving behind RC, I turned and threw to Don and caught RC off guard. Don made the easy catch and tag. That was my first pickoff in the majors. Picking a guy off second is pretty rare, and I liked seeing RC take that long walk back to the dugout.

In the bottom of the fourth inning, Dick Gray and Joe got singles with two outs. I came up to bat with Dick on third and Joe on first. Bob Friend was pitching for the Bucs, and I got ahold of the second pitch and sent it screaming right by his foot. He reached down to grab it, but I got it by him for a solid single and an RBI as Dick scored and Joe went to second. That made the score 2–0 in our favor.

In the bottom of the fifth, the Pirates got a couple of hits off me and had runners at first and third. They pinch hit Roberto Clemente to try to end my shutout. Joe and I had talked with Joe Becker, our pitching coach, about how to pitch to Roberto. We thought Roberto had trouble with a sidearm curve, so that was what I threw. Clemente went for it and popped it up to deep left field to Jim Gilliam. Jim made a nice catch to end the inning and keep my shutout going. That sidearm curve kept working for me against Roberto, and he never seemed to figure it out. He only got one single off me in eight at bats that year.

In the bottom of the sixth, I guess I was getting tired. I walked Bill Verdon, and then Bob Skinner got a double with runners on second and third. Next up was RC, and I couldn't keep it in the strike zone. I walked him to load the bases. Walt called in Johnny Klippenstein to relieve me. Johnny had just come over to us from the Redlegs in the trade for Newk. Johnny got us out of the inning without a score, so I left the game without an earned run. Johnny pitched well, and we ended up winning 4–1. That evened my record to 3–3, while the team was 26–35 and not playing well.

July 12. I pitched a few relief games and then got twelve days' rest before I got another start in the Coliseum against the Redlegs. The first inning started out badly when Walt Dropo, a six five, 220-pound stud, hit a two-run homer. In the third, Frank Robinson hit a double to score Johnny Temple. In the top of the third, I got a hit, and Duke hit me in for a score. After that, I held them scoreless until the eighth inning, when Walt called Clem in to close out the game. I went two for three at the plate that night and got the win to push my record up to 4–3.

Roberto Clemente started out in the Dodger organization, but Branch Rickey drafted him into the Pirates from the Montreal Royals in 1955. Roberto didn't develop his power until 1960, when he hit started hitting double-digit home runs.

August 13. Sandy Koufax started the game against the Cubs in the Coliseum. He was twenty-two years young, and '58 was the first year that he started more than twenty games. People debate about whether he was played too little before '58, but he was still fairly inexperienced, since he hadn't played in the minors. He had great speed, of course, but he was still a little wild in those days. Sandy was finding his control, though, and was 9–5 going into the game.

Frank Robinson was another Hall of Famer I faced. I struck him out once with my knuckleball.

We went up 5–0 in the third, and then the Cubs hit a three-run homer in the fourth, and Ernie Banks hit another one in the sixth. When Sandy let a couple guys get on base and then loaded the bases by intentionally walking Ernie, they called in Clem for relief. Clem let one run in to tie the game at 5–5. In the top of the ninth, Clem gave up a single, and they had me warm up in case things got worse. Clem walked Ernie again to have runners on first and second, and then they called number 26 into the game — that was me.

They wanted me to get Walt "Moose" Moryn out because he batted left. I warmed up and threw one pitch to Moose. He popped it high up to Don "Zip" Zimmer at short for the third out and an easy play. In the bottom of the ninth, Zip got a single, and then Elmer Valo hit a nice walk-off double. What is interesting and serendipitous to me about this game was that I got the win from that one pitch! By just holding the runners and having our guys score, I got the one-pitch win, and that moved my record to 5–4.

One of the funniest stories from the time in the Coliseum was about Don Zimmer betting that Duke Snider could throw a ball out of the Coliseum. We were hitting batting practice before many fans were in the stadium, and Zip was telling us how he had had a good day at the Hollywood Park racetrack. He said he'd also won at the poker table that day. He was always borrowing twenty dollars from me and others to get to the track with some extra cash. Don was always betting on something. Depending on where we were, he'd bet on the horses or some greyhounds or a couple rabbits he'd see in Vero Beach.

We were playing catch out in center field, and we brought it in for a game of pepper with Zip, Don Demeter, Joe P., and a couple others. Duke hit a ball high into the stands down the line, and the ball bounced up and hit the top wall of the stands. We all watched it after hearing that crack of the bat! Don kept looking at the top of the stands and said, "I bet I could almost throw a ball out of this stadium."

I said, "Don, there's no way you can throw it that high. Maybe Carl or one of the other outfielders, but you're an infielder." I reckoned Don was our shortstop, and he never had that powerful an arm.

Zip looked over to me and said, "I bet you're right. I bet Carl can throw it outta here." He rubbed his chin in thought. "I bet you five dollars that the

Reading Rifle could throw it right out of this stadium." He saw Carl Furillo nearby and yelled over to him, "Carl, we're betting that you could throw the ball out of this stadium. Would you try?"

Carl walked over to us. "Don, why would I want to do that?"

Not deterred, Don went on to Gino, but Gino said he didn't want anything to do with it either. Duke had finished batting practice and was walking by, so Zip said, "Duke, we got a friendly bet going here. I bet that you can throw a ball out of this stadium. Kipp here says that you can't." I looked at him with a befuddled look, but he went on. "I'm betting five dollars that you can throw it over that wall."

Zip pointed up to the stands to the left of the arches. Duke looked up and around and said, "Yeah, I bet I can do it. Sure." Duke was never one to step away from a challenge.

Zip got all excited and started hustling the other players, including me. He was making five- or ten-dollar bets, making a mental note of it since none of us had any money on us. Don was calling in the bets, and Duke started warming up his arm. We were a little past the China Wall, and he was eyeing that upper edge of the Coliseum. Over ten of us were standing next to third base when all the bets were in. Duke continued winding up for the throw. Zip said, "Throw it outta here, Duke!"

Duke backed up and then got a running start at it, as if he were throwing a javelin. The stadium was so high that he had to throw the ball at a very high and odd angle. Duke had a great arm, and the ball flew up and up and up and was going right toward the top of the stadium. Right as it was about to go out, the ball seemed to peter out and bounced off the top of the stadium wall and back into the stands. Everybody let out a sigh, and Zip patted Duke on the back. "Good try, buddy!"

As the players dispersed, Duke started rubbing his arm and saying how it didn't feel right. He thought he might have torn something. He tried to work it out by rolling his shoulder but ended up going to Walt and asking for the night off. Of course, Walt wasn't too happy about that. Duke iced his shoulder, and everyone asked him about it, and he reluctantly told a few inquisitive players. I was sitting near him on the bench when Buzzie Bavasi, our GM, came over. Buzzie wasn't usually in the dugout, so everyone sat up straight and stopped spitting tobacco on the ground when they saw him.

Duke Snider was a great man and very friendly. I always remember when he almost threw that ball out of the Coliseum.

Bald Buzzie went up to Duke and said, "I heard about your little game of throwing the ball out of the park. You're a leader of this team and shouldn't be doing stupid things like that. If you're not in the lineup tomorrow night, I'm going to have to dock you a day's pay. That's $287, by my reckoning."

Duke felt really bad and said, "I can play tonight if you like. It's not that bad. I'll be fine."

Buzzie looked down at Duke with a serious look and said, "You get your rest tonight, but I'll expect you out there tomorrow, or you're gonna pay!"

Duke nodded, and sure enough, Duke was back on the field the next day. His shoulder had made a miraculous recovery!

Here's an off-the-field story about the City of Angels. We usually ended the game about ten thirty or eleven at night and were hungry and wanting to have some fun. Many of us would go to the House of Serfas on La Brea Avenue and Stocker Street. It was run by Nick and Ernie Serfas. This was a true sports bar where fans, players, and beautiful women hung out and had a good time. The bar wasn't only for the Dodgers either. Players from the LA Rams, professional wrestlers, and weight lifters also went there to have a drink and relax.

One fun thing to do there was to look at the chalkboards that lined the walls with autographs from these stars. Everyone would walk around looking at who had signed, and I had my name up there in '58. Another unique thing about the bar was that it had a hotel in back. I stayed there quite a few times. The life of a baseball player is a migrant one, and Nick and Ernie would let us store our few belongings there while we were on the road. When we came back, we collected our stuff and checked into other rooms. We always had a good time and good food at the House of Serfas.

Lots of pretty women went to the House of Serfas, and I started dating one. I'd dated on and off through high school, college, and my years in baseball, but my priority was always sports. My traveling lifestyle prevented me from spending too much time with anyone but my teammates. The House of Serfas set a fun mood, and I met a beautiful woman there named Kathy Black. Kathy's father had been stationed in the Philippines when he met and married Kathy's mother, who was a native. We had some good times that summer together, but the season was coming to an end.

Through August, I had my ups and downs with the team and mainly pitched in relief. I had a 4–4 record, and I wanted to get that elusive complete game.

Highlights

- I moved to Los Angeles with the team and made the starting rotation.

- I attended the opening day festivities in San Francisco and Los Angeles, where the stars came out in broad daylight.

- The Dodgers and my pitching had mixed results that year, and my ERA was over 5.0 when we went into September.

- I enjoyed being a regular on the team and being a small star in the City of Angels.

13. ALMOST COMPLETE GAME AND SAINT PAUL — 1958–59

I want to talk about one crucial game — on Labor Day in 1958. The game was in San Francisco, and we were playing nine games against the Giants in one week! The Giants had been killing us all season and outscored us on the season 114–67. On Saturday, August 30, we lost both games in the doubleheader, and on Sunday they beat us down 14–2. The Giants had beaten us eleven out of fifteen games, and we had another doubleheader on Labor Day, September 1. I was slated to start the second game after not starting for over a month.

I watched the first game and saw Willie Mays hit a homer and a double. They were up 7–3 in the bottom of the seventh, and we ended up losing 8–6. This series of losses dropped us from fourth place to sixth place in three days. We all just wanted to go home, but we had to play our sixth game in four days at Seals Stadium. Everyone was worn out except me. I hadn't thrown a lick for four days and was ready to get on the field.

I warmed up well and was feeling good on the mound. The first batter was my teammate from the DR, Felipe Alou. Felipe was in his rookie season and was only hitting .222 when he came to the plate. He was hungry, and I got him to swing at some junk pitches, and then he popped out to center field. A couple of batters later, Willie came up. I didn't want to give Willie anything to hit, so I ended up walking him. The next batter, their left fielder Jackie Brandt, hit a grounder back to me, and I fielded it for an easy out. I got out of the inning without a hit.

Johnny Antonelli pitched for the Giants and was in his salad days as a regular All Star. He had the most starts and wins for the Giants that year, but the Giants weren't doing that great either except when they were playing us. Johnny was working us over pretty well, and neither side had a hit going into the fourth inning.

In the top of the fourth, Carl Fuillo got a single to end the double no-hitter, but nobody scored. After striking out two in the third, I had three up and three down in the bottom of the fourth through the meat of their rotation — Mays, Brandt, and Cepeda. In the fifth, Johnny gave up a couple hits, but no runs. I got out of the fifth with a double play and still no hits! Maybe this was finally going to be my first complete game. Pitchers were expected to finish games back then, and I hadn't finished one that year. I wasn't thinking about a no-hitter, but there it was.

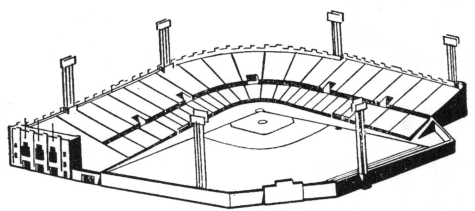

Seals Stadium, San Francisco—First N. L. Game Played in April, 1958

SEALS STADIUM COST $600,000 WHEN BUILT IN 1931

Until the San Francisco Giants' new 45,000-seat, $5,113,771 park at Candlestick Point is completed, the club will play its National League home games in Seals Stadium. Now 27 years old, Seals Stadium rated as the largest uncovered park in Organized Ball until the Dodgers moved into Memorial Coliseum this spring following their shift to Los Angeles. The big steel and concrete San Francisco arena, opened in April, 1931, was built at a cost of $600,000 by the triumvirate which then owned the Seals of the Pacific Coast League—Charles H. Graham, George Putnam and Charles (Doc) Strub. The park served as the home of both the Seals and the Missions until the latter club was shifted to Hollywood following the 1937 season. Improvements made by the Giants this year include construction of a pavilion in left field to boost the seating capacity.

Joe DiMaggio played in Seals Stadium before he moved on to the Yankees. It only held sixteen thousand fans, but they still made a lot of noise.

In the top of the sixth, Steve Bilko finally broke the stalemate by pounding a two-run homer over left-center field. Going into the bottom of the sixth, I had my no-hitter going when Antonelli came up to hit. Johnnie was a good hitter and solid athlete, and he didn't want to give me an easy win. He hit a single to right field, and Willie ended up hitting a homer to make the score 2–2 at the end of the sixth. I felt good, even though my pitch count was ninety-eight. I didn't know the pitch count at the time, and I was feeling pretty good.

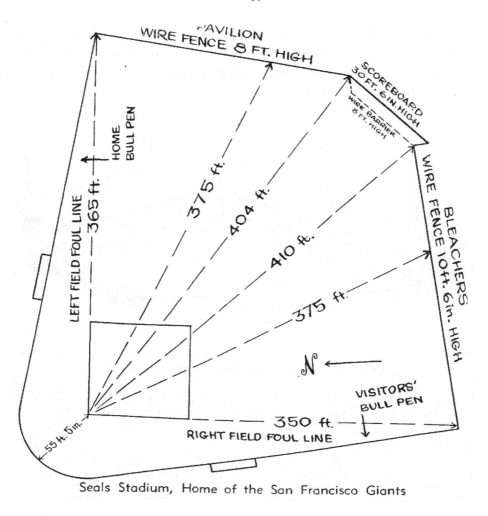

Seals Stadium, Home of the San Francisco Giants

Seals Stadium had deep foul lines but a modest center field at only 410 feet.

In the top of the seventh, I led off and bunted down the third baseline. Being a lefty, I had a couple-step advantage over righties getting to first base. I got a lot of hits that year drag bunting. I popped it down the line, and Antonelli bobbled the ball and got an error. Walt liked how Antonelli muffed the play, so he had Gilliam bunt again. I got to second, but Jim got thrown out at first. Next up was Gino. He hit a line drive over my head, and I took off running. I hightailed it around third for a score. Pitchers can make a difference in the score and be an offensive threat. Gil hit an RBI single a couple plays later to score Gino, and that was the end of Johnny. Forty-year-old Marv Grissom came in relief and got out of the inning with the Giants down 4–2.

In the bottom of the seventh, I gave away my only single to Orlando that year. Orlando was in his rookie year and batting .312, but he only went one for eight against me that year. He didn't get past first base. In the eighth, I had three up and three down and got my fifth strikeout of the game. My pitch count was up to 123 by the end of the eighth, and I was starting to feel it. I just wanted to get through one more inning.

In the bottom of the ninth, we were up 4–2 when Willie Mays came up to bat. He'd hit two homers that day already, and I wasn't about to give him another one. Walt had instructed me not to walk him, but I threw three balls, and he didn't go for one of 'em. I snuck a couple strikes by him after that, and he just watched them go by. I didn't mind taking him to a full count that way. My sixth pitch was right over the corner of the plate, and I thought I'd struck him out. But the umpire saw it differently, and Willie was soon walking to first.

With the tying run on first, Brandt hit a grounder to Bob Lillis at short. I was hoping they'd make a double play to end it, but they only got Willie out at second. Brandt was on first when Orlando came back up to the plate. I tried to get him to swing at a couple of outside pitches, but he didn't bite. I threw a knuckleball, and he swiped at it and missed. Then he watched a strike go by to give him a 2–2 count. On the fifth pitch, he popped it up to Carl in right field for the second out.

There were two outs in the bottom of the ninth when their catcher Bob Schmidt walked to the plate. Bob was in his rookie year and had worked his way up through different minor leagues. I had walked him the first two times up to bat, and he was aggressive at the plate. I wound up and threw a curve ball that didn't break well. Bob pulled it down the line foul. Joe P. called for another curve. Maybe my arm was worn out on that 140th pitch, because the pitch went high and didn't break much. Schmidt slammed it out of the park for a two-run homer to tie the score at 4–4.

I was one out away from a complete game, and I couldn't close the deal. It was very frustrating watching Bob jog the bases. I could have been walking off the field in victory, but instead I was stuck facing Eddie Bressoud, the next batter. When Eddie hit a single to left-center field, Walt came out and pulled me. Walt said, "I thought you were going to do it tonight, Kipp. You were close. You were damn close."

This picture from the 1959 All Star game features my teammate Charlie Neal and four of the best hitters I ever faced — a twenty-five-year old Hank Aaron, the legendary Ted Williams, Stan the Man, and Willie Mays — the only one to hit a homer off me.

I walked back to the bench, and my teammates congratulated me on a great game. "You'll get them next time." "Good try." I sat next to Babe Birrer, and he looked over and said, "You picked the wrong team to pitch a great game against. That would have been a complete game against any other team!"

Threw Wrong Ball, Says Kipp

Frank Finch, *Los Angeles Times*, September 2, 1958

Perhaps it was indelicate and impertinent to ask. It had been only a couple of hours since Freddie Kipp's gallant attempt to pitch his first complete game in the big leagues was derailed by Bob Schmidt's two-out, two-run homer in the last of the ninth.

But the rangy southpaw from Piqua, Kan., is a good-natured fellow so decided to chance it as the Dodgers' charter plane flew south from San Francisco Monday night.

"What," we inquired, "was your immediate reaction when you saw that homer sailing into the seats?"

Freddie grinned sheepishly, then replied: "I threw the wrong pitch. I should have thrown him my fast ball. It wasn't a very good pitch, the one Schmidt hit. It was a high curve ball, and I knew it was gone the moment he connected."

Was this the first time Kipp had been tied or defeated by a homer when he was only one out away from victory?

"No," said Fred. "When I was in Montreal I was leading Miami, 2–1, and got beat 3–2, in this situation. The moment the guy homered I said to myself, 'That's all, man. Let's go home.'"

Walk-off homers are a painful experience, but at least they have closure. This game was not over—not even close. We were in our fifth game in three days, and everyone was beat. But we couldn't leave. The extra innings went on and on like some Chinese water torture. Every pitch through the extra innings felt like another drip.

It wasn't until the thirteenth inning that we got two runners on base, but they didn't score. In the bottom of the fourteenth, the Giants loaded the bases before Johnny Podres struck out Valmy Thomas. In the fifteenth, the Giants loaded the bases again, and Bob Schmidt lined out to Duke in center field. In the sixteenth, we finally scored after eight scoreless innings. I thought we had it, but Whitey Lockman hit a homer to tie the game in the bottom of the sixteenth. A couple batters later, Ray Jablonski scored on an error to give us our fifth loss in a row!

We just couldn't get the win in Seals that long Labor Day weekend. We tried and tried and tried, but we couldn't close the deal against the Giants that year. If they would have relieved me in the ninth after 120 pitches, maybe I would have gotten the win. There could have been a happy ending to the game. I'd prefer that to the complete game. Instead I didn't get any credit for my eight and two-thirds innings.

Looking back after all these years, I go back to that game in Seals Stadium where I came so close to going the distance. I tend to think that the coaches today have it right. Pitching a complete game is too much for most players, and it makes more sense to bring in the relief.

September 5. I got the start against old Vinegar Bend in our first rematch since our time in the army. I pitched well again, and it definitely helped that Stan the Man was nursing an injury. Wally Moon was the only guy who earned a run against us that day. I lasted until the seventh inning, when they brought Stan in as a pinch hitter. Walt brought Clem in to get the Man out, and Clem held on to our 2–1 victory. I got my sixth win that night to raise my record to 6–4.

September 9. We were in Philly and had to finish a suspended game from July 27. The game resumed in the bottom of the sixth inning, and I was put in as a reliever in the bottom of the eighth. We tied the game up, and it went into extra innings. In the tenth, the Phillies loaded the bases before Walt called in Clem Labine to replace me. On Clem's second pitch, Wally Post hit a walk-off grand slam to give me my fifth loss.

September 15. Stan Williams started in County Stadium against the World Champion Braves, and he was having control issues right from the start. He walked the first two runners, and before he even got an out, I was on the mound with runners at first and second. The life of a reliever usually starts like this—runners on base and the momentum going the wrong direction. I was pretty shocked by being in the game so early and threw a couple extra pitches to warm up.

While I was up there, Walter and Gil came over to the mound, and Gil said, "Bruton"—the man on first—"wanders off the base pretty far, and he can't go to second. If I put my hand over the LA on my cap, it means that I'm going to sneak over behind the bag."

I said, "OK. When I turn my head to the plate, you break."

I gave a couple pitches to Eddie Matthews and noticed that Bruton had strayed away from first base. Gil gave me the sign, and I turned back to home as if nothing was up. I turned my head and threw the ball to Gil. Bruton didn't expect it at all, and Gil made the easy tag. That's the way I like to start an inning! That changed the momentum of the inning back to our favor, and I got out of the inning without a run scored.

Frank Howard and Gil Hodges show Gil Hodges Jr. how to play first base in Dodgertown. Gil was a great first baseman and helped me excel.

The Braves were hot, though, and I didn't get out of the game with a win. With a loss, my record dropped to 6–6. I pitched a little more relief after that game but was pretty much done for the season. I felt pretty good about pitching .500 in my rookie season—especially considering we had a losing record. Stan Williams was the only regular pitcher who had a winning record, 9–7, that year. Don Drysdale had a 12–13 record, and Sandy ended up with an 11–11 record. Sandy had started out the season well, but he sprained his ankle midseason and never recovered. Times were hard that year, and we ended up in seventh place—twenty-one games behind the Braves.

We were a young team going through transitions with a few wily veterans. It ended up being a story of threes for me. Three wins at home, three wins away. Three losses at home. Three losses away. Three wins at night. Three wins in the day. I had played rather well against left-handed hitters, who only hit .235 against me, so that was why they kept calling me in for relief against the opponents' lefties. I also batted .250—enough to get the Silver Slugger award for the best-hitting pitcher. I gave it all I had in '58 and got fifty-eight strikeouts in 102 innings. Not bad for a farm boy in the big City of Angels.

At the end of the season, I decided to continue my graduate degree in Physical Education at the University of Northern Colorado in Greeley. I studied for a few weeks before I got a telegraph from the Dominican Republic. They wanted me to pitch for them again, and I couldn't turn it down. For the second time, I wanted to play ball instead of study books.

Pitching in the Dominican Republic went well again. While I was there, I signed a contract with the Dodgers for $9,000. Some writers thought that missing that complete game cost me $1,000. A costly mistake.

Only 13 Dodgers Still Unsigned

Bob Hunter, *Los Angeles Examiner*, February 8, 1959

Roger Craig and Fred Kipp agreed to $10,000 and $9,000 contracts to bring to 26 the total number ready to start the campaign. Kipp's season was a comeback in itself, inasmuch as he had led the International League with 17 defeats in 1957. With the Dodgers, his 6–6 record was spaced at one victory a month, April through September.

However, he gave up 11 homers to the short left field fence in the Coliseum, but only five away from home. Kipp, a serious student of baseball and very possibly more talented than his record reflects, still is striving for his first all-the-way performance in the majors. He came within one out in San Francisco, when a two-run homer by Bob Schmidt tied the score, and the Giants finally went on to beat Johnny Podres in the sixteenth. That undoubtedly was at least a $1,000 pitch for Kipp.

I got back to Vero Beach in 1959 and everything went well in spring training. Pee Wee had retired, so the team was going through more fundamental changes. Pee Wee had been our captain and natural leader, so he was missed. Wally Moon was on our team now, and Don Demeter was hitting his stride. Young players I didn't know came up to me now and said hi and asked for pitching advice. I was twenty-seven and knew my way around the old naval base and knew most of the players. The young pitching staff was maturing. Don Drysdale turned twenty-one, Stan Williams was twenty-two, and Sandy Koufax was twenty-three. That shows how young some of our pitchers still were.

My pitching went well in spring training, but I guess my fastball didn't get any faster in '59. I got called into a meeting with the traveling secretary, and they told me I was being traded to the Phillies. They didn't know anything else about the trade, and the deal fell through. I'm not sure why they told me before it was final, but it threw my permanence with the team into question. The next thing I knew, they said I was going to play AAA ball for the Saint Paul Saints.

The Dodgers had too many pitchers that year, and they sent several other regulars to Saint Paul with me. Ed Roebuck, Larry Sherry, Jackie Collum, and even Don Bessent got sent down to the Twin Cities. We had more veterans on the Saints that year than the Montreal Royals did. Meanwhile, other major teams in the league seemed to be lacking southpaw pitchers. It was frustrating to be in an organization with so many great pitchers while other teams worked with skeleton crews.

I was twenty-seven and entering the prime of my career. I wanted to play in the majors and wasn't going to learn anything in the minors. When I look back on this demotion to Saint Paul, I think I should have refused to go down to the minors. I did casually talk to Buzzie Bavasi, our general manager, about being traded to a team where I could play, but I wasn't firm. Gaining experience in a great organization like the Dodgers was hard to beat, but now I wanted to play in the majors, and there wasn't much room. Instead of being traded, I got sent to the new American Association.

The American Association (AA) was quite different from the International League. The league split into two divisions of five teams that year instead of the eight teams of the year before. The league got a Texas twist that year with the addition of the Dallas Rangers, the Houston Buffs, and the Fort Worth Cats. I got to play against many players I hadn't faced, in new cities and stadiums. We traveled by train and bus more than planes, and we had fun.

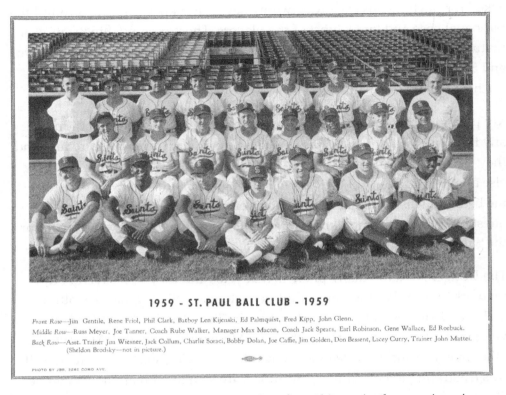

1959 - ST. PAUL BALL CLUB - 1959

Front Row—Jim Gentile, Rene Friol, Phil Clark, Batboy Len Kijenski, Ed Palmquist, Fred Kipp, John Glenn.
Middle Row—Russ Meyer, Joe Tanner, Coach Rube Walker, Manager Max Macon, Coach Jack Spears, Earl Robinson, Gene Wallace, Ed Roebuck.
Back Row—Asst. Trainer Jim Wiesner, Jack Collum, Charlie Soraci, Bobby Dolan, Joe Caffie, Jim Golden, Don Bessent, Lacey Curry, Trainer John Mattei.
(Sheldon Brodsky—not in picture.)

PHOTO BY JBR, 2282 COMO AVE.

We had a good club that year and I saw a lot of new hitters in the new American Association.

Rube Walker was my catcher for quite a bit of the season, and I was playing well. I became the main starting pitcher and started thirty games and pitched 213 innings. Ed Roebuck was the next most prolific after me, and he started twenty-eight and pitched for 196 innings. I pitched thirteen complete games and had five shutouts. I led the team in strikeouts with 125 and got the most wins on the team. I was 7–7 in the middle of the season and then won six games in a row. I ended up 14–11 and made the all-star team.

At the end of the season, I was the only pitcher from the Saints called up to the majors. When I joined the Dodgers on Labor Day weekend at the

Coliseum, we lost both games of a doubleheader to Chicago. We were in second place and three games behind the Giants. I fell into my second pennant race in my short career.

The '59 Dodgers were youthful and much different without Pee Wee as the captain. Wally Moon was hitting his moon shots over the China Wall, and Duke was leading the team with RBIs at eighty-eight. Don Demeter was a regular, and Maury Wills was in his rookie season—but not stealing many bases yet. We were an exciting and solid team, and we were hungry.

We were getting hot and won five games in a row after I got there (nothing to do with me) and came within half a game of first place by September 11. Then we lost two—including one to the Braves on September 14. That loss put us in third place—two games behind the Giants and one game behind the Braves. The Braves were getting hot too and trying for a "threepeat" of the pennant. They'd beaten the Yankees in the '57 World Series and lost to them in '58. We faced the Braves on the fifteenth, and it was our chance to catch up to them. I was starting to think that I was going to ride the bench, as I had done in the '56 pennant race. Every game was critical at this point in the season, and I was still doubtful that Walt would put me in at such a key moment.

In the top of the ninth, we were up 6–5, and Larry Sherry was having a little trouble. Larry gave up a double to start the inning, and then Felix Mantilla drove the runner in to tie the score. When a sacrifice bunt advanced Mantilla to second, they called me in to relieve Larry. The Braves were at the top of their order, and that meant two left-handed batters were coming up—Bill Bruton, their center fielder, and the future Hall of Famer Eddie Matthews. Walt had done his homework, and he knew that I did well against lefties.

I was a little nervous jogging out to the mound in the Coliseum for the first time that year. I warmed up with John Roseboro catching and thought I was ready. I did my double windup, which I had perfected that year, and threw two balls to get behind in the count against Bruton.

I didn't let that bother me. I straightened my fastball out and caught him watching a strike. I kept throwing strikes after that, and he started hitting foul balls all over the place—a grounder down the line, a pop fly into the stands, and another foul tip. I was warmed up now for sure. On the seventh pitch, he grounded one right at me. It was a steamer, but I grabbed it, checked Mantilla at second, and threw to first for the quick out. I was glad to get Bruton out, but you know the old saying—out of the frying pan and into the fire.

There were two outs in the bottom of the ninth, and Eddie Mathews walked up to the plate. I had tried to put the Bob Schmidt ninth-inning homer behind me, but a lingering doubt came back to me. I was determined to overcome that fear and get Eddie out. Eddie was my age—less than two weeks younger than I—and I'd faced him five times in '58 and had struck him out twice. Against most lefties, I mixed in some sidearm throws with my normal overhead throw to keep the pitches away from them. They weren't used to seeing that low ball coming at them from the left.

The riflemen of Milwaukee — Hank Aaron, Eddie Matthews, and Joe Adcock were the power hitters of the Braves.

I started with the sidearm and threw a ball outside. John called for a knuckleball. I'd been throwing that pitch well all year in Saint Paul. I

196

checked the runner at second and then threw the knuckler. I remember seeing the ball fall to the right when he swung, and it caused him to hit a chopper to Neal at second. Neal made a leaping catch and had time to throw it to Gil at first for the third out. I got us out of the inning, and now we were heading into the bottom of the ninth.

The players congratulated me and welcomed me back into the dugout. Walt told me "Good job!" and the double Ds—Don Drysdale and Don Demeter—patted me on the back. I had pitched in and done my part against the top of the order of the hot Braves. It was great to be back with my teammates from the year before. We ended up winning that night to tie the Braves.

On September 19, we were still tied with the Braves at two games behind the Giants. We swept the doubleheader in Seals Stadium to tie the Giants and left the Braves half a game back. On the twentieth, we pounded the Giants 8–2 to take a half-game lead over the Braves, and that gave us a one-game lead over the Giants. This was the first time we'd been in first place since April 26. The Giants were in free fall now and would never come back that year. We really broke them in that series, and it felt good to get them back for the pain of last year. The Dodgers-Giants rivalry had definitely made the trip out west intact. The next day, the Braves beat the Pirates to put them in a tie for first with us.

On September 22, we faced the Cardinals in Saint Louis and got into a slugfest. By the sixth inning, we were down 11–7 when Walt called me in to relieve. Stan Musial was up first, and I didn't want him to start a rally. I kept the ball away from him and worked the corners of the plate. He didn't swing once, and the count went full before the ref called a couple of strikes balls. I didn't mind walking him, but I thought I struck him out on some nice pitches. We got out of the inning without a score.

In the seventh, I started the inning off the wrong way. I gave up a single and a walk and then faced my old teammate Gino Cimoli with runners on first and second. Gino bunted down the first baseline. Gil and I charged the ball, and I got to it first. Gil ducked, and I threw it over his head to Charlie, who came over to cover first. The runners advanced to second and third with one out. I intentionally walked my old nemesis Ken Boyer to load the bases.

One of the worst scenarios I can think of is having the bases loaded with Musial coming up to bat in late innings. I couldn't walk Stan again with the bases loaded. Joe P. was catching and called for a knuckleball. I threw him one that danced just enough to make Stan foul it off. My next pitch was a curve, and Stan smacked it down the line to Jim Gilliam. Jim made a great catch and threw the force out at home. With the bases still loaded, Hal Smith came up, and he hit a high pop fly to end the inning. That inning was a lot of work, but at least I kept them scoreless.

I was coming up to bat in the top of the eighth when Walt pulled me. While I hadn't pitched that well in the seventh, I was going to be pitching to the bottom of the order and was hoping I could stay. I wished he'd let me get an at bat, but Walt was playing aggressively and put in Sandy Amoros to pinch hit for me. It wasn't until the bottom of the ninth inning when my Dominican teammate Frank Howard came up to bat that we got anywhere. Frank hit a line drive three-run homer to pull us to within one run. It didn't start a rally, though, and we lost 10–11 to put us one game back.

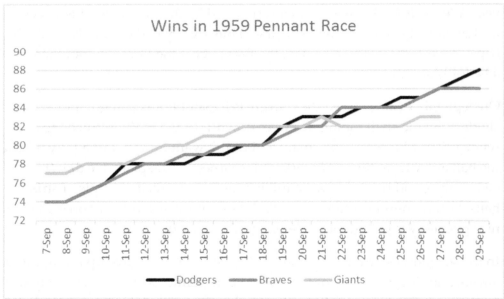

The Giants were leading in early September, but the Braves and Dodgers kept the steadier pace, and then we beat the Braves in the three-game playoff.

After that, the Braves lost a couple of games, while we won a couple. Then we reversed course again. On September 27, we beat the Cubs in Wrigley to end the season tied with the Braves. The tie forced a three-game playoff for the pennant.

This was only the third playoff in the history of the National League, and the Dodgers were in all three. We took a bus up to County Stadium, and Danny McDevitt started the game but got pulled in favor of Larry Sherry in the second inning. Larry had played with me in Saint Paul for the first half of the year and had been called up in July and started playing regularly in the rotation. Larry had a great arm and could throw one of the best sliders in the game. Larry was hot and shut them out for almost eight innings to lead us to the win in the first game of the playoff.

Larry was quite the emotional player and used to have sibling rivalries with his older brother Norm, who made it up to the Dodgers for the first time that year. Norm was my age and had been in the Dodger organization since 1950. Larry would get mad at Norm sometimes and throw pitches that Norm didn't call. It's hard enough catching major-league pitches, but it's even harder when you're expecting a curve ball and the pitcher throws a slider. When the uncalled pitch would break differently from what was expected and hit Norm, Norm would cuss out his younger brother, and I thought he was going to kill him. I've never seen a catcher go after a pitcher like a hit batter, but that's almost what happened. Larry was immature like that, but he had a lot of confidence on the mound, and he delivered.

In the second game of the '59 pennant race in the Coliseum, we went through almost all of our pitchers. I started thinking that I'd get on the mound. Drysdale started the game but was replaced by Podres in the fifth. Chuck Churn replaced Podres in the seventh. Then Sandy came in the ninth, and Clem Labine replaced him with the bases loaded in the top of the ninth. Clem struck Mickey Vernon out to finish the inning without a score, but we were still down by three runs.

> Before the second game in LA, I remember Walt Alston saying, "Bring your bags with you, because we're going to leave for Chicago right after we win!"

Lew Burdette of the Braves pitched the first nine innings and held us to two runs. He was going for his twenty-second win, but he couldn't get out of the inning. The Braves went through four pitchers that inning, including the legendary Warren Spahn. We wouldn't go down and tied the game at 5–5 to send it into extra innings. Walt put Stan Williams in after that, and he held the Braves scoreless until the twelfth inning.

In the bottom of the twelfth, thirty-seven-year-old pinch-hitter Carl Furillo came in with two outs and Gil on second and Joe P. on first. Carl hit a sharp grounder to short, and Felix Mantilla made a great catch but a bad throw to first. The ball ended up in our dugout. Carl could have been out, but he was safe at first, and Gil scored the winning run. We won in astonishing fashion, and LA had its first pennant.

We weren't expected to win the pennant that year, but we were going to the World Series to face the Chicago White Sox. I didn't go with the team in the World Series, so I watched from afar like everyone else. The Dodgers were an odd mixture of veterans and rookies, with one rookie shining over the others. Larry Sherry got saves in games two and three and then won games four and six. He was hot at the right time, and I always wonder if I could have done something like that in the right situation. Larry had started the year in AAA with me and ended up as the MVP of the World Series. Larry had a great fastball and slider and deserved that honor by performing on the ultimate stage in baseball—the '59 World Series.

I went back to Kansas City to visit my brother and see his children. I made it to Piqua and saw my family, but I spent more time in Kansas City. I ran across Ralph Terry, who was pitching for the Athletics. Ralph knew Bob Sight, an owner of a Chevrolet dealership, and they got a city judge to take me to a Rotary Club meeting to talk about baseball. Ralph and I started hanging out and playing basketball together.

Ralph's father was developing land near the Rio Grande down in Texas. He was planting orange orchards and watering them from the Rio. We drove down there to look at the land and picked up Ryne Duren, a Yankee pitcher, on the way. We had a great time driving through Texas and seeing Ralph's dad.

Highlights

- I pitched well against the Giants on Labor Day and went all the way to the bottom of the ninth with two outs before giving up a late homer to send the game into extra innings.

- I ended the season 6–6 while pitching a mix of starting and relieving.

- I spent the '59 season with the Saint Paul Saints and made the all-star team with a 14–11 record.

- I joined the Dodgers in September and played a couple of games in the pennant race, which we eventually won in a three-game playoff against the Braves.

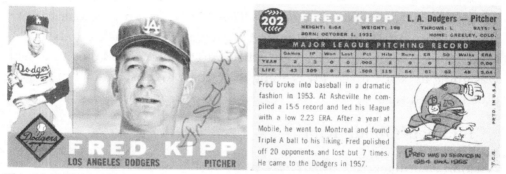

This 1960 Topps #202 card was released for the two games that I pitched in 1959.

14. TO THE YANKEES — 1960

In the winter season of 1959–60, I helped the Escogido Leones win the Dominican Republican championship again. I had a great time down there and showed up to Dodgertown in great shape and throwing well. Everyone was in high spirits from winning the World Series again, but I felt a little left out since I hadn't gone. I thought I could have had a bigger impact on the team and wanted to play in the majors. Everyone always played in the minors to get to the majors. The minors were a means to another end.

The Dodgers weren't willing to give me a raise after I had another solid winning season with the Saints. They didn't want to pay me what I thought I deserved — about $10,000 for the seven months from February to September. According to the *New York Times*, I was the only Dodger to not sign by February 24. Instead of going back to Saint Paul, I asked to be traded. Pretty soon afterward, I got called into the office, and they told me I was going to be a Yankee. I was going to go coast to coast again, but this time I headed east.

Bombers Obtain Kipp

John Debringer, *New York Times*, 04-03-1960

To prove that they can make a trade to someone other than their Kansas City pals, the Yankees completed a deal with, of all people, the Dodgers. However, the transaction isn't likely to be felt in either the National or American League pennant races.

The Yanks obtained Fred Kipp, a 28-year-old left handed pitcher who last season worked for the Dodgers' Saint Paul farm. In exchange, the Yankee farm at Richmond assigned two outfielders, Gordon Windhorn and Dick Sanders, to the Dodger farm at Montreal.

Among other things, Kipp has a deceptive knuckleball, something of a rarity among southpaws. He had a 14–11 won-and-lost record with Saint Paul last year and a 3.21 earned-run average. He struck out 125 in 213 innings.

I traded in the Dodger blue for pinstripes. Being a Yankee meant a lot in those days, and their dominance in the sport is dynastic. Carl Erskine used to say the Yankees were like the Roman Empire. They were the team that everyone feared. The statistics are mind boggling. From 1947 to 1964, the Yankees played in fifteen of the eighteen World Series and won ten of them. They were a dynasty, and I was going to be on the same team as Mickey Mantle, Whitey Ford, and Yogi Berra, to name a few. The new decade was starting, and I was excited about the change.

The first thing I did was drive to Saint Pete, where the Yanks were in spring training. I arrived the same day as Ralph Terry. Ralph had just gotten out of his service in the army. It was good to see Ralph, and we would eat together and hang out. The Yankee spring training was much different from Dodgertown. We only had the major-league team and tens of other likely players, as compared to the hundreds of players in Dodgertown.

Even though there weren't as many players around, the Yankee training camp felt like the big city instead of the small town that the Dodgers created. While the Dodgers were familial and friendly and again world champions in 1960, the Yanks had taken third place in '59 and were looking for a comeback. That was the lowest standing for the Yankees since I'd been in high school in '48. Manager Casey Stengel wanted change, and General Manager George Weiss brought in five new players, whom you can see on the cover of the book.

Because of the promotional picture on the cover of this book, I was associated with the other new players, who were Kent Hadley, Roger Maris, Elmer Valo, and Joe DeMaestri. Roger wasn't much of a home-run hitter until that year, when the Yankees showed him how to pull the ball down the first-base line, which was only 296 feet away in Yankee Stadium. Compared to the expansive left and center fields, down the line in right field was relatively short compared to most stadiums.

Roger was like a shooting star in '61, when he hit those sixty-one homers. The press really made hay with that record and put a lot of stress on Roger. Roger didn't deal with it well, and some said that pressure—the same pressure that Mickey had trouble with also—caused Roger to age quickly and lose some hair. I could relate to the hair-losing part. Roger never had another year like '61, but what a year he had.

In this 1960 All-Star Game photo, Yogi Berra has his arm around Stan Musial, and Joe Adcock looks on while Moose Skowron scowls.

Elmer Valo came over with me in '60 and was only one of three players who played for the Brooklyn Dodgers, LA Dodgers, and New York Yankees. Danny McDevitt was traded to the Yankees in '61 to become the third player to play for all three teams. I'm the only survivor as of this writing in 2017. While lots of players played for the Brooklyn Dodgers and the New York Yankees, Ralph Branca and I were the last two to walk this earth. Ralph passed in December 2016, so I'm the only one left. I'm the last Yankee Dodger.

I got to know the other Yankees pretty easily. Mickey was like a hero to everyone and easy to talk to. He was a down-to-earth, aw-shucks kind of guy who could hit like no other. He would chew the fat with just about anyone he ran into. Before games, Ralph and I would be shagging balls during batting practice, and Mickey would just walk up to us and start talking about what was going on.

Yogi Berra was great at teaching pitchers like Ralph Terry and me. He had a way of explaining things so that I could remember them.

He was the star, but he acted like the small-town bumpkin playing a game of pickup. That was the appeal of Mickey. I don't think he understood what he meant to others, especially the fans. New York elevated him to a stratospheric level of fame, and it was hard for him to deal with that pressure. I don't know how I would have handled it, but Mick handled it by drinking and walking around as if he were back in Oklahoma. He could drink like he could hit, and it would eventually lead to many problems with alcohol. He was the toast of the town, and he toasted to many people.

When Yogi was around, everyone would shut up so that he would talk more. He was always trying to get a laugh out of us, and he usually did. He'd try out sayings on us before he'd use them on the press. He learned his twisted style from Casey Stengel—who spoke in what we called Stengelese—but he took it to new levels. I liked his saying "How can you think and hit at the same time?" That summed up for me how players have to be hardwired to play this game. Baseball is split-second reactions, not a thinking man's game. There is plenty of time to think, but most of the time you don't.

Yogi was a natural at the plate. He could hit about anything. I'd watch him in batting practice, and he could connect no matter where the ball was thrown. Strikes, reasonable balls, and unreasonable balls were fair game to him. He was a great catcher as well. He squatted funny when he caught, and that was how he got his nickname "Yogi"—not from his philosophical musings, such as "He hits from both sides of the plate. He's amphibious!"

One crazy story from that spring break in Saint Pete was related to Ryne Duren. I'd been to Mexico with Ryne and Ralph, but I never got along with Ryne that well. He was a Jekyll-and-Hyde type of character. I had heard stories about his temper and saw it that first night in Saint Pete. We were staying in our hotel, and for some reason, Ryne got drunk and pissed off and threw a chair through an upstairs window. The chair and lots of shattered glass fell down onto the lawn in front of the hotel.

He climbed out on a ledge and was totally naked. He was yelling things at the world and especially George Weiss, the general manager. He was yelling that George was a tight ass because he wouldn't give a rais. This went on for a while before Ralph saved his life and pulled him back in the window. This never got out to the press, and Ryne didn't remember any of it the next day. There were other stories of him as a boy kicking rocks all the way home after a loss. I never had a temper like that and couldn't relate.

Ryne Duren was a tough guy to get along with, but my friend Ralph Terry was good with him and saved his life one night on the balcony of a hotel.

When the Grapefruit League, a series of exhibition games in Florida, was over that spring, we got on a train to Richmond, where we would play our farm team, the Virginians. When we arrived in Richmond, they had a huge breakfast for us at the John Marshall Hotel. Spring training usually had a lot of pomp and circumstance around it, and this was no exception. They fed us and nine hundred other people, including the governor of Virginia and mayor of Richmond. They held a parade for us on the Virginia capitol steps before the game.

I'd played in Richmond quite a bit in the International League, and I got my chance to pitch against the team that I would eventually relieve for. Casey pegged me as a reliever, and I got into the game to pitch the last two innings. We were well ahead, and I wished I would have shut them out. Instead, I gave up two hits and two runs and struck out two. Those runs bothered me and probably Stengel too.

Stengel was famous for his twisted sayings. Casey, who got his name from his hometown of Kansas City, came up with some funny sayings, such as the following:

"The secret to successful managing is to keep the five guys who hate you away from the four guys who haven't made up their minds."

"All right, everyone, line up alphabetically according to your height."

"Being with a woman all night never hurt no professional baseball player. It's staying up all night looking for a woman that does him in."

We got back on the train that night and took the sleeper up to New York. While it was only April 15, the Bronx was already a steamy eighty degrees, and we practiced for ninety minutes. I'd pitched batting practice there in '56, but it was quite different pitching there when I was wearing pinstripes. The grandeur of the stadium was overwhelming, and there was no other stadium like it. Left and center fields were huge, at over 460 feet, and few players hit it out that far. That also gave Mickey a lot of field to cover. If he hadn't trashed his knee in the '51 World Series on the drain in this stadium, Mickey could have been as good a fielder as he was a hitter. In Brooklyn, we used to joke that it felt like the Roman Coliseum in Yankee Stadium.

Two days later, on April 17, I pitched the final two innings of preseason against the Red Sox. This time, I shut them out and got three strikeouts. Casey said I looked good out there. Things were looking up, but Casey had thirteen pitchers on the roster, and that was too many. Casey told the press that he'd have to make a decision in mid-May, when the roster had to be pared down to twenty-eight.

We traveled up to Boston and had our season opener on April 19. Opening day in Fenway was electric. I looked around the field, and the contorted outfield reminded me of Ebbets Field. The thirty-seven-foot-tall Green Monster in left field reminded me of the China Wall in the Los Angeles Coliseum. The hand-operated scoreboard was classic even in the sixties and is still a great feature of that stadium today. People just can't help watching the person behind the scoreboard change those numbers.

The Red Sox and Yankees were ultimate rivals, so the air was thick with tension that night. Those Boston fans would yell all kinds of profanity at us. Ted Williams hit his second homer of the season in two games to put him in fourth place in the career home-run category. He pulled his calf muscle when he jumped out of the gate. At forty-one, he should have taken it easier.

I didn't get to play in the opener, where we pounded them 8–4, with Roger Maris going four for five with a single, a double, and two homers. Roger was our new leadoff hitter, and he made his presence known right away. He ended up winning the AL MVP award that year.

The next night in Fenway, on April 20, the Sox were pummeling us 7–1 even without Ted "Thumper" Williams. When the game was basically over, Casey called me in to relieve in the bottom of the eighth. I was facing the top of their order—Don Buddin and all-stars Pete Runnels and Frank Malzone. Elston Howard was catching, and he called for curves and fastballs. It worked, because I got all three batters out in quick succession—one grounder and a line drive to Tony Kubek at short, and another grounder to McDougald on third. My pitching was sharp, and I felt good about closing the game out. We beat the Sox the next night, with Ryne Duren getting the save. We were now 2–1, and Casey was pleased that we had gotten the better of the Sox in Fenway to start the season.

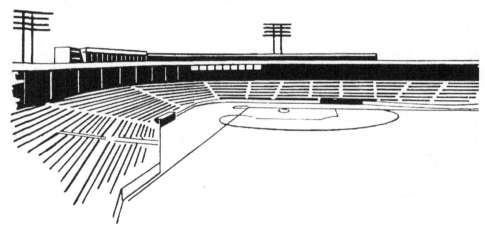

Fenway Park, Boston——First A. L. Game Played April 20, 1912

RED SOX' PARK NAMED FOR 'FENS' SECTION WHERE LOCATED
Fenway Park acquired its name from its location in a section of Boston's Back Bay known as the Fens, a name later changed to Fenway. The area commonly called the Back Bay consists chiefly of filled in land which once was flooded by a bay from the Charles River. Opened in 1912, Fenway Park was rebuilt in 1934 shortly after Tom Yawkey purchased the Red Sox.

h

Fenway Park has the character of the older stadiums that were squeezed into one square block.

We went back to Yankee Stadium for our home opener the next day against the Orioles. The stadium was only half full, with 36,686 fans. It was rather subdued compared to opening day in LA in '58, but that shows the benefits of being the new kid in town. The Yankees, surprisingly, didn't get much better attendance after the Giants and Dodgers left New York. Fans don't change their loyalties quickly.

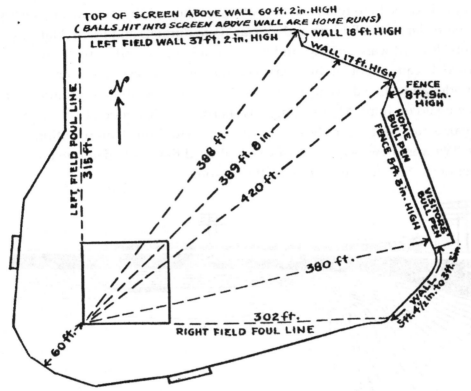

Fenway Park, Home of the Boston Red Sox

The Green Monster in left tried to equalize its shortcomings like the China Wall.

Whitey Ford got the opening honors, and he shut the Orioles out for the first seven innings. Ralph and I started warming up in the bull pen in the seventh, and we were ready to go. We were both excited to play in the season opener. Ralph got called in for the final two innings and shut them out. I was hoping that I'd get the call, but I learned to be patient. We beat them the next two games too to make our record 5–1.

About this time, I started living in New Jersey with Elmer Valo and a few others. We lived in New Jersey to save a few bucks, but it cost quite a bit of time and money to get there from the Bronx. If I could do it again, I would have stayed in the Manhattan Hotel on Times Square, where Mickey, Maris, Skowron, and Bauer lived. To show you what kind of guy Mickey was, he said I and others could visit their suite whenever we wanted to. We just had to tell the desk clerk that we were there to see Mickey, and they'd give us the key.

I would drop by his apartment, and it seemed as if Mickey was never there. I guess he was out partying somewhere or wandering around town. I'd go over with Ralph or others and hang out before or after a game instead of sitting around New Jersey. There wasn't much to do in New Jersey compared to New York City. Randomly visiting Mickey's suite worked for a while, but then the hotel manager said that too many people were coming and going. They cut us off. Mickey had a way of making you feel welcome. He'd make the hotel draw the line instead of drawing it himself.

On April 27, Whitey Ford got his second start, against the Washington Senators, and held them to one run until the eighth inning. Ryne and I were called to warm up in the eighth inning. I think Casey liked having a righty and a lefty ready to go. Whitey had amazing control but must have gotten tired when he gave up a three-run homer to Jim Lemon to put us behind 5–4. Ryne got the relief and struck a couple of guys out. Ryne was throwing smoke and was always fun to watch.

In the bottom of the eighth, Casey pinch hit Hector Lopez for Ryne, and I was the only one left warming up in the bull pen. It was nice to relieve in the top of the ninth with a clean slate. I was facing the rookie first baseman Don Mincher. Mincher was a solid hitter and would go on to be an All Star with the California Angels and the Seattle Pilots. He had already hit in a run that night, but we didn't know much about him yet, so early in his career. Elston was calling for some knuckleballs, and I gave it to him. I struck him out and then struck out Pedro Ramos too. The third batter was Billy Gardner, and I got him to groundout to Gil McDougald on third. Three up and three down. That's the way I like it. We couldn't get a tying run in the bottom of the ninth, and that was the end. Our record dropped to 5–3.

Mickey Mantle and Roger Maris were known as the M&M Boys and were a historic duo that had devastating effects on opposing teams.

On May 1, Ralph started against the Orioles in Baltimore. Ralph gave up a couple of runs in the second, and Casey started going through the bull pen—first Bobby Shantz, then John Gabler, Art Ditmer, and Johnny James. Gabler and Ditmar both came in with the bases loaded, and they gave up six runs in the fourth. By the time Casey put me in for the seventh inning, we were down 8–5.

Ron Hansen, the Baltimore second baseman, was the first batter I faced. He hit a solid single on me to start the inning. Next up was their pitcher Chuck Estrada. Chuck was a good hitter and had gotten a single already that night. He was pitching well and would end up completing the game and eleven more in 1960. He won eighteen and made the All-Star team that year. He laid down a bunt on me, and I charged the ball and threw him out at first. This advanced Hansen to second base, and I didn't like that.

With Hansen in scoring position, their second baseman Marv Breeding came up and popped up a curve ball to Bobby Richardson on second. With two outs, Al Pilarcik came up to bat. I'd played against Al in the International League in '56, and he was off to a good start and hitting over .400 early in the season. Pilarcik hit a single to Roger Maris in right field, and that let Hansen score. Next up was Gene Woodling, their left fielder, and he grounded out to second. That got us out of the inning.

When I went into the dugout, everyone was quiet, and I looked over and saw Casey sleeping away. Casey was sixty-nine, and they called him the Old Perfesser. He wasn't as motivated as he had been in earlier years, and this would turn out to be his last year with the Yankees — even though we made it to the World Series.

No one was talking in the dugout, but people were whispering back and forth to keep from waking Casey. I heard some people laughing and saw Bob Turley pretending to do his loud whistle. Bob could make a shrill whistle and was known for reading opposing pitchers' mannerisms and signaling batters about the coming pitch. After a few more chuckles and prodding, Bob gave out a sharp whistle to wake Casey up. That whistle echoed in the dugout, and old Casey jerked his head up and woke up quickly. Everyone just looked ahead as if nothing had happened. Then Casey slowly closed his eyes, drooped his head, and fell back to sleep.

We were down 9–5, and our second through fourth batters were coming up. Those batters were the three Ms — McDougald, Mantle, and Maris. I wish I had a great story to tell about how they powered some hits over the wall to help me get a win, but that would have to wait until '61. McDougal did hit the ball into deep right field, but not far enough. Mickey popped out, and Roger grounded out to end the inning.

In the bottom of the eighth, Bob Boyd, their first baseman, was first up to bat. He already had two RBIs that night, and I needed to keep him off base. Elston called for a mix of curves and fastballs, and I got him on a slider that was an easy groundout to third. Next up was Brooks Robinson, the future Hall of Famer. On this night, I got the best of him, and he popped out to Roger in center field. Next up was Jackie Brandt. Jackie got ahold of a knuckleball and sent it deep into right field. Roger was a great defender and ran under it for the final out. That ended my pitching night with only one run. My ERA was 2.25.

We won four games in a row after that, against the Tigers and the Athletics. On May 8, I played my last game in the majors. It was a gray, drizzly day in the Bronx. The White Sox were in town, and they were playing well. They were 11–6, and we were 10–5, so we could pull ahead in the standings if we won.

Art Ditmer was pitching for us and gave up a solo home run to Minnie Minoso. Art played well into the eighth, but our team couldn't get going. The Sox were leading 3–1 in the bottom of the ninth when Mantle and Maris came up. It was some classic Yankee play, where we picked up the pieces when we needed to. Mickey started the rally with a double, and then Roger hit him home with a single to center. The Sox brought in Gerry Staley. Bill Skowron hit a double off him right away, but Roger only made it to third on a good relay throw. The Sox intentionally walked Elston to load the bases with no outs.

> Brooks Robinson was coming into his own in 1960 and would be an All Star for the first time that year and the following fourteen years. He was known more for his prowess on third base, where he was known as the Human Vacuum Cleaner. He still holds the record for sixteen straight Golden Gloves. He played for the Orioles for twenty-three seasons, was the MVP of the 1970 World Series, and got his number retired.

Hector Lopez was up to bat and hit a grounder to third. They threw Roger out at home to keep the bases loaded with only one out. Casey pinch hit Yogi Berra, and I hoped he would make another clutch hit to score a couple of runs to win. Instead, Yogi hit one to first base, and they threw Joe DeMaestri out at home for the second out (Joe pinch ran for Skowron). Kent Hadley came up next and hit a line drive toward second, and Elston scored the tying run. With the bases loaded, Tony Kubek hit a line drive to right field and sent the game into extra innings. That put the game in my hands.

I'd been warming up during the bottom of the ninth, and they called me in to start the tenth. Yogi was catching now, and it was good to have his experience in there. Yogi was thirty-five and knew what pitch to call against the other veterans he had faced so many times. Yogi had such a great feel for the game, and he seemed to be able to read the mind of the batter and call the right pitch. Maybe he picked up on physical cues and knew what the batter would go for.

First up was the perennial All Star and future Hall of Famer Nellie Fox. They called him Mighty Mite, and he is supposed to be the third-hardest person to strike out in MLB history! He led the American League in singles for six consecutive seasons and was hard to get out. Yogi was chatting with Nellie before he called for a slider. I sent my slider in, and it dropped and caused Nellie to ground it to second base for an easy out.

Next up was Minnie Minoso, the "Cuban Comet." Minnie was the first African American to play for the White Sox and was known for "stealing first base." The expression meant that he crowded the plate to get hit by inside pitches. I couldn't afford to let him get to first like that, because it was hard to keep this speedster from stealing more bases in a crucial situation like this. Yogi called for a knuckleball, and that was what I gave him. The ball didn't release well, though, maybe because of the rain. Minnie found the slight knuckleball and hit it to center field for a good single. I thought he was one of the best players I saw play and think he should be in the Hall of Fame for his long, successful career.

With Minnie on first, Ted "Big Klu" Kluszewski came up to bat. I'd faced Ted a few times when he was in Pittsburgh and knew he'd chase outside balls. Ted was getting a little old, at thirty-five, but I still needed to be on my guard because he was a power hitter with loads of experience. Ted would often drive the ball right back at the pitcher, so I had to be ready to field the pitch.

While some pitchers would end up in all kinds of contorted positions after a pitch, I was ready to field, and this helped me be an excellent fielder. Throughout my career, I had a fairly unique fielding technique. After I released the ball, I hopped forward off the mound. I landed on the toes of both of my feet in a stance ready to field the ball. You can see it in the video on my website. With this technique, I never committed an error in the majors and only one error in 233 games after 1956. I'm proud of that achievement and can't stand to see modern pitchers out of position. I'm surprised more of them don't get hurt by 120-mile-per-hour balls coming back at them.

After a couple pitches to Klu, I got a little too aggressive in my hop off the mound and jumped all the way into the wet grass. My feet slipped on that wet grass, and I fell right on my ass!

I scrambled back to my feet and was glad that Ted hadn't driven the ball into me. I heard some laughter from the clubhouse and looked and saw Casey shaking his head. Now, this might be forgiven on many teams, and some people would laugh it off, but I think this little slipup put some doubts in Casey's mind. I didn't look professional when I was sitting down in the wet grass and scrambling to get up. The Yankees didn't want to look bad. With dirt stains on my ass, I sure didn't look good.

It didn't help that on the next pitch, Big Klu hit a single to right field. That was enough for Casey to pull me. It was a long and unfortunately final walk back to the bench with stained pants. I wish Casey would have given me the chance to get out of the inning. Jim Coates replaced me and proceeded to give up five runs and the game. Because I put the first two guys on base in that ninth inning, I got the loss, and that sent my major-league record to 6–7. I would never make it to the mound in the majors again.

I thought I had pitched well for the Yankees over the four games that I pitched. I didn't give up a homer or even an extra-base hit. While I'd only given up one run while pitching, my relief gave up two runners I put on base, and that bumped my ERA to an astronomical 6.23 for the Yankees. That stat doesn't really mean much when it's based on such a small playing time. I'm probably dwelling on these final stats too much, but when I look back and try to make sense of it all, I can't figure out why I didn't get another chance.

The bottom line is that I got my shot, and I didn't perform to the level that the coaches needed. I knew that to stay on the Yankees, I needed to play spectacularly, and I didn't. I played well and gave it my best shot. If I'd have done one or two things better, maybe I could have stayed with the Yankees for the rest of the season and gone with them to the 1960 World Series. That didn't happen. I gave it my all and have no regrets.

We lost a couple more games to Cleveland at home after that and then won two out of three in Washington. On May 18, when Casey had to cut the roster to twenty-eight players, I didn't make the cut. I was with the team for a total of six weeks, and it was very memorable. They sold me outright to the Richmond Virginians instead of optioning me to the team, as the Dodgers had. The Yankees basically severed ties with me on that day, and I was moving to Richmond.

Highlights

- The Dodgers traded me to the Yankees, and I joined them during spring training and played in some exhibition games.

- The Yankee organization was very different from the fraternal Dodgers, and on my first night, a naked Ryne Duren could have fallen to his death if Ralph Terry hadn't pulled him off the ledge of the hotel window.

- Pitching in the American League gave me a whole new set of competitors to face, and I pitched in Fenway Park, Baltimore's Memorial Stadium, and Yankee Stadium.

- After only four games of playing decently, I got traded to the Richmond Virginians and was never called back up to the majors.

15. TO RICHMOND AND RETIREMENT—1960 AND
BEYOND

I took the bus to join the Virginians in Richmond. We hit the road immediately, and I liked being in the International League again. Since I hadn't been in the Yankee organization long, almost all of my teammates were new to me. Minor-league players change quickly, and I hadn't played in the International League since 1957, so I was facing all kinds of new talent and flummoxing them with my sidearm knuckleball and overarm sliders.

The Virginians were a solid team, and we had some new players, such as Granny Hammer, whom I'd played against in Philly quite a bit. I was pegged as a reliever in Richmond and spent most of my time in the bull pen and away from the other players. I hit well that year and had three doubles in sixteen at bats. I relieved after a pinch hitter a lot of times and didn't get to bat much, but I hit .375 that year and became the closer.

Playing against the Dodgers' Montreal Royals was a big change for me. I'd often go over and talk to my old teammates and guys I had played with in spring training, such as Tommy LaSorda, Rene Valdez, Ralph Mauriello, and Babe Birrer. Tommy was in his last year of play and had been in the Dodger organization for a long time already. He had started playing when he was seventeen and played in the International League for nine years. Rene was also a veteran of the IL and had stayed in Montreal since '57. I didn't think that I'd be staying there for a few years.

Many great players were in the International League that year. The legendary Bob Gibson played quite a bit that year for the Rochester Redwings before getting called up. I saw him pitch in Omaha in the American Association and in Rochester. He was a wild pitcher back then and gaining the control that would lead him to stardom. He was still intense in those early years and was an amazing athlete—one of the quickest I've ever seen. He'd grown up in an orphanage in Omaha and played with the Harlem Globetrotters before turning his attention to baseball. His breakout year in Saint Louis was '61.

Another young talent I remember pitching to was Cookie Rojas of the Havana Sugar Kings. He couldn't hit a curve in those early days, so that was what I threw at him. He learned and overcame that challenge and was a great fielder. He would go on to have a great career in Kansas City, where I'd watch him with my family over the next decade.

Besides the players changing, the league was changing as well. In 1960, the Havana Sugar Kings became the Jersey City Jerseys because of a failed minor leaguer named Fidel Castro. Fidel had a love for baseball he pitched in an exhibition game in 1959 before the Rochester Redwings played the Sugar Kings. Fidel struck out two of the lackeys from the military police team. Those guys wouldn't

The day after Castro pitched, the Cubans got rather rambunctious watching an International League game and started making lots of noise, waving flags, and shooting guns. A stray bullet hit Redwings third-base coach Frank Verdi in the head and lodged in his shoulder. The Redwings left the game for good reason!

want to hit a homer and have Fidel stare them down as they ran around the bases. It would be a career-limiting move.

Fidel in an exhibition game in Havana. He never played in the minors but got some honors once he was dictator.

We played in Havana in 1960, before Fidel started nationalizing foreign-owned businesses. On July 18, baseball commissioner Ford Frick announced that the Sugar Kings would become the Jersey City Jerseys. The league was under pressure from the secretary of state Christian Herter. This move made our travel schedule much better. We had four teams in Canada or upstate New York and only Miami way down south.

I worked my way up in the Virginians' pitching staff and became their ace. Even with a late start in May, I pitched forty-seven games for them in 1960 and did well. I led the league with a 1.56 ERA over eighty-one innings and struck out fifty-three batters while giving up only fifty-seven hits and sixteen runs. The minor leagues obviously made my stats jump, and I moved to the top of the league. I thought the Yankees would call me up at the end of the year, but I never got the message.

Richmond was a nice city to play in, and I needed a car. I always thought that another convertible would be fun. I went to the local dealership, and an MG—Morris's Garage—caught my eye. While I was there buying the gray convertible below, I saw another lady buying a car there. We both ended up buying cars that day, and we ended up going out. I took her to a Richbrau picnic, and we drove our MGs around town on occasion. I liked the looks of that MG, but it wasn't that well designed for a big guy like me. For one thing, there wasn't any ventilation by my feet, and my feet would cook when the motor got hot. It was still a head turner of a car.

The season went well, but our team took second place behind the Toronto Maple Leafs, who won over a hundred games. I didn't feel like going down to play winter ball that year and drove my MG back to Kansas City. When I was crossing the Mississippi river and was almost into Saint Louis, that little car broke down right in the middle of the bridge. I got out and looked under the hood, but I didn't know what to do. No steam was shooting out, and I just sat there for a few minutes while it cooled. I thought someone might stop to help. After fifteen minutes, it started up, and I finished the drive over the Mississippi and got the points fixed the next morning.

I drove the car to Kansas City but decided it would be a better car for Los Angeles than the cold winter in the Midwest. After a few days of visiting, I continued my coast-to-coast trip and drove all the way to LA. The car didn't break down again, but I was always worried it would. I visited some of my teammates and saw some girls I knew, but I took a drive-away back to KC.

This 1958 MG was fun to drive, but it needed more time in the Morris's Garage than I liked. I drove it from Richmond to LA and sold it.

I spent the winter with my brother, Tom, and his young family in Kansas City. My cousin Hank Specht's wife, June, said she knew someone I might want to meet. June had gotten to know her children's kindergarten teacher and said she was a fine and beautiful single woman. June gave me Susan Kokoruda's phone number, and I called Susan and set up a blind date.

I had basically been married to baseball for several years. I didn't think that playing baseball and having a serious relationship were very compatible. Living on the road for multiple months a year and making a little salary were just not conducive to long-term relationships or raising a family. I wanted to settle down after I finished baseball and live a more normal life, like my brother and sister.

The date night finally arrived, and I wore my best sport jacket and picked her up at her house. The moment she walked in the room, she had my attention. Susan was very attractive, with gorgeous, bright-blue eyes and wavy, shoulder-length blond hair. Her father was a hairdresser, and she always had a fashionable hairdo in those days.

I melted when she smiled, and she was very easy to talk to and had plenty to say. She told me how she had grown up on Strawberry Hill in Kansas City, Kansas, and was in the homecoming-queen pageant. If there was one day that my life changed, it was that day.

When I dropped her off that night, she showed me her car. What a car it was—a 1960 convertible Corvette in Tasco turquoise. Susan lived at home and had saved up her money and bought this beautiful car. She told me how she had gotten a ticket for "exhibition of acceleration" when she raced her friend. She loved that car and zipped around town in it. Unfortunately, I couldn't fit in that little car worth a darn. It wasn't made for a man of my height.

Susan and I started dating, and we were regulars by Christmas. Susan was socially active and loved being with people. She and friends rented a hotel room in KCK for New Year's Eve, and that was our coming-out party to her friends. We made a very nice couple, and the stars were aligned. I met her family, and I even took her down to Piqua to meet my parents. Our relationship moved fast—I had never met anyone like Susan. I had some money saved and bought a one-karat emerald-cut diamond to propose to her. She accepted, and I went off to spring training in Florida engaged. We'd only been dating three to four months, but everything felt right.

The Virginians initially offered me a lowball contract that would allow me to go to spring training with the Yankees. They knew I wanted to get back to the majors, and that started with spring training, but I felt they were selling me short with a contract under $10,000. I told them I'd wait for more. Minor-league players didn't make much money, and they still don't. They eventually raised their offer, and I got down to the Virginians' training camp after the Yankees left.

I had such a good spring training that they decided to make me a starting pitcher again. I was glad to be back in a starting role and pitched well, but the '61 Vees weren't a very good team. While I started seventeen games and had eight complete games and three shutouts, my record was only 8–16. By midseason, my ERA had risen to 4.3, and I returned to being a reliever. The win-loss column was what I cared about most, and we ended up being seventh out of eight teams, with a 71–83 record. We had shoddy fielding, with many players having double-digit errors and one player even having forty-six! The best place to learn how to play the game is on the field, so we did have a lot of learning going on.

The following article did a great job of highlighting the troubles I was having.

Kipp Knows What Is Wrong, But Vee Reliever Can't Say Why

Shelley Roffe, *Richmond News Leader*, 1961

It's no mystery to Fred Kipp why he has been somewhat less than a mystery to enemy batters as a relief pitcher this season. As Kipp sees it, his chief problem is "getting behind on the hitters" and the "long ball." But Kipp's searching examination of Kipp stops short on at least one vital point. It's all very well to know what you're doing wrong. So far, neither the Virginians' tall, fidgety lefthander nor anyone else has been able to come up with the "why" answer.

The way Kipp, and the box score, tell the story, he comes in from the bullpen, fails his first few pitches over the plate, "has to make a pitch too good"—and boom!

This is not only contrary to what happened last year when Kipp was as fine a rescue man as there was in the International League but a complete break with his past. He's always considered a lefty whose control was as good as virtually any righthander's you could name.

Kipp's failure to subdue lefty batters is as much a mystery to him as the misplacing of his control. "I've got everything in my favor against them," he says. "My sidearm pitches, my curve, my fast ball. But I get behind." The Kipp examination of Kipp doesn't contain any alibis. Considering his performance last year, he might be pardoned if he fell back on the old one that hardly any relief pitcher ever is able to put good years together back to back.

As an afterthought, Kipp conceded there might be a clue at that on the overwork-underwork front. "You know, this is the first winter in the last four I didn't pitch winter ball," he said. Ah ha...maybe Kipp is the kind of guy who has to work 12 months a year to keep his control sharply honed.

Kipp's idea of a perfect reliever is a fellow who not only has impeccable control but also is favored by luck and the law of averages. In his defense, Kipp points out that his luck turned sour this year before his control did. As Exhibit A, Kipp points to a game he lost at Syracuse in April when a pinch-hitter, pitcher Bob Darnell, hit a grand slam against a pitch, "that was perfect from a pitcher's standpoint. A strike at the knees. I suppose he ought to get credit for hitting that kind of pitch, but..."

Since Kipp says he's a firm believer in the law of averages, it figures that eventually things should have begun turning his way. Batters would stop hitting perfect pitches. The Vees would begin scoring runs. Instead, things took a turn for the worse. Eventually, Kipp conceded the mental angle became a factor, one which might explain some of his difficulties. "Yes, I guess after a while a relief pitcher in a slump comes in and waits for something to happen," Kipp says.

Kipp is in full accord with manager Cal Ermer's plan to try curing him by using him as a starter. "A starter can make more than one mistake." Kipp said. "Not many more, but more. And maybe if I do well as a starter I'll keep on starting." Kipp is advised not to bet on this. The cure is designed to habilitate him for the bullpen.

The article shows how I just wasn't pitching as well as I used to, and maybe my luck had turned. My luck had turned good and bad before, so the law of averages should bring my next season around. The difference was that time wasn't on my side.

A bright spot in the '61 season for me was when Susan came to visit from KC. The first time she visited me was in Columbus, Ohio. We had a series in Columbus, and Susan came with her sister Carole and brother Jim. We had been writing letters back and forth, but there is still nothing like being there. About that time, we set the date to get married after the end of the season in October.

I like this profile shot of my throwing with the Virginians.

Susan came out again to Richmond to see me play and to visit. We had some great times, and she went to Washington, DC, to visit a friend and came back for another series when I returned to Richmond. Susan planned the whole wedding, and all I had to do was show up. At the end of the season, I returned to Kansas City to get married. We had a marvelous wedding, and we went to Puerto Rico for the honeymoon.

Cal Ermer, the manager of the Virginians, persuaded me to play for the Ponce Leones that winter in the Puerto Rican Winter League. Susan and I flew there early and enjoyed our honeymoon for a few days in San Juan. This was the first time that Susan had been out of the country, so I had a few things to show her. First, I showed her how to order food with poor Spanish by pointing my finger at the food I wanted. We had a nice time sightseeing before moving to where I was going to play.

Ponce is the second-largest city in Puerto Rico and on the south shore. We had to take a long, bumpy bus ride over the mountains from San Jose. Susan was a city girl, and she was out of her element when the bus stopped at a pit stop on the top of a green mountain to take a breather. She was motion sick and was glad to get off the bus. We had an hour to kill and plenty of time to eat.

The bus was full of locals, and they all got off the bus and ran to get in line for some barbecue pork. Susan wasn't hungry yet, so we walked around the mountaintop. The air was fresh until the wind shifted and a foul stench of pigs drifted through the air. I recognized the smell from growing up on a farm, but Susan didn't. She was curious about the pigs, and we walked over and looked at them rustling around in the muddy, stinky sty. It was fun watching the pigs run around until we saw the butcher grab one of the pigs, haul him up in the air, and slit his throat. Susan didn't like the blood too much, and those oinkers do have an amazing amount of blood.

We walked over to the kitchen area and saw how the farmer had twenty pig rotisserie ovens that were made out of half-open metal barrels. The farmer sold roasted pig all over the island, and he had trucks that delivered the finished product. When the wind shifted again and she smelled the roasted pork, Susan regained her appetite. We went upstairs to the restaurant to enjoy some fresh, delicious roasted pork. The restaurant would let us order any part of the pig, and one local sitting next to us was eating half of the pig's head. When Susan saw that head and the eye of the pig still in the socket, she lost her appetite again.

We went down the mountain and settled into a hotel in Ponce, and the season didn't go very well. My pitching seemed to be off, and maybe that was because my mind wasn't in the game as much as before. I had a wife now, and Susan had quit her teaching job to be with me. I attended to her as best I could, but she did feel a little out of place in the small town of Ponce, where she couldn't speak the local language. Most of the players were single, so Susan got a little lonely in little Ponce.

Puerto Rico was famous for baseball, with Roberto Clemente and Orlando Cepeda being stars at the time. The Santurce Crabs (Cangrejeros de Santurce) had been one of the most famous teams in the Caribbean when Willie Mays and Roberto Clemente played on the same team many years earlier.

My first wife, Susan, was a beautiful woman — inside and out.

The season got underway, and my Leones weren't playing well, and neither was I. A little more than a month later, Susan was pregnant, and we decided to pack our bags and move back to KC before Christmas.

We rented an apartment on the Plaza, and I was a substitute teacher for a while. We spent only a couple of months there before we went to spring training in Florida. I'd bought a '55 Cadillac for the ride down, and we left a day early to beat an eighteen-inch snowstorm that blew into Kansas City. Instead of freezing in KC, we headed south and were soon basking in the warm sun of Florida.

Susan's pregnancy was coming along well, but my career wasn't. In '62, I was stuck with the Virginians in the role of the reliever. I wasn't getting any better, and I didn't even get a start that year. I seemed to be working my way down instead of up.

When my first son, Chris, was born on July 20, 1962, I held him and knew that my life had changed again. My passion for the game was being converted into passion for my family. I had been able to focus on myself and baseball for almost ten years and had had a great career, but now I had other concerns.

To play at the major-league level, I needed high degrees of commitment, passion, and dedication. I was naturally gifted, but not like other players who could just casually show up. I needed to be focused on the game, but my vision was turning to my wife and new family. I had always thought that I wouldn't want to play baseball and raise a family at the same time. I believed in being with my family and not on the road. The phone wasn't ringing with offers to go to the majors either, so it was time to move on. My baseball career came to an end in '62, and there was no looking back.

We moved back to Kansas City, and I tried to sell insurance for a while on my fame. While clients liked hearing my stories, I'm not much of a salesman, and that job didn't work out. I started working construction with Garney Construction, and it felt right. In '63, I bought part of Bill Woodside's construction company. I'm still doing construction to this day, over fifty years later. We were a heavy-construction company, and we mainly installed sewers and water systems for new residential areas. Kansas City was growing consistently, and work was going well. In 1972, I started my own company, called Conduit Constructors. I built the company up to have a couple of crews and up to twelve workers. Nowadays, I mainly bid small concrete jobs for cities, consumers, or companies. I take cold winters off and work half days, but it keeps me off the streets.

In the summer of '63, I played some semipro ball for Graves Truck Lines. We were in a local Kansas City adult league. In '64, I played with the Service

Auto Glassmen, and we went to the National Baseball Congress in Wichita, Kansas, where we played against some great teams. John Gabler, who had played with me on the Yankees and in Richmond, pitched well, and we won the championship. We played teams from all over the United States, including Alaska, who had a couple of future greats in Graig Nettles and Tom Seaver. After that 1964 season, I pitched some batting practice for the Kansas City Athletics, but that was it. My baseball career was over.

In 1978, I attended the Giants-Dodgers Old-Timers' Game in San Francisco, which commemorated the twenty-year anniversary of the move to the West Coast. It was great to see my old teammates, and most of us were in good enough shape to hurt ourselves in an exhibition game. We pulled a few muscles and told a few old stories in the city by the bay.

My focus in the late sixties, seventies, and eighties was on raising my family, and we were enjoying every day. Susan and I always wanted a big family and had six children in nine years—five boys and one girl. I would wake up early, at about five in the morning, and be gone before the kids got up. I'd work all day and come home around three or four o'clock, and the kids would jump all over me as I made my way to take a nap. Susan did most of the child rearing, and I'm very proud of all of my children.

My family and I led a rather idyllic life in the suburbs of Overland Park, Kansas, until a fateful summer day in 1979. Susan had developed a lump on her left breast, and the doctors diagnosed it as stage-four breast cancer. Susan soon had a mastectomy, and the surgeons removed infected lymph nodes under her arm as well. After six months of chemotherapy, the doctors said Susan was cancer free. After such a long ordeal of seeing Susan suffer, our family went back to our normal suburban lifestyle for a few years before the cancer returned. After a long struggle and over a year in bed, Susan passed away in the spring of 1985.

Raising my family without Susan was one of the biggest challenges of my life. I wasn't very motivated at that time, and my career wasn't doing well either. I dated for a few years and met some wonderful women, but the relationships didn't stick. A good friend of mine, Marilyn Sell, said I should meet someone she worked with at Holy Cross Catholic Church. I met Lorraine Gillis in 1989 at a Catholic singles group, and I knew this could be a long-term relationship from the moment we met. Lorraine is very energetic, engaging, cute, and under five feet tall. I've got well over a foot of height on her, but that doesn't hold her back. I took her out to dinner a week later, and we hit it off well.

Here's my family in about 1972. Chris and Greg are in the top row. The middle row is me, Scott, and Susan. The bottom row is Mark, Karen, and Eric.

Lorraine and I fit each other well. She's very talkative, while I am rather laconic. Nine months later, we were married and have been for over twenty-five years. Lorraine had three children, so we would have made an interesting Brady Bunch with nine kids, but five of them had already moved out of the house. We moved into her home, where we still live today.

In 1996, I got inducted into the Kansas Baseball Hall of Fame. Luckily, Bill Russell, the career-long Dodger shortstop with four World Series rings, was inducted into the hall on the same day. This brought Tommy LaSorda out to the event to give a speech for both of us. Bill and Tommy brought in lots of Dodger fans, and we had a great induction ceremony. For my speech, I told another version of chapter one, where I beat the Cardinals and Stan Musial in the Coliseum.

In 2008, the Dodgers celebrated the fiftieth anniversary of the move to Los Angeles. Lorraine and I attended the glamorous event and were part of the 115,301 people who attended the preseason game against the Boston Red Sox. That's the largest crowd in baseball history and a world record. We had a great time seeing all my buddies and telling lies about the old days. In 2009, they had us back again to celebrate the fiftieth anniversary of our World Series victory. After these events, I started talking more about my baseball stories, and people seemed interested. I'm still surprised about how fans still have enough interest after all these years to send me pictures and baseball cards to sign about every week—usually for professional purveyors.

In 2015, for our twenty-fifth wedding anniversary, Lorraine and I went out to California, and the Dodgers let me throw the opening pitch. This was the first time I had pitched in Dodger Stadium, since it wasn't completed until '62. It was exciting to go out on the mound and look around the stadium. I was eighty-four years old and still did my warmup, as Tommy Holmes told me. I wound up and threw a good pitch to start the game. Tommy Lasorda was at the game too, so I talked to him for a while. He's been a good advocate for baseball and draws a lot of fans.

That's the story of my life, with an emphasis on my baseball career. I was a great minor-league pitcher and a good major-league pitcher. I was fortunate enough to play with the two most successful teams in the golden era of baseball and am one of the few still around to tell firsthand stories about it. I played one full year and four partial years in the majors and surrounded that with five years in the International League and one year in the American Association. I played in Japan in the Dodgers' goodwill tour and three winters in the Dominican Republic. I went coast to coast to coast with the Dodgers and Yankees, and I played on three continents with the best and against the best. I love reminiscing about the old days, and those days live on when I do.

When people ask me how I did it, I tell them it was a combination of having natural talent, being prepared, and working hard. I was very fortunate to be blessed with natural athletic abilities, but I nurtured that talent over many years of playing hard. I took chances and played wherever my knuckleball would take me. From the small towns of Nebraska to the big cities in Japan, I showed up and was ready to play. I made sure that I was physically fit and ready when the coach called my number. Working hard and being ready to do all that I could to help my team win is the way I have lived my life, and I suggest you do that too.

My wife, Lorraine, and I enjoying the fiftieth anniversary celebration of the Dodgers moving to Los Angeles, in 2008.

Highlights

- In Richmond, I was their ace reliever in '60 and led the league with a 1.56 ERA.

- I started seventeen games in '61, had eight complete games and three shutouts, and relieved in thirty-three games.

- I relieved fifty-three games in '62 and had my first son, Chris, during my last season.

16. SUMMARY AND STATISTICS

Major-League Highlights

I played with three major-league teams over five years. From Brooklyn to Los Angeles and back to the Bronx, I played with the two winningest teams of the 1950s and 1960s. Here is a quick recap of my pitching in the majors.

1956—Brooklyn Dodgers. I pitched in exhibition games against the New York Yankees and Boston Red Sox, played the season in Montreal, returned to ride the pine during the pennant race, pitched batting practice in the World Series against New York Yankees, saw Don Larsen's perfect game, and pitched forty-three innings—more than any other Dodger—in the goodwill tour of Japan.

This was the last great year of the Brooklyn Dodgers, with Jackie Robinson retiring after this season. Don Newcombe won the first Cy Young Award and MVP of the National League, with twenty-seven wins. Sal Maglie joined the team and had a big impact with his no-hitter in the pennant race. The Dodgers took the Yankees to game seven in the World Series but couldn't get the final win.

1957—Brooklyn Dodgers. I pitched in exhibition games against the Milwaukee Braves, Kansas City Athletics, New York Yankees, and Chicago White Sox; traveled with the team for the first eight games before playing with Montreal all season; returned to the Dodgers for the end of the season and got my cup of coffee in Chicago's Wrigley Field; and saw the last game at Ebbets Field.

With hearing rumors of the move to Los Angeles, playing home games in New Jersey, and losing Jackie, the team was in transition and got third place for the first time, in the fifties. Don Drysdale came into his own, with seventeen wins, and Clem Labine was our closer, with seventeen saves. Duke Snider hit forty home runs, but this was the year of the Milwaukee Braves, who beat the Yankees in the World Series.

1958 — Los Angeles Dodgers. I played the full season with the Dodgers and went 6–6 in forty games, with a mixture of starting and relieving. This was the highlight year of my career, and playing in the Los Angeles Coliseum and all the other National League stadiums was spectacular.

The move to LA took its toll on the team, and we had a losing record and finished in seventh place. The team had many of the stalwarts of the Brooklyn team, but we couldn't pull it together, and only Duke and Bob Lillis hit over .300.

Major-League Pitching

Year	Team	W	L	ERA	G	IP	H	SO	BB
1957	Brooklyn Dodgers	0	0	9.0	1	4	6	3	0
1958	Los Angeles Dodgers	6	6	5.0	40	102	107	58	45
1959	Los Angeles Dodgers	0	0	0	2	2	2	1	3
1960	New York Yankees	0	1	6.23	4	4	4	2	0
Total		6	7	5.08	47	113	119	64	48

1959 — Los Angeles Dodgers. I played the full season for the Saint Paul Saints and joined the Dodgers in the pennant race in September. I pitched well in two games during the home stretch and watched the Dodgers win a special three-game playoff against the Milwaukee Braves. We won the pennant and then the World Series against the Chicago White Sox.

The Dodgers were hot at the right time and, surprisingly, won the Series. Some said we were the weakest team to win the World Series, but a win is still a win. Larry Sherry was the star and MVP of the Series and peaked at the right moment.

1960 — New York Yankees. Instead of playing in Saint Paul again, I asked to be traded and was soon with the New York Yankees. I joined the Yankees on

April 3 and played in exhibition games against the Red Sox and the Richmond Virginians. I played four regular-season games before being traded to the Virginians on May 18. I was the closer for the Virginians, but the Yankees never called me up.

Minor-League Highlights

I played eight years in the minor leagues, and six of those years were in AAA leagues. I led my league in ERA in 1953 and 1959 and was an All Star in 1956 and 1959. I got twenty wins in 1956 for Montreal and won rookie of the year in the International League. In my last three years, I was the closer for the Virginians and pitched in 150 games.

Minor-League Pitching

Year	Team	W	L	ERA	G	IP	H	SO	BB
1953	Miami Sunsox	0	1	10.0	3	9	11		
1953	Asheville Tourists	15	5	2.24	22	165	122		
1955	Mobile Bears	4	2	2.34	10	50	48		
1956	Montreal Royals	20	7	3.33	40	254	220	127	118
1957	Montreal Royals	8	17	4.09	32	187	196	99	83
1959	Saint Paul Saints	14	11	3.21	35	213	198	125	93
1960	Richmond Virginians	5	3	1.56	47	81	57	53	22
1961	Richmond Virginians	8	16	4.31	50	163	170	96	52
1962	Richmond Virginians	4	5	3.39	53	85	73	53	39
Total		78	67	3.31	292	1211	1095	553	495

Semipro Highlights

I played for a variety of teams outside the minor leagues, including five seasons overseas. I started with the small-town team in my hometown and ventured out into new fields—first in the Midwest and later in Latin America. Without traveling, I would not have seen the variety of competition that helped me grow as a pitcher. I found a way to play baseball during every season of the year.

Semipro Pitching

Year	Team	Season	Highlight
1946 –49	Piqua	Summer	These teenage years were formative and fun.
1950 –53	Emporia Hornets	Spring	I pitched a no-hitter my freshman year and a one-hitter the next.
1950	Emporia Rangers	Summer	I played on the town team and traveled wider.
1951	Chamberlain Chiefs	Summer	I spent the summer in the South Dakota League and played the Cubans.
1952	Superior Knights	Summer	I pitched in Nebraska and got in *Life Magazine* for some on-field antics.
1955	Caracas, Venezuela	Winter	I pitched poorly for a few weeks and left after one month.
1957 –58	Escogido Lions	Winter	I went 11–3 in the DR this first season, and we beat the Estrellas Orientales in the championship.
1958 –59	Escogido Lions	Winter	I pitched well, and we lost the championship to the Licey Tigers.
1959 –60	Escogido Lions	Winter	We beat the Estrellas Orientales in the championship.
1961	Ponce Lions	Winter	I went to Puerto Rico on my honeymoon, but I only stayed a month.
1963	Graves Truck Lines	Summer	I pitched that summer for Graves and struck out a few people.
1964	Service Auto Glassmen	Summer	We won the National Baseball Congress in Wichita.

ABOUT THE AUTHORS

The whole book is about Fred, so here is a little about Scott. People often ask me, "What was it like growing up while your father was a baseball pitcher?" I have to say that I had no idea. He was retired by the time I was born, and I can't remember my father telling a single story about baseball in my youth.

My father is rather reserved, humble, and laconic. I started researching his baseball career before a family reunion in 2008 and teased the basic facts out him, but he didn't tell many stories. In 2015, I rented out a public-access-TV studio in Santa Barbara and interviewed him about his career. I've rarely seen him so excited, and he opened up and finally told many stories. In 2016, I decided to write this book and started grilling him about his life and the stories that I turned into this book. Bonding with my father over baseball brought us together, like so many other fathers and sons.

I had planned to finish the book in the summer of 2016, but my wife, Grace, was diagnosed with pancreatic cancer. I could barely write while I took care of her. The cancer consumed her, and she passed in early 2017. My father went through a similar experience with my mother, and he and many others helped me through this tragedy. I'm an electrical engineer and write as a hobby. I hope writing will become a source of income at some point.

Made in the USA
Monee, IL
14 June 2024

59390190R00136